understanding **Nietzscheanism**

Understanding Movements in Modern Thought
Series Editor: Jack Reynolds

This series provides short, accessible and lively introductions to the major schools, movements and traditions in philosophy and the history of ideas since the beginning of the Enlightenment. All books in the series are written for undergraduates meeting the subject for the first time.

understanding **Nietzscheanism**

Ashley Woodward

ACUMEN

First published in 2011 by Acumen

Acumen Publishing Limited
4 Saddler Street
Durham
DH1 3NP
www.acumenpublishing.co.uk

ISBN: 978-1-84465-292-1 (hardcover)
ISBN: 978-1-84465-293-8 (paperback)

British Library Cataloguing-in-Publication Data
A catalogue record for this book is available from the British Library.

Typeset in Minion Pro.
Printed in the UK by the MPG Books Group.

Contents

Acknowledgements

First, thanks are due to the series editor Jack Reynolds for inviting me to write this book. Thanks also to Tristan Palmer at Acumen for both his continual patience and understanding, and his generous words of encouragement. Acknowledgement must also be given to the anonymous readers of the initial book proposal and the reviewers of the manuscript in its first draft form. At both stages many useful suggestions (as well as heartening words of encouragement) helped to make the book what it is. Warm thanks also to Catherine Cameron and Jon Roffe for generously reading and commenting on chapters of the book. Material for several chapters of the book was trialled in the subject "Nietzsche's Legacy: Existentialism, Poststructuralism, Transhumanism" I taught at the Melbourne School of Continental Philosophy in the summer of 2010, and I would like to thank all the students who attended for giving me the opportunity to do this. Special thanks to Chloe Bo-kyung Kim for her patience and support during the writing of this manuscript. Of course, as always, responsibility for all the book's faults and limitations rests with me.

Abbreviations

Editions of Nietzsche's complete works in German:

KGW   *Kritische Gesamtausgabe: Werke*, G. Colli & M. Montinari (eds) (Berlin: Walter de Gruyter, 1967–).

KSA   *Sämtliche Werke: Kritische Studienausgabe*, 2nd edn, G. Colli & M. Montinari (eds) (Berlin: Walter de Gruyter, 1980).

References to Nietzsche's works give the abbreviated book title as shown in the following list, followed by the abbreviated title of the chapter, number of the part or section, or when required, a combination of these. For example, HAH 97 refers to section 97 of *Human, All Too Human*, while Z: 2 "Of Poets" refers to the section titled "Of Poets" in *Thus Spoke Zarathustra*, book 2. Wherever possible, I have referred to the Cambridge University Press editions of Nietzsche's works in English translation.

A   *The Anti-Christ*, in *The Anti-Christ, Ecce Homo, Twilight of the Idols, and Other Writings*, A. Ridley (ed.), J. Norman (trans.) (Cambridge: Cambridge University Press, 2005).

AOM   *Assorted Opinions and Maxims*, in *Human, All Too Human*.

BGE   *Beyond Good and Evil*, R.-P. Horstmann (ed.), J. Norman (trans.) (Cambridge: Cambridge University Press, 2001).

BT   *The Birth of Tragedy*, in *The Birth of Tragedy and Other Writings*, R. Geuss (ed.), R. Speirs (trans.) (Cambridge: Cambridge University Press, 1999).

CW   *The Case of Wagner*, in *The Anti-Christ, Ecce Homo, Twilight of the Idols, and Other Writings*.

D   *Daybreak*, M. Clark & B. Leiter (eds), R. J. Hollingdale (trans.) (Cambridge: Cambridge University Press, 1997).

DS   "David Strauss, the Confessor and the Writer", in *Untimely Meditations*, D. Breazeale (ed.), R. J. Hollingdale (trans.) (Cambridge: Cambridge University Press, 1997).

EH   *Ecce Homo*, in *The Anti-Christ, Ecce Homo, Twilight of the Idols, and Other Writings*.

EN   *Writings from the Early Notebooks*, R. Geuss & A. Nehamas (eds), Ladislaus Löb (trans.) (Cambridge: Cambridge University Press, 2009).

GM   *On the Genealogy of Morality and Other Writings*, 2nd edn, K. Ansell-Pearson (ed.), C. Diethe (trans.) (Cambridge: Cambridge University Press, 2006).

GS   *The Gay Science*, B. Williams (ed.), J. Nauckhoff & A. Del Caro (trans.) (Cambridge: Cambridge University Press, 2001).

HAH *Human, All Too Human*, R. J. Hollingdale (trans.) (Cambridge: Cambridge University Press, 1986).

HL   "On the Uses and Disadvantages of History for Life", in *Untimely Meditations*.

LN   *Writings from the Late Notebooks*, R. Bittner (ed.), K. Sturge (trans.) (New York: Cambridge University Press, 2003).

NW   *Nietzsche contra Wagner*, in *The Anti-Christ, Ecce Homo, Twilight of the Idols, and Other Writings*.

SE   "Schopenhauer as Educator", in *Untimely Meditations*.

TI   *Twilight of the Idols*, in *The Anti-Christ, Ecce Homo, Twilight of the Idols, and Other Writings*.

TL   "On Truth and Lying in a Non-moral Sense", in *The Birth of Tragedy and Other Writings*.

WB   "Richard Wagner in Bayreuth", in *Untimely Meditations*.

WP   *The Will to Power*, W. Kaufmann (ed.), W. Kaufmann & R. J. Hollingdale (trans.) (New York: Vintage, 1967).

WS   *The Wanderer and His Shadow*, in *Human, All Too Human*.

Z   *Thus Spoke Zarathustra*, R. Pippin (ed.), A. del Caro (trans.) (Cambridge: Cambridge University Press, 2006).

introduction

Nietzsche and Nietzscheanism

> I know my lot. One day my name will be connected with the memory of something tremendous, – a crisis such as the earth has never seen, the deepest collision of conscience, a decision made *against* everything that has been believed, demanded, held sacred so far. I am not a human being, I am dynamite.
>
> (EH "Destiny" 1)

I can think of no better way to begin this book on the influence of the philosopher Friedrich Nietzsche (1844–1900) than with this well-known assessment of his own significance. As he himself foretold, Nietzsche has indeed been one of the most influential figures in modern thought since the end of the nineteenth century. Nietzsche's work, however, is also notoriously ambiguous. It has been interpreted in a great variety of ways, and has influenced starkly contrasting movements and schools of thought, from atheism to theology, from existentialism to poststructuralism, and from Nazism to feminism. This book will chart Nietzsche's influence, both historically and thematically, across a variety of these contrasting disciplines and schools of interpretation.

While Nietzsche's importance to modern thought cannot be reduced to a single idea or point of interpretation, if there is one over-arching theme that helps us to understand his tremendous influence, then arguably it is *nihilism*, the devaluation of the highest values of Western culture. More than any other thinker of his age, Nietzsche analysed the significance of the vast changes wrought in culture since the Enlightenment at the level of *values*. In other words, he analysed changes in beliefs and traditions with respect to the meaningful sense of existence they supported. Nietzsche's contention was that the "highest values" that had been proposed in Western culture, and which had been supported by philosophical and religious traditions (primarily Platonism and Christianity), were being undermined by the advancements of Enlightenment-inspired thought. He believed that most people had not yet realized the radical implications of contemporary developments in thought, and still clung to values that no longer had any support in belief structures (for example, professed atheists still espoused a Christian morality). Nietzsche's importance, then, may be understood to lie in his attempt to accelerate the processes of modern thought, drawing the extreme conclusions from their tendencies. The rich variety of ways in which he mounted criticisms against traditional modes of thinking, valuing and living, as well as his radical proposals for new alternatives, have been vastly influential in a wide variety of areas. Understanding Nietzsche's thought and its influence is thus crucial to grasping many aspects of contemporary thought and culture.

How to read this book

This book is introductory in tone, presuming no prior knowledge on the part of the reader of either Nietzsche or the schools of thought he has influenced. As far as has been practicable, the chapters have been designed to be readable independently, and in any order. Thus, if you are only interested in Nietzscheanism and feminism, for example, you can read Chapter 4 on its own. However, both in order to avoid repetition, and to also make the book readable from cover to cover as a coherent whole, the reader is sometimes referred to material covered in other chapters. Those with no prior knowledge of Nietzsche's life, work and influence should read this introductory chapter first. It gives a brief overview of Nietzsche's life and work, introducing basic concepts (such as nihilism, the will to power and the eternal return) that will then be examined in greater depth, and from a variety of different viewpoints, in the following chapters.

The introduction then turns to the issue of Nietzscheanism. It briefly outlines Nietzsche's reception in his own lifetime and shortly thereafter, and gives a brief summary overview of the different "schools" of Nietzscheanism to be examined in the following chapters.

This introductory chapter is intended to provide enough information on Nietzsche to enable readers with no prior knowledge to navigate the chapters that follow. However, it remains the case that this is a book on Nietzsche*anism*, and is not primarily focused on Nietzsche's philosophy itself. Those readers with little knowledge in this area may wish to supplement their reading of this book with a more extended introduction to Nietzsche's philosophy. Several recommendations are made in the Further Reading, which also contains suggestions for further study on the topics covered in each chapter of the book. To further facilitate study, the chapters are peppered with key points, and a summary is provided at the end of each chapter. Questions for discussion and revision for each chapter can be found at the back of the book.

Finally, it has become standard for introductory textbooks in the humanities to warn the reader against relying solely on the introduction itself, and to exhort the reader to also read the original texts the book is introducing. I cannot repeat this sentiment strongly enough here. Nietzsche's own texts demand to be read, and his own superb and seductive writing is one of the keys to his enduring popularity and influence. However, as Walter Kaufmann notes, "Nietzsche's books are easier to read but harder to understand than those of almost any other thinker" (1974: 72), thus making secondary texts invaluable as well. Moreover, many of Nietzsche's interpreters covered in this book, from the existentialists to the poststructuralists to contemporary Nietzsche scholars, are exciting and demanding thinkers in their own right, and also deserve to be read in the original. To study Nietzsche and his influence is to embark on an adventure, and I hope that reading this introductory text will fill you with the enthusiasm to take this adventure further.

Nietzsche's life

Friedrich Wilhelm Nietzsche was born in the small village of Röcken, Saxony, a province of Prussia. (Röcken is now part of the town of Lützen in present-day Germany). His father, Karl Ludwig Nietzsche, was a pastor. His mother was Franziska Nietzsche, *née* Oehler. Friedrich was the oldest of three children; his sister Elisabeth was born in 1846, and his brother Joseph in 1848. Nietzsche suffered the loss of his father and brother at a young age, Karl Ludwig dying of a "softening of the brain" in 1849, and Joseph dying in 1850 before reaching the age of two. Nietzsche attended the prestigious grammar school Pforta, then studied theology at the University of Bonn. He quit theological studies and concentrated on philology (the study of ancient texts, mainly Greek and Roman, often today called "Classics"), following his favourite teacher

Friedrich Ritschl to the University of Leipzig. In 1868, Nietzsche met the great composer Richard Wagner, who was to be a decisive influence on the young man. Nietzsche subsequently became a close friend of the family, often visiting the Wagner's residence at Tribschen, where a room was kept reserved for him. Ritschl was so impressed with the young Nietzsche's aptitude for philology that he recommended he be appointed to the professorship in philology at Basel University, a position Nietzsche took up in 1869. He was twenty-four, a remarkably young age to be appointed to a professorship.

In 1870 Nietzsche caught diptheria and dysentery while serving as a medical orderly in the Franco-Prussian war. The after-effects of these illnesses, as well as other severe and chronic health problems, were to plague him for the rest of his life. In 1872 Nietzsche published his first book, *The Birth of Tragedy*, in part an exercise in Wagnerian propaganda. Devoid of scholarly references and an academic tone, the book disappointed the expectations of the philological community and effectively ended Nietzsche's promising career as a philologist. However, he continued to teach philology at Basel for the next seven years, often to very small classes, and battling serious health problems. Nietzsche became increasingly disillusioned with, and estranged from, Wagner over the period 1876–8. A decisive event in this estrangement is Nietzsche's early departure – ostensibly owing to health problems – from Wagner's Bayreuth Festival in 1876. (Wagner had an opera house especially built to showcase his music-dramas, and the premier of the festival that centres on it was in 1876. The festival has continued, and been consistently sold out, to the present day.)

Nietzsche continued to write and publish, and in 1879 resigned from his teaching position owing to health reasons. He then travelled around Europe, favouring Switzerland and Italy in particular, relocating according to the seasons because he believed certain climates to be more conducive to his health. He generally stayed in cheap boarding houses, supported by a university pension and by packages containing food, socks and so on sent by his mother. Nietzsche's health problems were often very severe. He recorded vomiting fits that lasted for days, and severe migraines that left him bed-ridden and unable to read or write for extended periods. He wrote of his intense suffering, and the frequent temptation to take his own life to end it. Instead of resting, however, as soon as he felt well enough he continued to write, and in the ten-year period from 1879 to 1889 – that is, from resigning from his teaching position to his final collapse – he produced a quantity of written material that would be extremely impressive even for someone in perfect health. In 1881, Nietzsche experienced something like a visionary revelation of the idea of the "eternal return" while walking on the shores of Lake Silvaplana in Switzerland. The desire to communicate this insight spurred him to renewed efforts in his thinking and writing.

Nietzsche remained unmarried, despite making several proposals. His only notable romantic entanglement concerned the twenty-year-old Lou Salomé, to whom he was introduced by his close friend, the moralist Paul Rée, in 1882. Apparently unaware of Rée's own romantic intentions concerning her, Nietzsche proposed to Salomé twice, and was both times declined. She did not want to marry anyone, and instead proposed an intellectual *ménage à trois* with Nietzsche and Rée in which they would live and work together. After a short period of this, Rée and Salomé left together. Nietzsche was deeply wounded by the experience of being spurned.

In Turin, in January 1889, Nietzsche suffered a complete mental breakdown from which he never recovered. The story famously goes that his collapse was occasioned by the sight of a horse pitilessly being whipped by its owner in the street. Nietzsche embraced the horse to protect it, and was returned to his hotel room, raving, by the owner of the hotel who had witnessed the incident. He then wrote a series of infamous letters to his friends, displaying a broken mind. Nietzsche was admitted to a psychiatric clinic at the University of Jena, but was shortly released into the care of his mother, who looked after him at their family home in Naumburg. In 1897 his mother died, and he was taken to Weimar to be cared for by his sister Elisabeth. He died there on 25 August 1900.

The cause of Nietzsche's illness and mental collapse has long been a matter of mystery and controversy. Until recently the most widely accepted opinion among Nietzsche scholars was that he had syphilis, contracted from a prostitute during his student days. However, this theory has been undermined by more recent studies, some by medical professionals (see e.g. Cybulska 2000; Sax 2003). While syphilis can cause insanity, Nietzsche's other symptoms do not accord with this diagnosis. A number of alternative theories have been proposed, but Nietzsche's illness remains an unsolved mystery. Other theories include a hereditary deficiency (as previously mentioned, his father had died of "softening of the brain"), and the possibility of a brain tumour. Some have even maintained that it was Nietzsche's own philosophy – rather than any physical cause – that finally drove him insane.

Nietzsche was the antithesis of the clever, successful academic who builds and maintains a reputation on a single idea carved out in narrow field and defended for life, without that single idea ever disturbing the rest of the academic's life, or interrogating the rest of the world or human existence. Arguably, Nietzsche's uncompromising drive to think widely and penetratingly caused him to fail as an academic, destroyed his health and caused shockwaves that have reverberated throughout the world ever since.

Nietzsche's philosophy

The following brief summary of Nietzsche's philosophy is intended to orient the reader unfamiliar with his work, and to provide points of reference concerning his main ideas, to which the reader can refer to aid in understanding discussions of those points in the following chapters. It is not intended to be comprehensive or definitive and, given that Nietzsche's philosophy is subject to multiple and disputed interpretations on so many points, in the chapters to come we shall sometimes see some of the points made here called into question.

Nietzsche's philosophy is standardly broken up into three periods, to which his major writings accord as follows: the "early" (*The Birth of Tragedy*; *Untimely Meditations*), the "middle" (*Human, All Too Human*; *Daybreak*; *The Gay Science*) and the "late" (*Thus Spoke Zarathustra*; *Beyond Good and Evil*; *On the Genealogy of Morality*; *Twilight of the Idols*; *The Anti-Christ*; *The Case of Wagner*; *Ecce Homo*). In addition, a collection of notes called *The Will to Power* was published posthumously (for more on the status of this volume, see below). Many of Nietzsche's views change radically between the different periods of his works, and sometimes he even seems to contradict himself within the same work. However, as indicated in the opening paragraphs of this chapter, Nietzsche's philosophy may be seen to have a degree of coherence in so far as it revolves around the central concept of nihilism. While Nietzsche did not use this term until relatively late in his writing career, we may retrospectively see his earliest works as expressing the same concerns with other names. In this introductory summary of Nietzsche's philosophy, we shall employ the expedient of using the term "nihilism" to name his core concerns throughout his career. Broadly speaking, then, we may consider Nietzsche's thought as beginning, first, with a diagnosis of the nihilism – or at least, the *seeds* of nihilism – he perceives as already existing within the society of his time. Second, he acutely *radicalizes* this nihilism; he makes the pre-existing seeds blossom. Third, he proposes to *overcome* this radical nihilism through a "revaluation of all values".

What, then, is nihilism? In fact, it is an ambiguous concept, to which Nietzsche gives various definitions and typological classifications. We shall unfold these definitions through an explication of Nietzsche's story of nihilism, which will follow the cycle of his thought through the three stages of nihilism he identifies: diagnosis, radicalization and overcoming.

KEY POINT *Nihilism: some definitions*
- The radical repudiation of value, meaning and desirability (WP 1).
- The highest values devaluate themselves (WP 2).
- Man rolls from the centre towards *X* (WP 1).

Diagnosis of nihilism

Nihilism occurs when all the highest values previously posited become devalued. Nietzsche's diagnosis of nihilism in modernity is not that all values *have already been* devalued, but rather that modern thinking has produced the seeds for such a devaluation. In the preface to *The Will to Power*, Nietzsche writes, "What I relate here is the history of the next two centuries. I describe what is coming, what can no longer come differently: *the advent of nihilism* … This future speaks even now in a hundred signs, this destiny announces itself everywhere" (WP "Preface" 2). So in a sense Nietzsche's diagnosis of nihilism is prophetic; it is an extrapolation from contemporary conditions of European culture. Nietzsche's vision of nihilism is a diagnosis of the existing illness of modernity, and a prognosis of the course the illness will take.

Nihilism (although not named as such) can be seen as a constant concern from Nietzsche's early period. His early philosophical thought took shape under the twin influences of the philosopher Arthur Schopenhauer and the composer Richard Wagner. Broadly speaking, this period of Nietzsche's thought resonates with the Romantic tradition; that is, it emphasizes feeling over reason and art over science as more conducive to life and a healthy culture. Nietzsche's first book, *The Birth of Tragedy*, develops an "artists' metaphysics" through an original interpretation of the meaning of ancient Greek tragedy, and proposes the "rebirth" of this tragic art in Wagner's music-dramas. Guiding Nietzsche's analysis is the view that much of Western culture has been – and remains – decadent. Nietzsche's primary concern is the meaning and value of life, and his contention is that the ancient Greeks knew something important that we have lost, but which we might rediscover through Wagner.

Ancient Greek tragedies, such as the works of Aeschylus, Sophocles and Euripides, were also "music-dramas"; they included a much stronger musical element than is typically appreciated today. Actors would play out a narrative, surrounded by a singing and dancing chorus. Nietzsche contends that the tragedy combines two types of aesthetic that are usually kept separate in the other arts: the *Apollonian* and the *Dionysian*. Apollo is the god of beauty, and associated by Nietzsche with dream, harmony, form and the plastic arts (such as sculpture). Dionysus is the god of wine, and is associated with intoxication, disharmony, formlessness, sublimity and music (traditionally, Dionysus was worshipped with orgiastic festivals in which participants would engage in drunkenness and sexual promiscuity). Nietzsche also associated these two aesthetics with metaphysical principles: Dionysus is the principle of the deepest underlying reality in which "all is one" and there are no distinctions between things, while the Apollonian is the principle of individuation, the distinction of things according to parts and structured forms.

KEY POINT
- The *Apollonian*: beauty, dream, harmony, form, the plastic arts, individuation, illusion.
- The *Dionysian*: sublimity, intoxication, disharmony, formlessness, music, oneness, reality.

Simply put, Nietzsche's "artists' metaphysics" in *The Birth of Tragedy* proposes that the Dionysian touches the true nature of reality as a sublime undifferentiated oneness, while the Apollonian covers over this reality with the soothing illusion of beautiful forms. With respect to life, both have their limitations, and Nietzsche sees the combination of both aesthetics in tragedy as the ideal form of art, a form that best allows us to cope with and affirm life. The beautiful forms acted out in the narrative are energised by the orgiastic power of the chorus; we are both intoxicated with reality and soothed with illusion.

Nietzsche proposes that this artistic wisdom was "corrupted" by the advent of philosophy in ancient Greece, typified by the figure of Socrates. In short, Nietzsche argues that the tragic aesthetic was usurped by the Socratic ideal of reason, which has increasingly dominated Western culture ever since. The irrational forces of the Dionysian, in particular, have been increasingly eclipsed and devalued. From the point of view of life, the problem with the dominance of reason is that it demands that life be rational, and – what is the same thing for Socrates – good. What is most distinctive about tragedy is that "bad things happen" on stage, but are transformed aesthetically: as such, tragedy teaches us how to cope with and even affirm life in full recognition of the suffering it contains. Socratic rationalism, however, denies the reality of the irrational and of suffering, and consequently devalues life as it is lived here and now in the name of "higher ideals" that embody the rational and the good. Nietzsche thus proposes – and this is a central point of all his philosophy – a *"higher" form of pessimism*, which accepts the suffering in life, but, rather than slumping into nihilism, is able to affirm life nevertheless.

For Nietzsche, Socratic rationalism came to dominate Western culture through its alliance with Christianity. (Many early Christians were Greek, and they considered Socrates and Plato "Christians before Christ".) At the heart of this tradition is what he identifies as a kind of "religious nihilism", which centres on the idea that there is a "true" metaphysical world behind the world of our sensory perception. From religious notions such as the kingdom of heaven to philosophical ideas such as Plato's world of the Forms, Nietzsche sees this positing of a metaphysical world other than that in which we live as an essential part of all systems of the highest values in the Western tradition. This "other" world is unanimously posited as superior, as the truth or reality behind this inferior, flawed and illusory world in which we live. In positing this higher world, Nietzsche claims, we are passing sentence on – we are condemning and devaluing – the world in which we live. Nietzsche sees this belief in a metaphysical world as nihilistic because it views the perceptual world as "not good enough"; it devalues our lives here and now in relation to the other-worldly ideal.

In his later works, Nietzsche develops this early criticism of Western culture through the idea that the "highest values" invented with the decline of tragedy begin to break down, threatening the collapse of all values. For Nietzsche, modern thinking has devalued the highest values by destroying the basis on which they ultimately rest. Furthermore, these values have devalued *themselves*. Nietzsche is very specific about the *cause* of nihilism. According to him, the highest values posited by Western man are *all* rooted in, and depend on, the "Christian-moral" interpretation of life. Nietzsche does not see any existing systems of value as independent of this paradigm, including philosophy, science, politics, economics, history and art. According to Nietzsche, *all* the highest values posited by the major traditions of thought throughout Western history have relied on a kind of *deification of nature*. Religion, philosophy and even science have relied on a metaphysical view of the world that is either identical with, or akin to, positing a God who structures and controls the world. Given this, the diagnosis of nihilism as the devaluation of the highest values revolves around Nietzsche's famous dictum, *God is dead*. In the context in which this proclamation appears (i.e. the first part of book three of *The Gay Science*), its meaning is clear: Nietzsche proclaims not just the death of the Christian God (in the sense of the death of *belief in the existence* of God), but the death of all similar metaphysical explanations of life.

In modernity, the highest values have devalued themselves through the *development* of various values, particularly the value of *truth*. Truth is posited as a virtue within the Christian-moral paradigm along with the various other virtues such as goodness, faith, love, charity and so on. Truth is the virtue motivating philosophy, science and the various other endeavours to increase human knowledge. It is an important assumption of both religion and Enlightenment thinking that the virtues they posit are complementary: that the advancement of truth will advance the good of humankind, for example. It is one of Nietzsche's most important contentions that this is, in fact, not the case. The virtues of the Christian-moral paradigm, pushed far enough, are antithetical. In particular, the virtue of truthfulness – the virtue at the heart of the Enlightenment project and of modernist thinking – has uncovered the lies of various other virtues.

Nietzsche has in mind the discoveries made in the pursuit of truth that undermine core Christian beliefs, for example the Copernican revolution in cosmology, which unsettles the belief that the earth, and thus also humankind, is at the centre of (and of central importance in) the universe. Most significantly, the widespread acceptance of the theory of evolution owing to Charles Darwin's research undermines the theory of creation and thereby the necessity of a creator God. Although he engages in a barrage of attacks on science and on doctrines such as rational explanation and cause and effect, we might quite generally say that in Nietzsche's eyes the Enlightenment search for truth that characterizes modern thinking undermines Christian-moral virtues and beliefs (particularly belief in God) by providing an alternative, scientific worldview. This, then, is Nietzsche's diagnosis of nihilism in modernity: the modern quest for truth is undermining belief in God.

Radicalization of nihilism

While probably the vast majority of Europeans still believed in God in Nietzsche's time, many intellectuals and artists repudiated his existence. Nietzsche complained, however, that while they did not believe in God, for the most part they still believed in many of the values of the Christian-moral interpretation. For Nietzsche, the idea of God is the *basis* for all the highest values, and without God, *they cannot exist.* Remove belief in God, and all values should be devalued. Furthermore, it was Nietzsche's practice to look for the underlying *emotional* and *psychological* motivations behind ideas and beliefs and, according to them, to classify these beliefs into types. Thus, the idea of God for Nietzsche was not simply the theistic God, but represented all metaphysical beliefs that give order and meaning to the world. Nietzsche's radicalization of nihilism, then, involves (i) expanding the notion of God's death to the death of all metaphysical beliefs, (ii) *demonstrating* the untenability of these other metaphysical beliefs, and (iii) showing that the devaluation of the posited *other* world (heaven, Plato's Forms, etc.) leads to a necessary devaluation of the values of *this* world (morality, etc.). Most of Nietzsche's works from *Human, All Too Human* (thus, from the beginning of his "middle period") onwards effect at least in part a radicalization of nihilism. Nietzsche conducts this radicalization through methods of philosophical questioning and assertion that undermine the previously held principles and beliefs of both the philosophical tradition and of common culture.

While in *The Birth of Tragedy* Nietzsche effectively hoped that the nihilism of modern culture would be overcome through Wagner's rediscovery of the tragic aesthetic, *Human, All Too Human* marks an abrupt shift. Nietzsche rejects his early romanticism, criticizes art and metaphysics, and embraces reason, science and psychological explanation. In effect, the earlier views he held as a counter to nihilism come to be seen as part of the problem of Western thought and culture that he wishes to attack. The motivations for this radical change in perspective are complex, but at least two decisive influences may be mentioned. First, Nietzsche became disillusioned with Wagner and broke his ties with the composer, believing his music was succumbing to the demands of popular taste, and to nationalism, anti-Semitism and Christianity. Second, Nietzsche came under influence of a new friend, Paul Rée (1849–1901), whose major work *The Origin of the Moral Sensations* ([1877] 2003) explored human psychology in a way that deeply informed Nietzsche's own psychologizing and critique of morality. In a more general way, we may understand Nietzsche's embrace of the scientific spirit in his middle period as motivated by the realization that it contributes to demythologizing the "highest values", and paves the way for a revaluation.

The range of topics attacked by Nietzsche's polemics is far too wide to summarize, so we must content ourselves with listing just a few of his most important, and most repeated, targets.

Morality
Famously, morality is one of Nietzsche's central targets. In many of his writings, and especially in his book *On the Genealogy of Morality* (1887), Nietzsche seeks to undermine current moral values by showing how they have origins that are less than noble. He distinguishes two main types of morality: "master morality" (also called "noble morality") and "slave morality" (or "herd morality").

KEY POINT
- *Master morality*: Masters are the strong types who are able to affirm themselves, cope with the tragic nature of life and legislate their own moral values.
- *Slave morality*: Slaves are the weak types who cannot cope well with suffering, and develop a belief in a moral order of the universe to compensate.

Nietzsche explains the development of slave morality through three basic psychological and existential attitudes, which are also manifestations of an "incomplete" form of nihilism (they allow the slave to live, but only a very diminished or nihilistic form of life). These attitudes begin with an attempt to answer the question, Why do I suffer? First, the slave reacts with *"ressentiment"* (resentment) against the master, and against life itself, blaming them for his or her suffering. Second, the slave may internalize *ressentiment* in a "bad conscience", telling themselves that they suffer because they are a bad person and deserve to suffer. Third, the slave may embrace an "ascetic ideal", depriving himself or herself of pleasure in this life in the belief that he or she will be rewarded in an afterlife. For Nietzsche, Christianity embraces each of these three attitudes. Moreover, because of *ressentiment* against the masters, it tries to diminish their power, and labels master morality "evil". Nietzsche's critique of morality and attempt to move "beyond good and evil" is really a defence of master morality and an attempt to create new moral values, rather than the rejection of all morality as such.

Truth

Nietzsche's relationship to the idea of truth is ambiguous and still hotly debated, but there is no question that he attacked the notion of truth at some points in his writings, and in some respects. One notable point of Nietzsche's deep questioning of "truth" concerns its value for life. Since Socrates, truth has typically been closely associated with the good: what is true has been assumed also to be good for us. At times Nietzsche strongly calls this assumption into question, suggesting that perhaps *untruth* is a condition of life: that it is in fact untruths that enable us to live and which are conducive to happiness. Nietzsche writes:

> We have arranged for ourselves a world in which we are able to live – by positing bodies, lines, planes, causes and effects, motion and rest, form and content; without these articles of faith no one could endure living! But that does not prove them. Life is not an argument; the conditions of life might include error. (GS 121)

The debated issue of Nietzsche's relation to truth will receive some further discussion in Chapter 7.

The "true world"

Complementing Nietzsche's questioning of the epistemological notion of truth is his attack on the metaphysical notion of a "true world". As we saw above, Nietzsche views belief in a "true world" as religious nihilism. He believes that this idea is one of the key ones to be abolished by the scientific search for truth (since, in short, we have not been able to discover any scientific evidence for its existence). With the loss of a grounding for meaning in a "true world", there are two ways in which we might see meaning in the "apparent" world. Nietzsche abolishes them both. The first of these is to posit a kind of cosmic *order*, a network of rules and laws, underlying reality. This is the game of science, philosophy and morality. Nietzsche rejects such an order, asserting that all apparent order in the world is of human creation; it is part of the untruth that allows us to live. For Nietzsche, the world is a chaos of dynamic becoming; there is no static being, no permanent order.

Second, given the view of the world as becoming, one might posit meaning through the idea that becoming has some *goal*. Again, Nietzsche rejects this. He rejects the idea that the world – and humanity – progresses towards some kind of goal, as the dialectical histories of Hegel and Marx, or the Enlightenment project of the emancipation of humanity, suggest. Nietzsche does not see history as progress, writing that "the nineteenth century does not represent progress over the sixteenth ... 'Mankind' does not advance" (WP 90). For Nietzsche, the world of becoming has no goal. He writes, "becoming aims at *nothing* and achieves *nothing*" (WP 12(A)).

In summary, once we have lost our faith in the true world (and this loss of faith is a form of the death of God, the de-deification of Nature), we may try to posit meaning in this world. This is the stage of *partial nihilism*, in which God is dead but morality and other "highest values", ways of positing meaning through order and goals, live on. This is the stage of nihilism diagnosed by Nietzsche in the modernity of the late nineteenth century. *Radical nihilism* follows from the realization that once the true world is abolished, all the values of the apparent world are abolished too. This is because, according to Nietzsche, all notions of order and goal are rooted in and depend on a deification of nature. Kill God, and all the highest values hitherto posited must also perish.

For Nietzsche, nihilism is a lamentable state of weakness and despair. (Sometimes he calls the languishing in despair *passive nihilism*, and opposes it to the *active nihilism* that tries to radicalize the destruction of the highest values and prepare for a revaluation.) However, nihilism is only a transitory, transitional state, and Nietzsche asserts that it can eventually be overcome. But why radicalize nihilism at all? Why not leave nihilism in its partial, more bearable state? The answer to this question is found in Nietzsche's theory of *decadence*: in other words, his critique of modernity. According to Nietzsche, European culture of the late nineteenth century had become decadent. Decadence is Nietzsche's term for *cultural degeneration*; it is a state of sickness and weakness that afflicts society. Decadence itself Nietzsche sees as a consequence of the Christian-moral paradigm; it manifests in religious nihilism, slave morality, *ressentiment*, bad conscience and so on, as we have seen above. In short, then, Nietzsche welcomed the advent of nihilism as a necessary "purge" that would destroy decadence and restore strength, health and vitality to European culture.

Overcoming of nihilism

As well as radicalizing nihilism, Nietzsche provides us with guiding principles for a new valuation, a revaluation of all values that must follow nihilism. These guiding principles include three well-known but gnomic ideas: the will to power, the eternal return and the *Übermensch*. Each of these ideas provides not a new set of values as such, but a new principle that Nietzsche sees as enabling a more life-affirmative interpretation of the world, and a guide to creating our own new values.

The will to power

The will to power is a view of the world and of life. Nietzsche's view is not that the will to power *is* life (he rejects Schopenhauer's view that life is an expression of will; asserting that will is a phenomenon of already-living things only); rather, it is the *will of* life. The will to power is the desire for greater strength, greater abundance; it is the desire for increase and growth. According to Nietzsche the basic desire of life is not for life itself, for mere existence and preservation (for how could what does not live desire life?). The concern for self-preservation, Nietzsche contends, issues from a state of weakness. The state of strength manifests the will to power as a desire for *more* power, *regardless* of preservation. In a truly strong and healthy state, the will to power demands an increase of power regardless of consequences, even if it means death. Nietzsche writes: "To wish to preserve oneself is a sign of distress, of a limitation of the truly basic life-instinct, which aims at *the expansion of power* and in so doing often enough risks and sacrifices self-preservation" (GS 349). The will to power is also manifested as a self-overcoming. Living things seek to become greater than they are; again, to extend, grow, increase. Nietzsche has Zarathustra proclaim, "this secret life itself spoke to me: 'Behold,' it said, 'I am that *which must always overcome itself*'". For Nietzsche, the will to power is the fundamental drive of all life. Zarathustra further declares: "Wherever I found the living, there I found the will to power" (Z: 2 "Of Self-overcoming").

Arguably, the will to power can be given a strongly fascistic interpretation, and it was certainly one of the elements of Nietzsche's philosophy that was appropriated by Nazism. We might see the German invasions of other European countries under the Nazi regime – and, indeed, imperialism and colonialism quite generally – as manifestations of the will to power. Certainly they are movements of growth and expansion. Nietzsche seems to lend support to this interpretation in passages such as *Beyond Good and Evil* 259, where he asserts that life itself is necessarily a process of appropriation, injury and overpowering of the weaker.

More recently, however, influential interpretations of Nietzsche have tended to focus on the will to power as self-overcoming rather than as exploitation, domination and intolerance. Furthermore, it is significant that Nietzsche considered the *worst* crimes to issue from states of weakness, rather than states of strength and abundance. We might suggest, then, that it is the *frustrated* will to power that actually *seeks* harm to others as a last recourse to any kind of power; the strong, healthy, abundant will to power merely demands increase, and is indifferent to the effects of such increase.

The will to power, as a view of life and the world, provides Nietzsche with the basis for a new valuation, a new criterion for determining values. This criterion is neatly expressed as follows:

> What is good? – Everything that enhances people's feeling of power, will to power, power itself.
> What is bad? – Everything stemming from weakness.
> What is happiness? – The feeling that power is *growing*, that some resistance has been overcome. (A 2)

Nietzsche's idea of the will to power has a further important dimension: it is a metaphysical theory – a description of the most fundamental nature of reality. In this sense, the will to power describes the world according to a quasi-atomic theory, in which the fundamental unity of reality is a centre of force, which strives to expand itself outwards (to increase its power). In doing so, it comes into contact with other forces, with which it struggles for domination or forms alliances. The will to power describes the world as constituted, at a fundamental level, of a multitude of competing forces; the seemingly stable objects in the world (including ourselves) are products of the temporary alliances of forces. This is an immanent theory of the world as one of constant becoming, thus providing an alternative to the metaphysics of transcendent being: it explains how things come to be in the world through processes of change, without having to appeal to another world in which things supposedly have their origin in fixed designs. (The physics of the will to power is taken up in more detail in Chapter 7.)

The eternal return

Nietzsche's idea of the eternal return (or eternal recurrence of the same, as it is sometimes called) is that every event that has ever happened, and will ever happen, is repeated eternally. From an individual point of view, this means that everything that happens in one's life has already happened and will happen again *exactly the same*, down to the minutest detail, again and again, *ad infinitum*. Nietzsche seemed to believe that this is an actual fact about the universe: a conclusion that could be drawn from certain principles of physics. The eternal recurrence as an actual physical fact is based on the assumptions of infinite time, finite matter and the law of conservation of energy. Given that these assumptions are true, Nietzsche believes, the eternal recurrence can be proved. Nietzsche argues that in an infinite amount of time, a finite amount of matter must arrange itself in the same patterns an infinite number of times. Thus, the physical circumstances of which our lives consist must reoccur in exactly the same way an infinite number of times. Nietzsche expresses the physical aspect of the eternal recurrence as follows:

> If the world may be thought of as a certain definite quantity of force and as a certain definite number of centers of force – and every other representation remains indefinite and therefore useless – it follows that, in the great dice game of existence, it must pass through a calculable number of combinations. In infinite time, every possible combination would at some time or another be realized; more: it would be realized an infinite number of times. (WP 1066)

It is relatively uncontroversial that Nietzsche is wrong if he believes the eternal recurrence to be a physical fact on the basis of this argument. (See Chapter 7 for further discussion of the physics of the eternal return.) However, the physical actuality of the eternal return is arguably not of prime importance. The importance lies in the *experience* of the idea, and the existential consequences such an experience may have. Nietzsche poses the question:

> What if some day or night a demon were to steal into your loneliest loneliness and say to you: "This life as you now live it and have lived it you will have to live once again and innumerable times again: and there will be nothing new in it, but every pain and every joy and every thought and sigh and everything unspeakably small or great in your life must return to you, all in the same succession and sequence .... (GS 341)

The eternal return is a kind of thought experiment that acts as a *catalyst* for nihilism. The idea itself is the most extreme form of nihilism;

it is Nietzsche's most extreme *radicalization* of nihilism; it is a vision of absolute meaninglessness; an eternal return of events without aim and without end. According to Nietzsche, this is potentially the most paralysing of ideas. It is an idea that might crush one: that might force one to succumb to the abyss of meaninglessness.

KEY POINT *The eternal return*
The eternal return is the idea that time is cyclical, and everything that has happened will happen again an infinite number of times. It has at least two significant meanings in Nietzsche's thought. First, it is a quasi-scientific theory about the real nature of time. Second, it is an existential "thought experiment".

The eternal return is an idea that one might also endure. But in order to endure it, Nietzsche believes that one must overcome nihilism by the revaluation of values. The eternal return teaches another principle of this new valuation: *amor fati*, the love of fate. Nietzsche acknowledges the inescapable pain of life, a fact that the eternal return forces us to confront. How do we react to the idea of having to experience this suffering again and again and again, infinitely? The only way to bear it, Nietzsche asserts, is to affirm it. For Nietzsche, the pain of life is inseparable from its joy. It is the natural tendency of joy to want more of itself; it is easy to affirm joy, to want it again. But if we want the joy again, then we *must* affirm the pain and suffering, for they are inalienable from joy. This is what the eternal recurrence teaches the strong: the affirmation of life, including its suffering. In this way, one overcomes *ressentiment*: the resentment against the inadequacies of life that motivate the positing of God, the "true world", morality and all the bases for the old values. The eternal return is also a motivation to take responsibility for our experiences: to make every event of our lives such that we can affirm its eternal return.

There is also an important sense in which the eternal return is an alternative theory of time to that which dominates in Christianity, in which life is given a meaning indexed on an end point in historical time (the Last Judgement, in which each of us will be either rewarded or punished for the way we chose to live our lives). This Christian view of time is well expressed by a minister in James Joyce's *A Portrait of the Artist as a Young Man*: "Time is, time was, but time shall be no more" (1993: 366). Nietzsche rejects this view of time because it underpins an illusory meaning of life and, worse, a life-negating morality (the ascetic ideal). He replaces it with the challenge of the eternal return, in which time itself must be affirmed without finding any meaning in an end point or goal: time is, time over again.

The Übermensch

Nietzsche's term "*Übermensch*" has been variously translated as "superman", "overman" and "overhuman" but, owing to the potential misunderstandings these terms invite, many contemporary commentators prefer to leave the term untranslated. Consistent with his view of modernity as decadent, Nietzsche insists that modern man, too, is inadequate. He asserts that mankind should not be preserved, but should be *overcome*. He posits a higher type of human: the *Übermensch*. Nietzsche's *Übermensch* is a superior type who will come in the future; present mankind is a bridge between animal and *Übermensch*. Nietzsche writes, "Mankind is a rope fastened between animal and overman – a rope over an abyss" (Z "Prologue" 1). Supposedly, man will be to the *Übermensch* as the animal is to man. The *Übermensch* is no Darwinistic idea of necessary biological evolution, however. Rather, the *Übermensch* must be consciously *willed* into existence by mankind; we must make of ourselves deliberate bridges to the *Übermensch*. (For further discussion of the *Übermensch* and evolution, see Chapter 7.)

So what is the *Übermensch*? Essentially, the *Übermensch* is an affirmer and creator. He or she is one who has survived nihilism, has affirmed life (together with suffering) at the ultimate level demanded by the eternal return and expresses his or her will to power through *the active creation of values*. The *Übermensch* is one who legislates values and creates a view of the world through active interpretation. Furthermore, the *Übermensch* creates *himself or herself*. Nietzsche does not believe that there is some pre-given, unitary self that can simply be an object of knowledge, as the Greek dictum "Know thyself!" suggests. Rather, Nietzsche proclaims "*Will a self*" (AOM 366): we must *become* who we are through *self-creation*. Nietzsche insists that we must, in a sense, form ourselves as an artist forms a work of art. He writes, "*One thing is needful. – To 'give style' to one's character – a great and rare art!*" (GS 290). He writes of forming the character by removing parts of one's original nature, adding aspects of second nature, concealing the ugly where it cannot be removed and accentuating the beautiful, all through "long practice and daily work at it" (*ibid.*).

Nietzsche does not believe that any examples of the *Übermensch* fully realized have yet existed. (He certainly does not claim that he himself is an *Übermensch*). However, he believes that certain cultures have given birth *by accident* to certain *higher types*, which, although not *Übermenschen*, are suggestive of what types may come in the future. Among Nietzsche's examples of higher types are Alcibiades, Cesare Borgia, Napoleon, the Hohenstaufen Friedrich II, Leonardo da Vinci, Goethe and Jesus Christ. All these men have been, according to Nietzsche, powerful creators of themselves, of values and of influential interpretations of the world.

Nietzsche's conception of the *Übermensch* seems to be quite elitist. While at times he seems to suggest that the *Übermenschen* will replace humanity as we know it today, at others he insists that greatness is only meant for the few: that the higher types will be few in number and will legislate values for "the herd". He writes: "I teach: that there are higher and lower men, and that a single individual can under certain circumstances justify the existence of whole millennia – that is, a full, rich, great, whole human being in relation to countless incomplete fragmentary men" (WP 997). Moreover, Nietzsche clearly states that the "lower men" must play a politically subordinate role: "in the absence of spiritual greatness, independence ought not to be allowed, it causes mischief, even through its desire to do good and practice 'justice.' Small spirits must *obey* – hence cannot possess *greatness*" (WP 984). If the elitist interpretation of Nietzsche's *Übermensch* is right, then we must consider his whole story of nihilism from an elitist point of view; it is only the select few who will suffer the trials of nihilism, survive and create values. The masses of society – "the herd" – will be saved from nihilism because they will believe in the values the *Übermenschen* (or the *higher types*, at least) will have created. (The question of Nietzsche's elitism, and his politics in general, is pursued in Chapter 3.)

For Nietzsche, "Not 'mankind' but *overman* is the goal!" (WP 1001). It is questionable, however, whether Nietzsche considers it an achievable goal. The point may be simply that it is a *constant* goal. On this interpretation, it is the striving towards greatness itself that makes great. This interpretation is supported by Nietzsche's view of the universe as a constant becoming, without a static end point. It also makes sense in terms of the will to power: the *Übermensch*, like all life, is a constant self-overcoming, a constant striving for growth and ever more abundance. As a principle for the revaluation of values, then, Nietzsche's ideal of the *Übermensch* teaches self-creation, the creation of values and the creative interpretation of the world, and sets up the creative self as a goal not to be finally achieved, but towards which to be constantly striving.

> **KEY POINT** *The* Übermensch
> The "superman", "overman" or "overhuman" is a higher type of human being who is able to affirm the tragic nature of existence, master himself or herself and create new values.

In summary, Nietzsche tells a story about nihilism that begins with a diagnosis of the seeds of nihilism (partial nihilism) in modernity, proceeds through a prognosis of radical nihilism in the course of the two centuries to come – a course that Nietzsche himself spurs on with his "nihilistic" observations and arguments – and ends in the overcoming of nihilism, which is outlined by several guiding principles. Nihilism, for Nietzsche, is the radical repudiation of meaning and value brought about by the death of God. Radical nihilism is the realization that without God, none of the highest values hitherto posited hold; morality and all forms of the deification of nature disappear. There is no reason to believe in a "true world", and the "apparent world" is seen to be without order or goal. For Nietzsche, nihilism is a necessary step in the development of both the individual and society. For Nietzsche it is an opportunity to eradicate the *decadence* that he sees as characterizing modernity through the influence of the Christian-moral worldview. Nietzsche provides three broad principles for the overcoming of nihilism. The will to power supplies a yes and a no: yes to all that is strong, expansive and powerful; no to that which is weak and reactive, that which diminishes power. The eternal return is a test that demands a radical affirmation of life in order to be endured; it teaches us to love even suffering, and to act so that we *may* affirm life. The *Übermensch* is a goal for us to strive towards, and it teaches us that in the very face of nihilism we must actively create ourselves and our values.

The advent of Nietzscheanism

Nietzsche remained relatively unknown within his sane lifetime. His books, some of which he self-published, sold few copies and had few readers. Perhaps some of the hyperbole of his writing style can be attributed to the frustration of a man who felt he had deeply important things to say, but to whom no one was listening. In any case, things took a dramatic turn around the time of Nietzsche's break with sanity, and within a few decades he was arguably the most famous and influential writer in Europe, whose influence extended across the globe. The first use of the term "Nietzschean" was probably by Herman Conradi in his 1887 novel *Phrasen*, where he speaks of "we Nietzscheans" (Diethe 2006: xxii). Now, the term can be used to cover a vast array of thinkers who have in some sense embraced Nietzsche, or followed in his footsteps.

In 1888, the literary scholar Georg Brandes gave the first lectures on Nietzsche's work, in Copenhagen. Brandes then published an important article on Nietzsche, "Aristokratismus Radikaler", in 1890. This article is often cited as the beginning of Nietzscheanism in Germany, as it ushered Nietzsche into mainstream intellectual discussion (*ibid.*: xxii–xxiii). While the prevailing tone was enthusiastic, Nietzsche also had his detractors in these early days of fame, the most notable example being Max Nordau in his *Degeneration* (1893). Another critical work worth mentioning if only for its wonderfully unambiguous title was Hermann Türk's *Nietzsche and His Pathologically Wrong Paths* (1891). Nietzsche's sister Elisabeth Förster-Nietzsche was an opportunistic anti-Semite and, following Nietzsche's breakdown, she dedicated herself to using her brother's work and growing reputation to further her own racist, nationalist agenda. In 1892, she began to publish the first collected edition of Nietzsche's works, edited with Peter Gast. In 1894, she replaced Gast with Fritz Koegel as editor of this collected edition, known as the *Grossoktavausgabe*. In the same year, Lou Salomé published a book on Nietzsche (Salomé 2001), and Elisabeth set up the Nietzsche Archive in Naumburg. In 1896, Elisabeth moved the archive (and a year later, Nietzsche himself, who she sometimes displayed in his stupefied state to visitors) to Weimar, where it remains today.

It is now very well known that Elisabeth edited her brother's works to suit her interests (notably omitting comments against anti-Semitism and German nationalism, as well as at least one personal slight against her). The most infamous, influential and controversial product of her editorial efforts is the volume *The Will to Power*, a collection of Nietzsche's unpublished notes placed out of chronological order and thematically grouped according to Elisabeth's vision of her brother's work. The book first appeared in 1901, and a much expanded edition was published in 1906. *The Will to Power* powerfully influenced the reception of Nietzsche's works because of Elisabeth's portrayal of it as Nietzsche's *magnum opus*, the summation of his most important thought, despite its incomplete character. It has divided Nietzsche interpreters, some (such as Heidegger) using the posthumous material almost exclusively, some using the published and unpublished material indifferently, and some insisting that anything he did not himself select for publication should be entirely bracketed from Nietzsche interpretation. (Nietzsche's posthumous notes are now available in a much less distorted form in the Colli–Montinari edition of Nietzsche's complete works, and some of the material from *The Will to Power* is published with greater fidelity to its original form in English translation in *Writings from the Late Notebooks* [LN]).

Much of the early reception of Nietzsche took place among artists and writers, and in what can broadly be termed the "cultural scene". For the first decades of the twentieth century, Nietzsche was understood more as a poet, mystic and visionary than as an academically respectable philosopher. He influenced practically all of the early-twentieth-century avant-garde and modernist art movements, but notable admirers include the writers August Strindberg, André Gide, Thomas Mann and Hermann Hesse, the poet Stefan George and his "Circle", the composers Richard Strauss and Gustav Mahler, and the dancers Vaslav Nijinsky, Isadora Duncan and Mary Wigman. Despite this undeniably important dimension of Nietzscheanism, in keeping with the prevailing tone of the series of which this book is a part, our scope here is restricted to the primarily *academic* disciplines and movements that Nietzsche has influenced. I refer the reader interested in Nietzsche's influence on literature to John Burt Foster's *Heirs to Dionysus* (1981). For a broad survey of literary, artistic and cultural Nietzscheanism generally, see Carol Diethe's *Historical Dictionary of Nietzscheanism* (2006). Another notable area of Nietzsche's influence that I have unfortunately not been able to cover here is psychotherapy. Nietzsche was of great interest to each of the three founding figures of psychoanalysis, Sigmund Freud, C. G. Jung and Alfred Adler, and has also been important for the tradition of existential psychotherapy. I refer the reader interested in exploring this area to the volume of essays *Nietzsche and Depth Psychology* (Golomb *et al.* 1999), and to the more specific comparative study *Freud and Nietzsche* (Assoun 2006).

Until 1900, much of the attention given to Nietzsche focused on his biography and the literary value of his work (both his madness and his writing – and perhaps the curious combination of the two – seems to have exerted a peculiar fascination). Elisabeth Förster-Nietzsche was again influential in this respect, publishing a three-volume biography of her brother between 1895 and 1904. In the first decade of the twentieth century, however, numerous books appeared attempting to give a comprehensive survey of his thought (Vattimo 2001: 170). These works began to take Nietzsche's philosophical thought more seriously, and often compared him with major philosophers, such as

Kant. Notable works in this period include Hans Vaihinger's *Nietzsche as Philosopher* (1902), Arthur Drews's *Nietzsche's Philosophy* (1904) and Georg Simmel's *Schopenhauer and Nietzsche* ([1907] 1991). Nietzsche also exerted a widespread cultural influence in Germany in the early twentieth century, and was adopted by a diverse range of interest groups, including nationalists, vegetarians and naturists. Notably, from his earliest reception, Nietzsche was enthusiastically read and endorsed by representatives of both the far right and the far left of the political spectrum.

A popular story has it that by the First World War, Nietzsche was considered such an important figure of German culture that a copy of his book *Thus Spoke Zarathustra* was included in every soldier's rucksack. While, as Diethe (2006: xxvii) reports, this story is not true, cheap editions of the book were made widely available. The most important book on Nietzsche to be published between the two world wars was Ernst Bertram's *Nietzsche: Attempt at a Mythology* ([1918] 2009). This work portrayed Nietzsche as responding to a particular problem: how to unify a nation's people in the horizon of religion's decline. Bertram understands Nietzsche as attempting to create a new mythology to fulfil this task. Moreover, he self-consciously creates a mythologized version of Nietzsche himself, a version that "would make Nietzsche a mirror of the German soul, its suffering, its upsurges, its creative power, and its destiny" (Safranski 2003: 331). This highly influential interpretation of Nietzsche positioned him firmly in the tradition of right-wing romantic nationalism, and paved the way for his infamous adoption by National Socialist ideologues in the 1930s. The most important "Nazi interpretation" of Nietzsche was Alfred Baeumler's *Nietzsche, der Philosoph und Politiker* (Nietzsche, the philosopher and politician) (1931). Elisabeth famously presented Hitler with her brother's walking stick during his visit to the Nietzsche Archive, and during this period Nietzsche's name became tarred with the brush of Nazism. Quite quickly, however, some important scholars began to defend Nietzsche from the Nazi interpretation, and in doing so developed what would become highly influential interpretations of Nietzsche's thought, the influence of which would extend from the Second World War to today. These interpreters included Martin Heidegger, Karl Jaspers and Karl Löwith in Germany, and Georges Bataille in France.

While we shall sometimes have occasion to return to late-nineteenth- and early-twentieth-century Nietzscheanism, for the most part the chapters that follow will take up the story of Nietzscheanism from the mid-1930s, when the important interpretations by Heidegger, Jaspers and Löwith began to establish Nietzsche as a philosophically respectable figure. It is these later works, which have in general removed the romantic, nationalistic and mythological resonances that deeply inflected many of the earliest strands of Nietzscheanism, that remain most influential, and of most relevance to the contemporary student of Nietzscheanism.

During the Winter of 1880–81, Nietzsche lived and worked in Genoa, the birthplace of Christopher Columbus. He imagined himself as a second Columbus: an explorer of the mind and the spirit rather than of the external world (Safranski 2003: 206, 219). While Kant famously imagined reason as an island from which we should not venture, Nietzsche can be seen as setting out to explore the surrounding seas (*ibid.*: 350). We can imagine his voluminous and heterogenous writings as reports of his discoveries, indicating that we are not, after all, living on a lonely island, but are situated rather in a vast archipelago. "Nietzscheanism" consists of all the attempts that have been made, and might yet be made, to follow Nietzsche to the mysterious islands he discovered, many of which remain to be explored. This book may be understood as a kind of map, the chapters of which chart some of the most prominent islands in the Nietzschean archipelago to which some explorers in the realms of thought have followed him, and have begun to chart.

one

Nietzscheanism and existentialism

> As we thus reject Christian interpretation and condemn its "meaning" as counterfeit, *Schopenhauer's* question immediately comes at us in a terrifying way: *Does existence have any meaning at all?* A few centuries will be needed before this question can ever be heard completely and in its full depth.
>
> (GS 357)

Existentialism is one of the most widely known forms of philosophy outside the academic world. While now frequently considered passé, it enjoyed a great deal of popularity in the middle decades of the twentieth century. Moreover, it remains one of the intellectual and cultural trends with which Nietzsche's name is often associated in the popular imagination. The accuracy and usefulness of characterizing Nietzsche as an existentialist is now a matter of debate, and some contemporary Nietzsche scholars would prefer this association to be forgotten (for further discussion of this point, see Ansell-Pearson [2011]). Nevertheless, there is no doubt that in an important chapter of Nietzsche's reception and influence, he was understood as an existentialist, or at least an important precursor to existentialism. In a work entitled *Reason and Existence*, for example, the German existentialist philosopher Karl Jaspers (1883–1969) identifies Nietzsche (alongside Kierkegaard) as one of the original existential thinkers:

> The contemporary philosophical situation is determined by the fact that two philosophers, Kierkegaard and Nietzsche, who

did not count in their times and, for a long time, remained without influence in the history of philosophy, have continually grown in significance.   (Jaspers 1955: 23)

Similarly, the American philosopher Walter Kaufmann argues that "In the story of existentialism, Nietzsche occupies a central place: Jaspers, Heidegger, and Sartre are unthinkable without him, and the conclusion of Camus' *The Myth of Sisyphus* sounds like a distant echo of Nietzsche" (1975: 21). These examples index the fact that in the period following the Second World War, the image of Nietzsche as a proto-existentialist dominated in both continental European and Anglo-American scholarship. Moreover, the impact of Nietzsche's thought on twentieth-century existentialist philosophers means that, in many of its forms at least, existentialism was a form of Nietzscheanism: one of the most influential forms of Nietzscheanism of the last century.

In this chapter, we shall trace the reception of Nietzsche as an existential thinker, framing the existentialist interpretations of his work with precursors and successors to that movement. First, we shall consider Nietzsche's deep influence on two important trends in German philosophy that pre-dated existentialism: life-philosophy and value-theory. We shall then introduce existentialism as such, and examine Jaspers's reading of Nietzsche. Following this we shall consider Nietzsche's influence on French existentialism, focusing on the presence of Nietzsche in the thought of Jean-Paul Sartre and of Albert Camus. Then, we shall consider the Anglo-American reception of Nietzsche as an existentialist through the works of Kaufmann, his most important post-war translator and interpreter. We shall then summarize the rationale for positioning Nietzsche as an existentialist, before concluding the chapter with an outline of Heidegger's Nietzsche interpretation. While Heidegger holds an important place in existentialist thought because of his early work, his Nietzsche interpretation coincides with his turn away from existentialist themes, and lays the foundation for post-existentialist readings of Nietzsche.

Before existentialism: life-philosophy and value-theory

Before Nietzsche became widely associated with existentialism, in Germany his work was extremely influential in two movements that can be understood as precursors to existentialism: life-philosophy (*Lebensphilosophie*) and value-theory. These movements and the philosophers primarily associated with them are not usually included in histories of existentialism, and most of the twentieth-century existentialists were not directly influenced by them. However, they deserve a brief mention here because some of the central themes in Nietzsche's works that were taken up by the existentialists first found an audience with the life-philosophers and value-theorists. Thus, rather than having any direct line of influence, life-philosophy and value-theory may be considered precursors to existentialism because of their common source in certain Nietzschean themes, and their common impulse to respond to particular needs and problems.

While little known today, life-philosophy was the dominant trend in German philosophy (as well as culture more broadly) between roughly 1870 and 1930. Its origins can be traced back to critical reactions to the Enlightenment in the works of philosophers such as J. G. Hamann (1730–88) and J. G. Herder (1744–1803), and movements such as "Storm and Stress" (*Sturm und Drang*; late 1760s to early 1780s) and German Romanticism (late eighteenth and early nineteenth centuries) (Gaiger 1998: 488). According to Herbert Schnädelbach (1984), however, the history of life-philosophy proper only began with the late works of F. W. J. Schelling (1775–1854), in which the principle of "life" is opposed to the principles of philosophical idealism (typified most famously by the philosophy of G. W. F. Hegel [1770–1831]). Its most important "fathers" were then Arthur Schopenhauer (1788–1860), French philosopher Henri Bergson (1859–1941) and Nietzsche.

What, then, *is* life-philosophy? In a very general sense, life-philosophy is "a philosophy which asks after the meaning, value, and purpose of life" (Gaiger 1998: 487). More specifically, however, life-philosophy turns "life" into a foundational and all-encompassing principle, and understands this principle as something fundamentally irrational: life is thus opposed to rationality. (This is why Schnädelbach identifies its origin with Schelling's opposition of life to idealism; since philosophical idealism elevates reason.) Accordingly, life-philosophy rejects theoretical abstractions, giving preference to a philosophy of feelings and intuitions. Moreover, as Schnädelbach (1984: 141) further suggests, life itself is understood in a metaphysical sense by the life-philosophers, so life-philosophy may be defined as a *metaphysics of the irrational*. Life-philosophy is associated with a movement in biological science known as "vitalism", which opposed purely mechanistic understandings of life (the idea that living beings are just complex arrangements of inorganic matter) by asserting that there is something unique that living beings possess: a "life force". (Notable proponents of vitalism included the embryologist Hans Driesch [1867–1941] and Bergson.) Life-philosophy privileges a metaphysics of life based on a biological model rather than the model of physics, and this biological or organic model is extended to all forms of life (for example, the author of the hugely influential book *The Decline of the West* [1932], Oswald Spengler [1880–1936], understood human societies as organisms with a life cycle of growth and decline).

Finally, and perhaps most significantly, life-philosophy construed "life" as the ultimate normative criterion for making any and all types of judgement, whether concerning knowledge, aesthetics, ethics or politics. Life-philosophers typically developed systems of evaluative oppositions, opposing life to death, growth to decay, dynamism to stasis and so on. In short, the *healthy*, that which enhances life and is identified with the true and the good, is opposed to the *sick*, that which diminishes life and is identified with falsity and evil. Schnädelbach notes that for most, if not all, life-philosophers, this normative antithesis inclines towards "a glorification of the healthy and the strong, of force and of man as a robber-beast" (1984: 145). These normative antitheses were often deployed as the basis for a cultural critique, allowing aspects of culture to be criticized as sick or decadent, others to be praised as life-enhancing, and allowing an overall political programme of cultural renewal or regeneration in the name of eliminating sickness and promoting health (a programme realized in numerous ways both culturally and philosophically in this period in Germany, from nudism to National Socialism).

Nietzsche was an essential reference and inspiration for life-philosophy for a number of reasons. First, he can be credited with introducing life as an ultimate criterion for all judgements and values. Already in his first book, *The Birth of Tragedy*, the central problems are posed as the respective values of knowledge and art *from the point of view of life*. In a later commentary, he identifies one of its main novelties, the identification of Socratic rationalism, as the introduction of decadence into Hellenic culture: "'Rationality' *against* instinct. 'Rationality' at any price as dangerous, as a force undermining life!" (EH "The Birth of Tragedy" 1). Throughout his works, life acts as a criterion for his evaluations of historicism, culture, morality, religion and so on. Nietzsche is particularly notable in this regard for placing truth and knowledge in the service of life, for questioning their value from the perspective of life and for defending error over truth if it is life enhancing. Moreover, Nietzsche often associates that which is life enhancing with the irrational: the body, the unconscious, the emotions, music and art, states of intoxication and so on. Moreover, he analyses the way rationality and consciousness can turn against life, stifling it in rigid metaphysical and moral categories, and negating its value through the belief in a superior world of rational Ideas (as with Platonism). Nietzsche is also responsible for introducing the normative antithesis between the healthy and the sick or decadent central to life-philosophy (although, arguably, this distinction is far more subtle in Nietzsche than it was for most of the life-philosophers). Nietzsche employed these criteria for a full-scale critique of culture, and he was interpreted by some life-philosophers (e.g. Wilhelm Dilthey [1833–1911]) as essentially a cultural critic rather than a philosopher. Finally, Nietzsche associated dynamism with life and stasis with death, and his doctrine of the will to power could be understood as a dynamic and irrational metaphysics of life.

Many of the important currents of twentieth-century continental philosophy have engaged in a critique of rationalism in a way that seems indebted to life-philosophy, even if unconsciously. We can sum up what is essential to life-philosophy by noting, with Schnädelbach, the nature of this debt:

> [S]ubject and object, consciousness and what it is conscious of, are themselves seen as derivative and grounded in an ante-cedent whole, which it is possible to ascertain only by means of intuition. Pre- and non-objective lived experience, moods, the neutrality of what is experienced are supposed to precede all objectivity; analysis, dichotomisation, the hiatus between intuition and concept – all are supposed to come about only by means of secondary exposition of that whole, which up until Heidegger was called "life". (1984: 147)

Despite its one-time prominence, and more recent philosophy's unconscious debt, life-philosophy declined to the point where it is today all but forgotten, for two main reasons. First, many of the streams of life-philosophy (both philosophical and cultural) fed into the disaster that was National Socialism. In particular, the combination of biologism and cultural criticism centring on the antithesis of the healthy and the sick paved the way for a racist politics that could justify exterminating Jews, gypsies, invalids and so on, in the name of "cultural hygiene". Consequently, life-philosophy, and particularly its biologistic and critical-cultural tendencies, were suppressed and forgotten with the post-Second World War de-Nazification of Germany. (Nietzsche's relation to National Socialism will be further considered in Chapter 3.) Second, the more general impulses towards developing a philosophy that seeks out the value and meaning of life were taken up in existential-ism, which thereby superseded life-philosophy. (This will be taken up shortly in the following section.)

Value-theory can be treated more briefly, since while it was inspired by Nietzsche's rhetoric of nihilism and the "revaluation of all values", the primary proponents of value-theory were themselves far more influ-enced by philosophers such as Kant and Hegel than by Nietzsche's own approach to the problem of values. The term "value" was taken over from political economy (where it referred to the monetary value of goods, etc.) by Rudolf Hermann Lotze (1817–81) in the 1840s. However, it was Nietzsche's work that gave rise to the prominence of this concept in philosophy. For Nietzsche, nihilism – the decadence of the current age – can by understood as a crisis of values, brought about by the fact that *"the highest values devaluate themselves"* (WP 2). Briefly put, for Nietzsche the highest values so far posited in Western culture consisted of a combination of belief in a transcendent metaphysical world (Plato's world of the Forms, etc.) and "slave" morality, a combination he some-times referred to with the shorthand expression, the "Christian-moral interpretation". One of the key values of the Christian-moral interpreta-tion is truth, but Nietzsche believed that in his own era the pursuit of the value of truth had undermined the Christian-moral interpretation itself because it had revealed that we have no sound reason for believing in the existence of the true world. This results in nihilism because it is no longer possible to believe in anything. Thus, he calls for a revaluation of all values to renew culture by placing our values on a firmer footing.

Following Nietzsche, many philosophers tried to find a new founda-tion for values. Lotze's own value-theory is a form of idealism, in which values (what *ought* to be the case) have an ideal existence above and beyond the "real" existence of the universe as examined by science in terms of mechanistic materialism. This position is indebted to (although distinguished from) the idealism of Plato and Hegel. Transcendental philosophies of value, exemplified by the works of Wilhelm Windelband (1848–1915) and Heinrich Rickert (1863–1936) were a form of neo-Kantianism that attempted to ground values by examining the sub-jective conditions necessary for objective values to be posited. A final important school of value-theory, the phenomenological, sought to use Edmund Husserl's phenomenological method (a rigorous examination of consciousness) to isolate the essences of values and arrange them hierarchically. The most important representatives of the phenomeno-logical philosophy of values were Max Scheler (1874–1928) and Nicolai Hartmann (1882–1950). Arguably, although inspired by Nietzsche, none of the major proponents of value-theory followed his own radical views on value. The value-theorists all wanted to ground values as *objective*, as more than things posited by subjective, willing individuals. As we shall see, it was this far more subjective approach to values that was taken up by the existentialists.

The philosophy of existence

As mentioned above, one of the reasons that life-philosophy disappeared in Germany was that its impulse towards an authentic form of life was taken up in a more profound way by existentialism. This transition is marked explicitly in Fritz Heinemann's book *New Paths in Philosophy* (*Neue Wege der Philosophie*; 1929). Heinemann later contended that here he was the first to use the term "philosophy of existence" (*Existenzphilosophie*), the original term used to refer to what became known as existentialism. Heinemann argued that the philosophy of existence went beyond life-philosophy by integrating within the concept of "existence" the antitheses of "life" and "reason" (see Schnädelbach 1984: 157). Thus, the philosophy of existence continued the impulse towards life, but was not so radically opposed to rationality as was life-philosophy. (It should be noted, however, that *some* philosophers generally now classified as existentialists are in fact strongly anti-rationalist.) The term "philosophy of existence" was used explicitly by philosophers such as Jaspers and Gabriel Marcel (1889–1973). Later, the term "existentialism" was adopted by philosophers such as Jean-Paul Sartre (1905–80), Simone de Beauvoir (1908–86) and Maurice Merleau-Ponty (1908–61), and applied to others who did not accept this description themselves, most notably, Albert Camus (1913–60) and Martin Heidegger (1889–1976).

Like life-philosophy, the origins of existentialism (or the philosophy of existence) can be traced back to the late works of Schelling, and the critical reaction to idealism they contain. Schelling developed an original interpretation of the philosophical concept "existence", which was taken over by the Danish philosopher and theological writer Søren Kierkegaard (1813–55), generally regarded as the first existentialist. Kierkegaard reacted critically to Hegel's absolute idealism, defending the individual from what he saw as the individual's negation in a totalizing system, and defending the value of personal subjective faith against the hegemony of reason. The second primary nineteenth-century philosopher often regarded as an existentialist, and a forefather to twentieth-century to existentialism, is Nietzsche. We shall examine Nietzsche's own "existentialist credentials" in a later section of this chapter. For now, before examining how Nietzsche was interpreted by twentieth-century existentialists, and how his own philosophy may be interpreted as existentialist, it will be useful to summarize existentialism according to its main themes.

Of course, "existentialism" is only a very general concept used to group a number of diverse thinkers and philosophies with certain themes in common. If we wanted to express the heart of existentialism concisely, we could perhaps say that it is that philosophy that is centrally concerned with *the existing individual, standing alone in the face of a meaningless universe*. To elaborate existentialist themes further, we can organize them around three main points: how existentialism sees the world, how it sees the self and what it sees as the correct way of thinking and writing about existential issues. First, the central point to be made about the existentialist view of the world is that it is objectively meaningless. Meanings and values are not given by the world or by anything outside humankind. This meaninglessness, and the predicament of humanity in facing a meaningless world, is what existentialists mean by *absurdity*. In this, existentialists rebel against the tendencies in traditional philosophy to posit meaning in the objective structures of the world or in transcendent ideas such as God or Platonic Forms. Second, existentialism places a certain conception of the self at the heart of its philosophy. Importantly, for existentialist philosophers the word "existence" has a narrower meaning than it has had in traditional philosophy. Traditionally, *existence* has been opposed to *essence*. Essence has been understood as "whatness" (*quidditas*): what a thing is as opposed to other things. Existence has meant the very fact of being: simply *that* a thing is ("thatness"). As such, the term "existence" could be said to apply to anything that has being, or exists. For existentialists, however, existence means only *human* existence. Human beings are thought to exist in a way that is completely different from, and perhaps at odds with, the ways that inanimate objects and less conscious animals have being.

Given this focus on human existence, existential philosophy places central importance on "the subject" (roughly, the philosophical name for our self-consciousness). The existentialist subject, however, must be distinguished from the Cartesian subject as "thinking thing". The existentialist subject is not reduced to rational thought, but encompasses the entire range of human faculties and experiences, including emotions, sensations, and the body (though not in a scientific, biological sense). Furthermore, a central focus of the subject in existentialism is on *agency*; the ability of the human being to make choices and act freely. Given the existentialist view of the world as objectively meaningless, the human subject is held to be the sole source of meaning and value. This focus on the human realm as constitutive of meaning defines existentialism as a form of humanism (albeit a limited one, since it denies humanity a fixed essence), and in this way can also be seen as a radical extension of the Enlightenment desire to reject all claims to an authority beyond humanity and place man in a central position in the world. Finally, existentialism focuses almost exclusively on the individual in their personal experience of existence, which is considered to be particular and unique (see Oaklander 1992: ch. 1). The individual is the unit of existential analysis, and the secrets of existence are thought to be unlocked by the solitary contemplator in an *authentic* relation with himself or herself and the cosmos. Authenticity – understood as a particular way of being or existing – is the dominant norm of existentialism, and is arguably a new category, differing from traditional philosophical categories such as psychology or ethics (Crowell 2010). Collective modes of human life, such as social groups, crowd behaviour and intersubjective relations, are mostly considered negatively, as phenomena that take the individual subject away from his or her authenticity. For the existentialist, philosophical truth unfolds in isolation, and the individual is the privileged site of the happening of this truth.

John Macquarrie (1972: 14) suggests that existentialism is best thought of as a *style* of philosophy (rather than a school of thought), and it is perhaps in the existentialist's approach to philosophizing that existentialism most significantly departs from traditional philosophy. First, existentialism rejects the possibility of gaining an adequate understanding of the world through purely rational philosophical concepts, particularly in the form of a system. For many existentialists, the tendency towards rational system-building is associated with the kind of philosophy that focuses on essences to the denigration of existence. Traditional philosophy is criticized for building systems of thought that are overly rational, universal and abstract; such systems are thought to forget the importance of the particular individual in their concrete existence. Furthermore, existentialism embraces the emotional dimensions of life that philosophy has traditionally rejected as hampering rational thought. Existentialists, on the contrary, hold that emotions are an essential part of our existence and certain emotions and moods reveal insights into the nature of existence that purely rational and abstract thought cannot penetrate. In particular, existentialism focuses on feelings that often appear as primarily negative: anxiety, shame, guilt, alienation and despair. Such moods are thought to reveal dimensions of existence such as finitude, contingency and the inevitability of death, which are constitutive of human existence.

Instead of abstract rational thought, then, existentialism privileges personal inner experience as the mode of access to truth, and advances a form of philosophy that is a testimony to such experience. Since they deny that traditional philosophical forms of thinking and writing can access or express what is existentially significant, they engage in a writing style that is closer at times to literature than academic philosophy. Such writing attempts an "indirect communication" (Kierkegaard) with the reader, in an attempt to record inner personal experience in such a way that the reader will be moved to have such experiences themselves. Existentialist philosophizing and writing attempts to convey an "affective force" with "existential effects". That is, it attempts to effect changes in existence, increasing the authenticity of the lives of individual human beings. Philosophical ideas that do not have any relation to life as it is lived in its concrete everydayness are dismissed as existentially irrelevant (see Oaklander 1992). To summarize, we may say that the existentialist style of philosophizing attempts a unity of life and thought that is found lacking in philosophy's traditionally dominant forms (and it is in this sense that it takes over the fundamental impulses of life-philosophy). For existentialists, the central problem of philosophy remains the meaning of life, and how we, as individuals, are to respond to a meaningless world.

Jaspers: Nietzsche's philosophical activity

According to Brian Leiter (2001), the existentialist reading of Nietzsche derives from Jaspers, in particular the section called "Man as His Own Creator" from his monumental work *Nietzsche: An Introduction to the Understanding of His Philosophical Activity* ([1936] 1965). We can agree with Leiter and go further: Jaspers was the first to identify Nietzsche as an existential philosopher, and this major work contains the quintessential presentation of Nietzsche as an existentialist, not just in relation to the theme of self-creation, but to many other existentialist themes as well. Before we elaborate these themes, however, we must note that the importance of Jaspers's Nietzsche interpretation resides not only in the interpretation itself, but in the fact that it was published in the context of Nazi Germany and the dominance of Nazi-aligned interpretations such as those of Richard Oehler, Alfred Baeumler, and Ernst Bertram, and that it presented a non-Nazi interpretation. Moreover, Jaspers was an eminent philosopher, and his work acted to assert the autonomy of Nietzsche's thought from its Nazi appropriation. Against Nazi tendencies, Jaspers emphasized Nietzsche's rejection of disciples and encouragement of individualism. Moreover, as Kaufmann notes, passages in the book such as the following seem to speak out against National Socialism (albeit without directly naming it): "Nietzsche can be used by all the powers which he fought: he can serve … the violence which mistakes the idea of the will to power as an order of rank for a justification of any brutality" (quoted in Kaufmann 1957: 426). Jaspers was banned from teaching from 1937, and his books banned from 1938, by the Nazi regime.

Kaufmann calls Jaspers's *Nietzsche* "one of the most fascinating books ever written by one philosopher about another" (1975: 30). Yet, Kaufmann argues, Jaspers most accurately describes the book when he admits that it is really an introduction to his own philosophy: "My *Nietzsche* was to be an introduction to that shaking up of thought from which *Existenzphilosophie* must spring" (quoted in Kaufmann 1975: 32). Thus, we must approach Jaspers's Nietzsche interpretation via his own philosophical project.

Jaspers was trained in psychiatry before turning to philosophy, and one way of understanding his "philosophy of existence" is as a critical response to the objective, empirical methods of studying human beings prevalent in psychiatry. Drawing in particular on Kant, Schelling, Kierkegaard and Nietzsche, Jaspers develops a philosophy in which human existence, the world and Being exceed objectivity and can be clarified only through philosophical reflection. For Jaspers, however, philosophical reflection itself cannot comprehend existence by remaining abstract and cognitive, but must embrace the irrational and must have its source in lived experience. Jaspers insists that philosophical concepts cannot present objective knowledge of existence in cognitive definitions, and that, in order to have value, they must be made meaningful in the context of the life of each individual interpreter. Approached correctly, philosophy can clarify existence, and the writings of philosophers can be "existentially appropriated" to increase our own self-understanding and sense of meaningfulness in life.

In Jaspers's philosophy, a number of basic concepts outline his conception of human existence. First, the central concept of "existence" (*Existenz*) refers to the human being or human reality in the entire range of its existing, including the facts of subjectivity and irrationality. According to Jaspers, existence cannot be grasped by objective, empirical psychology, and can be illuminated only by a thought that itself embraces the subjective and the irrational (although not to the exclusion of rationality). Jaspers argues that human existence is dependent on a "transcendence" (*Transcendenz*), such that existence is "suspended" between itself and transcendence. In some of his writings, this transcendence is associated with God. Moreover, in a formulation not dissimilar to Heidegger's (as we shall see), Jaspers understands Being (sometimes called "the Encompassing" [*das Umgreifende*]) as that which gives or makes possible objects and things in the world, but which cannot itself be reduced to something objective. Throughout his works, Jaspers insists that existential concepts such as these cannot be understood through rational reflection alone, and reason must be "shipwrecked" – that is, brought to an experience of its own limits – in order to break through into the realm in which authentic philosophical thought is possible. He calls the type of experience that makes such a breakthrough available a "boundary situation" (*Grenzsituation* – sometimes translated as "limit situation" or "ultimate situation"). Such experiences include suffering, guilt and confrontation with death.

Briefly put, Jaspers's deep concern with Nietzsche lies in Nietzsche's ability to make the reader experience the limits of reason and make the illumination of existence possible. This core concern coincides with a unique approach to Nietzsche's texts. First, Jaspers notes that the peculiar thing with Nietzsche is that he is in danger of being misunderstood because his books *seem* so readily comprehensible. This is only the case, however, if single aphorisms or essays are taken in isolation. Jaspers insists that in order to understand Nietzsche, we need to read the whole of his works in a comparative fashion; it is only through this process that their difficulty, but also their special value, will emerge.

Jaspers situates Nietzsche's work between the aphoristic and the systematic, and between the philosophical and the writerly. He suggests that it may be described with the following image: "it is as though a mountain wall had been dynamited; the rocks, already more or less shaped, convey the idea of a whole" (Jaspers 1965: 3). The task of the interpreter of Nietzsche's work is to reconstruct the whole from the pieces, but not in order to present it as an objective philosophical system or set of doctrines. For Jaspers, true interpretation aims towards the self-involvement of the interpreter (*ibid.*: 6), and the interpretation of Nietzsche aims at both the whole and its collapse. In the case of Nietzsche, he writes:

> [W]e must experience both the systematic possibilities and their collapse. Only then do we become aware of the powerful incentive which Nietzsche provides for posterity, not by offering them a place of refuge but by awakening them and indicating

the path they should follow, viz., participation in the elevation
of human existence which he made possible.   (*Ibid*.: 4)

Jaspers then follows immediately with a line worth isolating for emphasis:
"No one will envisage the quintessential in Nietzsche unless he achieves
it himself" (*ibid*.). Thus, for Jaspers, interpreting Nietzsche means integrating the multiplicities of his works into a whole as far as possible, but
recognizing that the whole towards which Nietzsche's thought strives
necessarily falls apart. For Jaspers, the collapse itself is precisely the site
of the greatest value in Nietzsche's work, since it allows the interpreter to
cross the boundary of reason into authentic philosophizing.

An important point of Jaspers's reading can be gleaned from the
subtitle to his book, "An Introduction to the Understanding of His
Philosophical Activity": significantly, it announces itself as an introduction not to Nietzsche's *philosophy*, but to his *philosophical activity*.
For Jaspers, the most interesting and significant thing about Nietzsche is
his *manner* of philosophizing; he sees Nietzsche's philosophical activity
as a means, not as an end. In fact, Jaspers goes so far as to conclude that
there is little of value in Nietzsche's work as far as positive philosophical
claims, positions, arguments or doctrines are concerned. According to
him, Nietzsche's well-known positive ideas such as the will to power,
the eternal return, the Dionysian, and the *Übermensch* are no more than
"a pile of absurdities and vacuities" (quoted in Kaufmann 1957: 419).
Nietzsche's value, rather, lies in his revelation of the limits of reason, and
his ability to lead reason to its "shipwreck". Jaspers writes:

> One must know what it means to be concerned with Nietzsche,
> and how this concern leads to no conclusion … Nietzsche is
> interpreted in two ways. One interpretation finds his impor-
> tance in an achievement he completed. He becomes the founder
> of a philosophy … the philosophy of the will to power, the eter-
> nal recurrence, the Dionysian grasp of life. For quite another
> interpretation, which we profess, Nietzsche's importance lies
> in his loosening function. His exciting force, which leads the
> human being to the authentic problems and to himself, does
> not instruct the reader, but awakens him.
>
> (Quoted in *ibid*.: 423)

Thus, Nietzsche's value lies in his capacity to produce "boundary
situations" in his readers, and *understanding* Nietzsche's "philosophical
activity" does not at all mean rationally comprehending his work as a

set of conceptual doctrines, but, rather, existentially appropriating his texts. Nietzsche's works "abandon us without giving us any final goals and without posing any definite problems. Through them, each one can only become what he himself is" (Jaspers 1975: 208). (Jaspers's last phrase here is a reference to Nietzsche's well-known adoption of a saying by the ancient Greek philosopher Pindar, which appears in the subtitle to his book *Ecce Homo*: "How One Becomes Who One Is". See below for Jaspers's interpretation of this Nietzschean idea.)

For Jaspers, the single most important fact about Nietzsche's corpus considered as a whole is that it abounds in *contradictions*. This is precisely why the whole falls apart. At first, "One finds it insufferable that Nietzsche says first this, then that, and then something entirely different" (Jaspers 1965: xi). Jaspers claims that for almost any proposition in Nietzsche, it is possible also to find its opposite in his works. Jaspers, however, gives these contradictions a positive value, and asserts that "*Self-contradiction* is the fundamental ingredient in Nietzsche's thought" (*ibid.*: 10). He argues that these contradictions are neither confused nor whimsical, but necessary and inescapable. How could contradictions be necessary? Jaspers's suggestion is that single (non-contradictory) propositions are actually misleading simplifications of Being. Being, lying beyond the grasp of reason, cannot be elucidated by any single proposition, and can be only indirectly indicated by contradictions. Contradictions can give us the *feeling* that there is something that cannot be adequately thought by rational means alone. Thus, the contradictions are necessitated by the subject matter of Nietzsche's thought. According to Jaspers, then, to gain an authentic understanding of Nietzsche, the interpreter needs to search out contradictions, and directly experience their necessity (i.e. realize why neither of the contradictory propositions is sufficient to express truth). Jaspers summarizes the goal of this focus on contradictions as follows: "In the end, the contradictory elements and circles in the movements of Nietzsche's thought are simply the means to touch indirectly upon what lies beyond form, law, and the expressible. Nothing can be at this boundary, and yet everything must be there" (*ibid.*: 155).

As signposted above, a further important element of Jaspers's interpretation and its influence on existentialist philosophy is his emphasis on the theme of *self-creation* in Nietzsche. Jaspers explains that creation is the highest demand underlying Nietzsche's critique of morality. Creation is "authentic being" and "the ground of all essential activity" (*ibid.*: 151). Jaspers emphasizes that for Nietzsche, human beings are not like other beings, which passively undergo alterations; rather, they are free and have the power actively to develop themselves (*ibid.*: 154). (Of course, it is well known that Nietzsche often critiques the idea of free will, and this is a good example of exactly the kind of contradiction Jaspers sees abounding in Nietzsche's works.)

KEY POINT *Self-creation in Nietzsche*
Jaspers thematizes self-creation in Nietzsche according to the following three formulations (1965: 154–5):
1. *Values are not given, but must be created.* Self-realization and self-development depend on the freedom from belief in fixed values and the creation of new values. (Together, these points constitute the meaning of Nietzsche's "transvaluation of all values".)
2. *Self-transformation occurs through one's relation to oneself.* The relation one assumes towards oneself includes seeing oneself, evaluating oneself, self-deception and giving form to oneself. This change through self-relation does not remain on the level of the psychological, but takes place in, and reveals, the self as an incomprehensible depth.
3. *Through change, one becomes that which one really is.* While this may initially appear paradoxical, change brings about a realization of "what one really is" in so far as the very fact of change means that we are beings capable of change; in Japers's terms, we are beings open to existential possibilities. We "become that which we really are" when we realize and embrace our existential nature as beings capable of actively altering ourselves.

Despite this thematic elaboration, Jaspers asserts that creation is ultimately one of those ideas in Nietzsche that is never adequately conceptualized, and on which our thinking runs aground (*ibid.*: 152). Perhaps paradoxically, it is such running aground that leads to the genuine experience of creation through the personal development that comes with growing awareness of self and insight into existence.

Through Jaspers, Nietzsche was interpreted as an existentialist philosopher, and became (along with Kierkegaard) one of the most important influences on twentieth-century existentialism. The force of Jaspers's Nietzsche interpretation is perhaps best encapsulated in the following passage from the end of the introduction to his *Nietzsche*:

> *Our task* is to become ourselves by appropriating Nietzsche. Instead of yielding to the temptation to take the apparent univocality of doctrines and laws as proof of their universal validity, each of us should respond to his challenge by attaining individually the highest rank of which his nature is capable. We

should not subordinate ourselves to oversimplified principles and imperatives but, rather, through him find the way to the genuine simplicity of truth. (*Ibid.*: 23)

French existentialism: Sartre and Camus

While the philosophy of existence was developing in Germany through the works of Jaspers and Heidegger, it was also developing in France. Marcel developed the existentialist understanding of "existence" (focusing on contingency and the individual) independently, prior to his reading of Kierkegaard or Jaspers. This idea was first published his 1925 essay "Existence and Objectivity" (in Marcel 1952), then expanded in his 1927 *Metaphysical Journal*, which has been cited as the first existentialist book published in France (Schrift 2005: 32). Other French thinkers, such as Sartre, Beauvoir, Merleau-Ponty and Camus, developed existentialist ideas with more direct influence from authors such as Kierkegaard and Heidegger. Nietzsche, too, was a profound influence on French existentialism, but far more of an unconscious or subterranean one than in German existentialism. Unlike Jaspers or Heidegger, the French existentialists did not devote major works to him, yet their works are scattered with Nietzsche references, and the presence of key Nietzschean themes in their thought is undeniable. In this section, I shall restrict my focus to two thinkers whom we may take as indicative of the importance of Nietzsche for French existentialism: Sartre and Camus. Sartre is arguably the most well known of all the existentialists, and while his references to Nietzsche are often oblique, his philosophy expresses deep Nietzschean concerns. The case for characterizing Camus as an existentialist is somewhat more difficult, as he consciously distanced himself from the movement and is sometimes referred to as an "absurdist", as distinct from "existentialist". However, Camus is typically grouped with the existentialists despite his own disavowals, and his deep engagement with Nietzsche makes his consideration here essential.

Sartre

On 29 October 1945, Sartre presented a talk called "Existentialism is a Humanism" (1975) to the Club Maintenant in Paris. The lecture was subsequently published in a short, affordable edition, and sold well (the publisher later claimed credit for "making" Sartre's name). Up to then Sartre was a recognized novelist in literary circles (he had published

Nausea [1965] in 1937), and had already published the *magnum opus* of his existentialist philosophy, *Being and Nothingness* (1956). But it was in the immediate post-war period, 1945–50, and following Sartre's talk "Existentialism is a Humanism", that existentialism became an internationally famous phenomenon, and Sartre was promoted as its primary spokesperson. Sartre is now recognized as one of the foremost intellectuals of the twentieth century, and his work encompasses multiple genres of writing, as well as changing interests and themes. As well as novels and philosophical works, Sartre penned biographies, works of literary and artistic criticism, numerous political tracts, some very successful plays, and some less successful film scripts. In his later career, he changed his philosophical position significantly, from an individualist focus characteristic of existentialism, to a social and political focus deployed through the prism of Marxism. Nevertheless, at least in the English-speaking world, it is his existentialist philosophy for which Sartre remains best known, and no adequate discussion of existentialism can take place without recognizing his pivotal place in the movement.

Given Nietzsche's strong association with existentialism, the relationship of his thought to this most famous of the existentialists needs to be addressed. As Craig Beam (1998) notes, Nietzsche and Sartre are often grouped together as representatives of *atheistic* existentialism. Sartre asserts that "Existentialism is nothing else but an attempt to draw the full conclusions from a consistently atheistic position" (1975: 369), an assertion that resonates with Nietzsche's concern to unfold the full consequences of the "death of God". Despite this commonly noted association, it is not clear to what extent, or in what ways, Sartre may have been influenced by Nietzsche.

When asked directly in an interview whether he was influenced by Nietzsche in his early education in philosophy, he replied: "I remember giving a seminar paper on him in Brunschwicg's class, in my third year at the École Normale. He interested me, like many others; but he never stood for anything particular in my eyes" (Rybalka *et al.* 1981: 9; cited in Daigle 2004: 196). Sartre never published a book on Nietzsche, although there is some evidence that he wrote a long study on the German philosopher, begun in the period of 1947–48, which no one seems to have read and which may be lost (Sartre 1990, cited in Daigle 2004: 197). His published writings are peppered with references to Nietzsche, but they express a variety of attitudes towards him, ambiguous in sum. On the one hand, for example, he seems to admire Nietzsche as an atheist who "draws logically and strongly all the consequences from his atheism" (quoted in Daigle 2004: 196). On the other hand, he explicitly criticizes central ideas of Nietzsche's, such as the will to power, the eternal return and the *Übermensch* (*ibid.*). The question of Nietzsche's possible influence on Sartre admits of no easy answer, then, but several scholars have tried to draw out their philosophical commonalities, and one such scholar, Christine Daigle, has argued that "It remains more than possible that Nietzsche influenced Sartre's thinking" (*ibid.*: 197).

Daigle argues that Nietzsche and Sartre both address the same philosophical problem, and both propose a similar solution to this problem. The problem that acts as a starting-point for both is nihilism, or the meaning of life in the wake of the death of God. Both answer this problem with reference to the creative individual as a meaning-provider. Sartre agrees with Nietzsche about the alienating effects of the metaphysical–religious tradition, and embraces a thoroughgoing atheism. Daigle suggests that while Nietzsche presented the death of God polemically and attempted to hasten his demise with an active nihilism, Sartre tends to take atheism for granted: "Nietzsche attacks a crumbling tradition, whereas Sartre finds it already in ruins" (*ibid.*: 199). Like Nietzsche, Sartre views the world as lacking any meaning in itself, and once the role of God as meaning-provider has been made redundant, we face the problem of finding a new way of providing meaning. In the *Notebooks for an Ethics* (a posthumously published collection of notes for a never-completed work on ethics, announced at the end of *Being and Nothingness* and worked on in 1947–48), Sartre writes: "In this way, man finds himself the heir of the mission of the dead God: to draw Being from its perpetual collapse into the absolute indistinctness of night. An infinite mission" (quoted in *ibid.*: 200). Like Nietzsche, Sartre sees the death of God as a liberation from an alienating tradition, and as an opening of infinite human possibilities (which he sees, famously, as implying the radical freedom of human beings). But this freedom comes at the cost of the problem of meaninglessness, of having to find a meaning to fill the emptiness left by the loss of religious belief.

According to Daigle, both Sartre and Nietzsche give a similar response to the problem of nihilism by pointing to the creative powers of human beings as able to produce meaning. Significantly, she sees both as beginning with art as an exemplar of creative meaning-production, but moving towards a more generalized model of creativity in which the interpretation of the world through our daily living and engagement in life projects creates meaning. For Nietzsche, this is evident in his focus on ancient Greek tragedy as a meaning-giving, life-affirming art in *The Birth of Tragedy*. But already in that work – and more clearly in later works – creation is not just artistic. Rather, according to Daigle, Nietzsche sees the world of "brute matter" as an "innocence of becoming", meaningless in itself, which is transformed into a meaningful world through our human apprehension of it, and ascription to it of values ("good/bad"). Because Nietzsche sees the world as meaningless in itself, all interpretation and evaluation (and not simply art) are creative, meaning-conferring activities.

Daigle sees a similar line of thought in Sartre. In his first published novel, *Nausea*, Sartre presents the world as absurd and meaningless in itself; this absurdity gives rise to the protagonist Roquentin's feeling of "nausea" in the face of the sheer contingency of existence. The most celebrated example of nausea in that work is Roquentin's encounter with the formless mass of a tree root, which strikes home to him the meaninglessness of things with a merely material existence. By contrast, Roquentin finds relief from the feeling of nausea while listening to the jazz song "Some of These Days": the deliberate structures of a work of art provide a sense of meaning. However, Sartre further argues that appreciation of existing works of art is not enough to provide meaning and justification to our lives; we must ourselves become creators, and treat ourselves, our lives and the world as material for creative transformation. In his more overtly philosophical works, Sartre explains that it is only the creative activity of human consciousness that can confer meaning and value on an otherwise meaningless world.

The central role of creativity in Sartre's philosophy is evident in his well-known "slogan" of existentialism, *existence precedes essence* (Sartre 1975: 348; trans. mod.). This means that because human beings are endowed with consciousness, not subject to the constraints of deterministic laws of cause-and-effect, we are radically free to create ourselves. For Sartre, "man first of all exists, encounters himself, surges up in the world – and defines himself afterwards" (*ibid.*: 349). There is no essence, or preexisting blueprint, defining human nature and limiting what we can be. Therefore, we are radically free to create ourselves, and – more strongly – we have no choice but to create ourselves through our actions in the world. In "Existentialism is a Humanism", Sartre uses the analogy of art to indicate how self-creation is to take place through the creation of values:

> Moral choice is comparable to the construction of a work of art. … As everyone knows, there are no aesthetic values *a priori*, but there are values which will appear in due course in the coherence of the picture, in the relation between the will to create and the finished work.　　　(*Ibid.*: 346)

In the absence of God, there are no pre-existing values and no human nature. For Sartre, we must create ourselves through creating the values we are to live by, taking it upon ourselves to construct the meaning of our own lives in a process analogous to an artist's construction of a work. In summary then, as Daigle sees it, both Nietzsche and Sartre replace God as meaning-provider with the creative human being as meaning-provider.

KEY POINT

Nietzsche and Sartre express similar existentialist ideas by beginning with the same problem (nihilism, or the meaning of life in the wake of the "death of God") and proposing a similar solution to this problem (the creative production of meaning by human beings).

While avoiding questions of influence, Beam (1998) has similarly attempted to draw out commonalities between Sartre and Nietzsche, but has also highlighted what he believes to be some significant differences between their philosophies. Summarizing briefly, while recognizing (like Daigle) that both address the same problem of nihilism, Beam argues that Sartre is "both a less radical and less life-affirming thinker than Nietzsche" (*ibid.*). Beam sees Sartre as retaining a fundamentally pessimistic view of human nature that contrasts with Nietzsche's affirmation of the possibility of joy in existence, and also sees Sartre's ontology as retaining many elements of the Platonism Nietzsche overturned, including a denigration of nature and the world of becoming. Nietzsche's relation to Sartre remains an issue for further investigation and debate, but their shared place in existentialism is clear, and is well expressed by Beam when he writes, "Of those modern thinkers who resolutely face the fact that God is dead and the universe contains no inherent meaning or purpose, Sartre and Nietzsche are among the most important" (*ibid.*).

Camus

Camus was a French Algerian journalist and writer, and a sometime associate of Sartre and other French existentialists. He was a passionate moralist whose appeals to his readers to take stock of their lives in the condition inaugurated by the death of God continue to be widely read today. Like Sartre, Camus takes the same beginning point as Nietzsche: the problem of nihilism – how are we to live without belief in a transcendent meaning and a given code of values? While Nietzsche arguably remains elitist (see Chapter 3), and Sartre develops complex and esoteric philosophical theories, Camus can be understood as *humanizing* and *democratizing* the problem of nihilism bestowed by Nietzsche. An anecdote told by Colin Wilson (an early popularizer of existentialism in England) about his meeting with Camus illustrates this point nicely. Wilson explained to Camus his own theories on how life has a meaning that exists outside us, with which we might be united through mystical experience. He recounts Camus' reaction as follows:

> The idea seemed to worry Camus. He gestured out the window, at a Parisian teddy boy slouching along the other side of the street, and said: "No, what is good for him must be good for me also." What he meant was clear enough: that any solution to this problem of "absurdity" must be a solution that would be valid for the man in the street as well as for mystics and intellectuals. (Wilson 2004: 173)

In contrast to Sartre, the influence of Nietzsche on Camus' thought is both readily apparent and deep. Nietzsche has a significant presence in Camus' two main theoretical works: in *The Myth of Sisyphus* ([1942] 2000) he is a constant reference, and *The Rebel* ([1951] 1971) contains a section devoted to the German philosopher, "Nietzsche and Nihilism" (in the English edition this section title is omitted, and the text appears under the section title "Absolute Affirmation"). In addition to Camus' explicit discussions of Nietzsche, a number of scholars have noted many Nietzschean themes in his plays and novels. I shall focus here, however, on the theoretical works.

The Myth of Sisyphus and *The Rebel* develop and explore the problem of nihilism from an individual and a collective perspective, respectively. In *The Myth of Sisyphus*, nihilism is developed as the idea of the absurdity of existence, and is explored in terms of the individual and the problem of suicide. In the latter, nihilism is developed in the context of social relations between individuals, and explored as a problematic justification for murder and bloody revolution. If nihilism is understood as a negation of life, then Camus dramatizes the problem and presses its urgency by interpreting it as literally and practically as possible, through suicide and murder. He explores the way that philosophical nihilism can potentially justify each, and he is concerned to show how such justifications may be rejected and the problem of nihilism overcome.

Camus famously begins *The Myth of Sisyphus* by asserting, "There is but one truly serious philosophical problem and that is suicide" (2000: 11). For Camus, suicide is to be understood as the judgement that life is not worth living, whether or not this judgement is a conscious one. According to Camus, what tempts us to suicide – at least in the philosophical sense in which he is interested – is absurdity. Accordingly, much of Camus' analysis of the problem of suicide is carried out through a development of Camus' own theory of the absurdity of existence. William E. Duvall writes:

> [Camus'] understanding of the absurd is from the beginning grounded in Nietzsche's diagnosis of nihilism, his lucid awareness of the lack of meaning, truth and finality which results from the death of God, and his consciousness of the reality of human suffering which accompanies this silence. (1999: 40)

Camus believes life to be meaningless because there is no objective structure to the universe, divine or otherwise. The world does not make sense and is resistant to all attempts to explain it. More precisely, what matters for Camus is that even if God did exist, or the world had some other objective structure or significance, *we could not know it*. He writes: "I don't know whether this world has a meaning that transcends it. But I know that I do not know that meaning and that it is impossible for me just now to know it. What can a meaning outside my condition mean to me? I can understand only in human terms" (Camus 2000: 51).

Understanding is everything for Camus. Meaning can be accepted only in terms of what can be understood. As he puts it, the challenge is to "live without appeal" (*ibid.*: 53): without appeal to God or any other transcendent meaning that we cannot understand, or the validity of which we cannot be assured. However, Camus has a quite specific understanding of absurdity, which is misunderstood if we take it to mean simply the meaninglessness of existence.

KEY POINT *Absurdity*
For Camus, the absurdity of life is not simply the meaninglessness of life, but a tension between two terms: objective meaninglessness and the human desire for meaning.

For Camus, to understand is above all to unify. The inability of reason to understand the world amounts to the failure of the possibility of unity.

Furthermore, it is the very fact of *consciousness*, and with it the desire to understand the world rationally, that thwarts the possibility of unity. Camus believes that if we had no more consciousness than the lower animals, there would be no division in the world. We would be part of it, at one with it. There would be no tension between the human desire for meaning and the world, and life would not be absurd. Likewise, if the universe thought and felt as we do (i.e. if there were a God, who manifested a divine order), there would be no division either and absurdity would not take hold. What, then, does Camus think we ought do in the pursuit of meaningful lives? How should we respond to absurdity? Can this kind of nihilism be overcome?

Camus concludes *The Myth of Sisyphus* with a famous analysis of the titular myth. Sisyphus was condemned by the gods to rolling a stone to the top of a mountain only to see it roll back to the bottom, and to have to roll it to the top again, *ad infinitum*. As Camus notes, the gods apparently thought (not without good reason) that the most dreadful punishment is futile and hopeless labour (*ibid.*: 107). For Camus, this myth acts as an analogy for the absurdity of human life; in fact, he places the lot of factory workers on a par with Sisyphus' futile labours. However, for Camus, Sisyphus is also an absurd hero, a figure who holds the secret of victory over absurdity. Camus emphasizes the following points about Sisyphus. First, his fate is a tragic one precisely because he is *conscious* of the futility of his labour. Such a consciousness is double-edged for Camus: on the one hand it might enhance suffering, but on the other he asserts that "crushing truths perish from being acknowledged" (*ibid.*: 109). Consciousness allows Sisyphus to acknowledge and to *affirm* his fate, and in this way to master it. Camus sees in Sisyphus' scorn for the gods a corollary of contemporary atheism, and the liberation that results from it. A lucid acceptance of an atheistic, absurd universe makes life difficult to bear because it evacuates it of divine meaning, but such awareness also holds the key to overcoming the nihilism absurdity threatens: "It drives out of this world a god who had come into it with dissatisfaction and a preference for futile sufferings. It makes of fate a human matter, which must be settled among men" (*ibid.*: 110).

As quoted earlier, Kaufmann has suggested that "the conclusion of Camus' *The Myth of Sisyphus* sounds like a distant echo of Nietzsche" (1975: 21). How is this echo to be heard? First, Sisyphus' ceaseless rolling of the boulder, an eternally futile labour aimed towards accomplishing nothing, echoes Nietzsche's eternal return, in which the universe repeats itself without aim or goal, rendering everything that happens apparently futile. Second, like Nietzsche, Camus emphasizes the superiority of a *tragic* view of existence – one that acknowledges the absurdity of life as well as its joy – over false optimism. For Camus, lucidity has its own power to master fate. According to him (still echoing Nietzsche), this mastery takes place not only by acknowledging fate, but by affirming it ("The absurd man says yes and his effort will henceforth be unceasing" [2000: 110]). Thus, Camus presents a Nietzschean answer to the problem of absurdity by arguing that it is enough to affirm this world and our place in it to overcome absurdity with a sense of meaning:

> The universe henceforth without a master seems to him neither sterile nor futile. Each atom of that stone, each mineral flake of that night-filled mountain, in itself forms a world. The struggle itself towards the heights is enough to fill a man's heart. One must imagine Sisyphus happy. *(Ibid.:* 111)

Nietzsche continues to be a powerful influence shaping Camus' later book *The Rebel*, but here he receives both a more extended, and a more critical, discussion. If there are resonances of Nietzsche's absolute affirmation as a response to nihilism in *The Myth of Sisyphus*, it is precisely this theme that comes under attack in *The Rebel*. Nevertheless, as Duvall has argued, despite the overt criticisms of Nietzsche that appear in the book, as a whole it must be understood as motivated by deeply Nietzschean concerns. In this work, Camus examines the theme of rebellion or revolt in two related dimensions, the *political* and the *metaphysical*. Politically, he is interested in the history of rebellions since the end of the eighteenth century, and the specific moral problem that arises from this bloody history: is murder ever justified? Metaphysically, he is interested in the way whole cultures, often following the lead of specific philosophers (such as Marx and Nietzsche), have rebelled against the religious beliefs that have traditionally guided and constrained their lives. Camus relates the problem of murder in political rebellions to metaphysical rebellion because, first, he believes that many of the political rebellions have in fact been accompanied by metaphysical rebellions, and, second, because the nihilism to which metaphysical rebellion can lead offers a potential philosophical justification for murder. Camus is concerned to examine the internal "logic" of rebellion, and to try to show that according to its own standards, rebellion can never justify murder.

Once again, Camus' starting-point is thoroughly Nietzschean: it is the problem of nihilism. Metaphysical rebellion is akin to Nietzsche's active nihilism; it stems from a rejection of the "highest values" embodied in a transcendent order presided over by God. Camus cites the origin of this rebellion in a dissatisfaction with the metaphysical worldview: "Metaphysical rebellion is the justified claim of a desire for unity against the suffering of life and death – in that it protests against the incompleteness of human life, expressed by death, and its dispersion, expressed by evil" (1971: 30). The metaphysical rebel rebels by "denouncing God as the origin of death and as the supreme disillusionment" (*ibid.*). Camus draws a link between this metaphysical rebellion and political rebellion by pointing out that once metaphysical values are deposed, the values on which an existing social order has been structured are also undermined, and the rebel becomes aware that responsibility for this order falls from God to human beings. Therefore, society can be restructured according to a new and different set of values:

> When the throne of God is overthrown, the rebel realises that it is now his own responsibility to create the justice, order, and unity that he sought in vain within his own condition and, in this way, to justify the fall of God. Then begins the desperate effort to create, at the price of sin if necessary, the dominion of man. (*Ibid.*: 31)

The problem of murder then arises because the metaphysical rebellion, which justifies political rebellion, also seems to lead to a nihilism in which "nothing is true, everything is permitted", including murder.

Against this, Camus presents an argument, inspired by Descartes, about the very logical nature of rebellion. To rebel metaphysically, he suggests, means recognizing that all others are in the same metaphysical situation as are we ourselves (that is, we are all abandoned, without God and without transcendent values to give meaning and purpose to our lives). He expresses this as a reformulation of Descartes' famous *cogito, ergo sum*: "I *rebel* – therefore we *exist*" (*ibid.*: 28). According to Camus, being true to the initial impulse and inner logic of rebellion means affirming solidarity with our fellow humans, and rejecting murder outright. It is only when this impulse is forgotten or perverted, Camus argues, that rebellion can devolve into bloody revolution and the philosophical justification of murder.

Beyond the central Nietzschean theme of *The Rebel*, Duvall has argued that the history of rebellion Camus presents is a kind of Nietzschean genealogy, the moments of which can be mapped on to Nietzsche's genealogy of morality (Duvall 1999: 42). Camus tries to show how rebellion has frequently become decadent, degenerating into what he terms "revolution", in which murder becomes rampant and the original impetus of rebellion is betrayed. Moreover, Duvall argues, Camus' discussion of art in chapter 4 of the book is deeply influenced by a Nietzschean aesthetic (*ibid.*: 43). Despite Camus' evident debt to Nietzsche, however, the section of the book most explicitly devoted to Nietzsche, "Nietzsche and Nihilism" (which was also published as a standalone essay), is predominantly hostile to the German thinker. Taking what, we may note, is a characteristically existentialist perspective, Camus insists on interrogating Nietzsche not only according to the explicit content of his ideas, but according to the implications of living by those ideas (*ibid.*: 51). On this score, Camus finds Nietzsche guilty of generating ideas that helped to shape twentieth-century totalitarianisms.

The crux of Camus' critique of Nietzsche is that the absolute affirmation of existence he proposes as a response to nihilism cannot say no to murder. In the terms of Camus' discussion in *The Rebel*, Nietzsche's philosophy is thus culpable in the straying of rebellion from its own foundations and its decadent sliding into bloody revolution. First, Camus argues that while Nietzsche's rejection of transcendent values appears to embrace freedom, it in fact embraces a kind of servitude. His argument is predicated on the idea that free actions require some degree of direction; some constraints, and some goal. Without such constraints, a generalized relativism ensues: there is no more reason for doing one thing than another, and all action is paralysed. As Camus puts it (alluding to a Dostoevsky novel), with Nietzsche "[a] profounder logic replaces the 'if nothing is true, everything is permitted' of Karamazov by 'if nothing is true, nothing is permitted'" (Camus 1971: 63). According to Camus' reading, in rejecting transcendent values, Nietzsche chooses an absolute affirmation of this world, a fidelity to fate and history that makes no judgements of the world. With such an affirmation, thought submits passively to an assumed necessity in the order of things, and desires no change. This is how Camus understands Nietzsche's *amor fati*, which he terms a "deification of fate" (*ibid.*: 64).

Far more problematically than this servitude to fate, however, Camus sees Nietzsche's absolute affirmation as consenting to murder and evil: "This magnificent consent, born of affluence and fullness of spirit, is the unreserved affirmation of human imperfection and suffering, of evil and murder, of all that is problematic and strange in our existence" (*ibid.*: 63). After noting the well-known influence of misinterpreted Nietzschean thought on National Socialism, Camus insists that we must defend Nietzsche vigorously from such misinterpretations. Nevertheless, he asserts that Nietzsche's work *can* be used as a philosophical justification for murder, and to this extent, it is not innocent. In short, his judgement of Nietzsche is that "[t]o say yes to everything supposes that one says yes to murder" (*ibid.*: 68).

Whatever one makes of Camus' critique of Nietzsche, it is notable that he refers in this essay almost entirely to a particular section of *The Will to Power*, and, as Duvall (1999: 51) points out, this material is not representative of anything in his published works. In conclusion, then, Camus' relation to Nietzsche is ambivalent: his deep debt to the German thinker is without question, but while recognizing Nietzsche as the most profound diagnostician of nihilism, Camus found his responses to the problem inadequate, even dangerous, and sought to formulate his own. In an interview, he presents his own work as primarily an engagement with this Nietzschean theme: "I have sought ... to transcend our darkest nihilism ... [out of] an instinctive fidelity to a light in which I was born, and in which for thousands of years men have learned to welcome life even in suffering" (quoted in *ibid.*: 47).

Kaufmann: Nietzsche with, and beyond, existentialism

As signposted in the introduction to this chapter, Kaufmann is largely responsible for positioning Nietzsche as an existentialist in the anglophone world. Kaufmann was a German-Jewish émigré who left Germany and settled in America in 1939. He completed a dissertation on Nietzsche and value at Harvard University, and from 1947 until his death in 1980 he was a professor of philosophy at Princeton University. Kaufmann's influence on Nietzsche scholarship in English can hardly be overestimated. He translated most of Nietzsche's books, and many of his translations, available in inexpensive editions, are still widely read. Moreover, his *Nietzsche: Philosopher, Psychologist, Antichrist* ([1950] 1974) was the major post-Second World War English-language publication on Nietzsche, and worked to redeem him from his Nazi associations and establish him on a serious philosophical footing. It is a book that is still often recommended as a good introduction, and is considered indispensable by many Nietzsche scholars. Kaufmann's Nietzsche became the Nietzsche most widely disseminated in both public and academic consciousness in the mid-twentieth century in the English-speaking world, and the widespread contemporary interest in Nietzsche owes a debt to him.

Nevertheless, much contemporary Nietzsche scholarship has presented Kaufmann's Nietzsche interpretation as an unfortunate *misinterpretation*. First, it is often suggested that in defending Nietzsche he presented a watered-down version of his philosophy, made palatable to liberal humanists. Kaufmann's Nietzsche has memorably been described as "King-Kong-in-chains ... under heavy sedation" (quoted in Ratner-Rosenhagen 2006: 243). Second, he is typically held responsible for the image of Nietzsche as an existentialist, especially by those who wish to dismiss existentialism as a passé fad. Recently, however, this image of Kaufmann's Nietzsche has been called into question (for some notable examples, see Pickus 2003; Ratner-Rosenhagen 2006). Following the insistence of these scholars that we should not take Kaufmann's reputation at face value, in this section we shall outline the existentialist dimensions of Nietzsche's philosophy in so far as they are explicitly discerned by Kaufmann in his own writings.

In a later essay on the reception of existentialism in the United States, Kaufmann claims that in *Nietzsche* he "presented Nietzsche neither as an existentialist nor in the perspective of existentialism" (1976: 101). However, it is arguable that there are elements of his Nietzsche interpretation that may be readily identified as existentialist. Jennifer Ratner-Rosenhagen describes these elements in terms of: "'the urgency of Nietzsche's task': after the death of God, when divine explanations are untenable and naturalistic explanations fail to give human experience any dignity or meaning, the solitary individual must confront his awesome aloneness in an indifferent universe" (2006: 262).

Like Jaspers, a key point of Kaufmann's interpretation is Nietzsche's ideal of self-overcoming and self-creation. In complete contrast to Jaspers, however, Kaufmann asserts the systematic coherence of Nietzsche's philosophy, and contends that the contradictions that seem to characterize his writings are more apparent than real. The emphases on self-creation and systematic coherence coalesce around an interpretation of the will to power as the core doctrine of Nietzsche's philosophy, on which the rest centres. Against the "proto-Nazi" image of Nietzsche, which understands the will to power as a "might makes right" apology for the desire to dominate others, Kaufmann asserts the primary meaning of the will to power as the self-overcoming of the individual. Nietzschean "power", on Kaufmann's reckoning, is the power individuals have over themselves: the power to free themselves from traditional, religious and social constraints, to overcome the weaknesses in themselves, and to create and live by their own values as sovereign individuals. Kaufmann presents Nietzsche as an Enlightenment thinker, and a follower of the great eighteenth- to nineteenth-century German Johann Wolfgang von Goethe, in so far as he sought to attain individual autonomy and self-perfection. This emphasis on the self-creation of the individual is a recognizable existentialist theme in Kaufmann's Nietzsche.

Moreover, in 1956, Kaufmann's name became linked to existentialism through his editorship of the book *Existentialism from Dostoevsky to Sartre* ([1956] 1975), which introduced European existentialism to anglophone readers through first-time translations of many prominent existentialist thinkers. Nietzsche is included in the book, following Jaspers's positioning of him as one of the key nineteenth-century existential thinkers. In his introduction to *Existentialism from Dostoevsky to Sartre*, Kaufmann pinpoints the following traits of Nietzsche's philosophy as justifying his characterization as an existentialist:

- the refusal to belong to any school of thought;
- the repudiation of the adequacy of any body of beliefs whatever;
- opposition to philosophic systems;
- dissatisfaction with traditional philosophy as superficial, academic and remote from life; and
- a preoccupation with extreme states of mind (1975: 20–21).

However, Kaufmann distinguishes Nietzsche from other existentialists by noting his lack of preoccupation with failure, dread and death. While he is preoccupied with suffering, his response to suffering emphasizes the affirmation of life, and the extreme states of love and laughter. Moreover, Kaufmann suggests that because of his lightness of spirit and style, Nietzsche is closer to the French existentialists than to the other Germans (*ibid.*: 21).

In an essay simply titled "Nietzsche and Existentialism" (the transcript of a lecture given in 1972; in Kaufmann 1976), Kaufmann identifies the following further aspects of Nietzsche's philosophy as able to be grouped under the heading "existentialism":

- literary criticism;
- an interest in psychology;
- a critique of "worldviews" (*Weltanschauungen*), including Christianity;
- the analysis of nihilism and a possible attitude towards an absurd world;
- a concern with authentic and inauthentic modes of being; and
- literary efforts and stylistic experiments.

Kaufmann devotes much of the essay, however, to highlighting the differences between Nietzsche and various other existentialists. Moreover, he suggests that we can identify three types of philosophy in Nietzsche: (i) metaphysics (speculations regarding the will to power and the eternal return); (ii) analysis (remarks concerning language and grammar); and (iii) existentialism. Here, as elsewhere, he is at pains to not only point out the existentialist themes in Nietzsche, but also insist that Nietzsche's thought can in no sense be *reduced* to existentialism. In fact, as Ratner-Rosenhagen (2006: 254) has argued, Kaufmann saw Nietzsche's philosophy, with its multifaceted character, as ideally placed to negotiate the opposition between Anglo-American "analytic" philosophy, and continental European philosophy, as well as the opposition between academia and public life.

As we have seen, then, there is good reason for pointing to Kaufmann as the interpreter in the English-speaking world most responsible for situating Nietzsche as an existentialist. His highly influential *Nietzsche* contains elements that may be understood as existentialist, and in several writings Kaufmann explicitly detailed Nietzsche's "existentialist credentials". However, Kaufmann in fact remained ambivalent about this positioning, pointing out differences between Nietzsche and other existentialists as well as similarities, and highlighting the rich variety to be found in Nietzsche's works. It is in the assumption that Kaufmann reduced Nietzsche to an existentialist that the error of the "Walter Kaufmannn myth" (see Pickus 2003) is to be found. The truth is that Kaufmann insisted that "Existentialism suggests only a single facet of Nietzsche's multifarious influence, and to call him an existentialist means in all likelihood an insufficient appreciation of his full significance" (1975: 22). In short, Kaufmann wanted to position Nietzsche as central to existentialism, but existentialism as peripheral to Nietzsche.

Heidegger: Nietzsche as the last metaphysician

Heidegger was undoubtedly one of the most significant and influential philosophers of the twentieth century, and one of the many areas in which his thought had a major impact was his interpretation of Nietzsche. While the specific points of Heidegger's interpretation are often disputed, he was greatly influential in positioning Nietzsche as a highly significant philosopher, who made original contributions to the traditional problems of philosophy, and who deserves a place in the Western philosophical canon. The early phase of Heidegger's work, characterized by his *magnum opus*, *Being and Time* ([1927] 1962), enabled him to be positioned as one of the major figures of existentialism. Here, he analyses the structures of human existence (or *Dasein*, as he calls it) in a way that was highly influential on Sartre and many others. However, his serious engagement with Nietzsche coincides with what is often called the "turn" in his thinking, away from existentialist themes – in which *Dasein* is central – towards a thinking of Being that displaces the importance of human existence. This in turn allows us to position our discussion of Heidegger's Nietzsche at the end of this chapter on existentialism, as a transition to the next chapter on poststructuralism (a movement that Heidegger's reading of Nietzsche in some respects influenced).

Heidegger's interpretation of Nietzsche was primarily presented in a series of lectures given at the University of Freiburg between 1936 and 1941, and published in two volumes in 1961. However, his essay "The Word of Nietzsche: God is Dead" (in Heidegger 1977) presents many of the key points of these volumes in a condensed and more easily digestible format. The following outline will focus on some of the main interpretive moves he makes in this essay (although occasionally range beyond it).

Heidegger's reading of Nietzsche is radical, and in many respects represents a reversal of Nietzsche's own stated views. As we have seen, for Nietzsche nihilism is the history of the devaluation of the highest values hitherto, and the response to nihilism consists in a revaluation of all values guided by the principles of the will to power, the *Übermensch* and the eternal recurrence. Heidegger turns Nietzsche on his head: value-thinking itself becomes nihilism, and Nietzsche himself the ultimate nihilist. How does Heidegger accomplish this dramatic reversal? To understand Heidegger's critical reading of Nietzsche, we must first understand a few key points of Heidegger's own thinking.

Famously, Heidegger's philosophical project was centred on the "question of Being". What is Being? For Heidegger, answering, and even posing, the question of Being is fraught with difficulty. This is because, according to him, the Western philosophical tradition has forgotten to ask about Being: or at least has forgotten to ask about it in the right way. Heidegger calls the kind of thinking that has forgotten to ask the question of Being *metaphysics*. For Heidegger, Being is what "gives" particular beings or entities to us; it is the condition for the possibility of things being at all, and for appearing to us as they do. For Heidegger, Being cannot be reduced to a particular being or entity. He calls the difference between Being and beings the "ontological difference", and criticizes metaphysics for forgetting this difference. In other words, according to Heidegger, the metaphysical tradition in the history of philosophy has tried to answer the question of Being by referring to a particular entity but, rather than adequately answer the question, this has obscured the question itself.

According to Heidegger metaphysics *is* nihilism, because it is the "becoming nothing", or forgetting, of Being. For him, Nietzsche represents the culmination of metaphysics and thus of nihilism. Nietzsche represents this culmination in the very fact that he believes he has overcome metaphysics, while in fact his thinking remains metaphysical. Thus his thinking forgets Being, while believing itself to be free of this forgetting. Nietzsche's thinking is therefore a double forgetting of Being. But why does Heidegger insist that Nietzsche's thinking remains metaphysical? Because he gives an answer to the question of Being, determining it as a being.

First, Heidegger argues that Nietzsche succeeds only in *reversing* Platonic metaphysics and, in so doing, he continues to think metaphysically. For Heidegger, such a reversal is insufficient to displace the problem of metaphysics itself; it still fails adequately to think Being. While Plato asserted stable and unchanging structures (the Ideas) as the true foundation of reality, and changing appearances as less-than-real, Nietzsche reverses this picture of the world by asserting that the changing flux of the will to power is the true nature of reality, while apparently stable structures are less-than-real. According to Heidegger, for Nietzsche Being is will to power. While Nietzsche privileges the flux of becoming that the will to power describes, and derides the very notion of (stable and eternal) Being as nihilistic, Heidegger takes the view that, for Nietzsche, Being and becoming are the same. When Nietzsche names the flux of becoming as the will to power, Heidegger takes it that he is naming "what is", which Heidegger understands as Being. Furthermore, Heidegger believes that Nietzsche's metaphysics fits into the traditional metaphysical formula of *essentia* (essence or possibility) and *existentia* (actuality, or the particular manifestation of *essentia* as it is). This formula is metaphysical in that it tries to think Being but succeeds only in naming it as a being, thereby excluding the question of Being itself. According to Heidegger, Nietzsche's will to power is *essentia* and his eternal reccurence is *existentia*.

Furthermore, Heidegger identifies Nietzsche with the metaphysics of subjectivity (which he calls *subjecticity*). According to Heidegger's reading of the Western philosophical tradition, modern metaphysics began with Descartes and the subjecticity inaugurated by his famous principle *cogito, ergo sum* (I think, therefore I am). Heidegger interprets the subject in its original meaning as "a ground lying at the foundation"

(1977: 148). Accordingly, the subject becomes, for Descartes, the seat of certainty: the one thing we can be certain of is our self-conscious existence. As such, the subject becomes a metaphysical understanding of Being in so far as it becomes the ground for all objectivity. Now, according to Heidegger, Nietzsche extends the metaphysics of subjectivity by interpreting Being as will to power. On Heidegger's interpretation, the will to power implies willing subjects; these are the "centres of force" that attempt to preserve and enhance themselves. Nietzsche sees the *Übermenschen* as human beings who have realized the "truth" of the will to power and attempt to extend their will to a domination of the earth.

Another integral aspect of Heidegger's interpretation of Nietzsche is his criticism of value-thinking. As we have seen, Nietzsche presents his theory of nihilism and its overcoming in terms of values. Furthermore, the will to power itself – and thereby Being, according to Heidegger – is understood in terms of value. What is value for Nietzsche? Heidegger quotes aphorism 710 of *The Will to Power*: "The point of view of 'value' is the point of view constituting the *preservation-enhancement conditions* with respect to complex forms of relative duration of life within becoming." Heidegger interprets this to mean that "values are the conditions of itself posited by the will to power" (1977: 75). That is, values are the conditions for the preservation and enhancement of the will to power. These conditions are thereby the ground of the will to power itself, and this allows Heidegger to identify will to power with value. And since, as we have seen, for Heidegger's Nietzsche will to power is Being, Heidegger can now interpret Nietzsche to be saying (or rather, *not* saying explicitly, but nevertheless implying) that *Being is a value*. For Heidegger, this is the ultimate degradation of Being. It has become a "mere" value, even if the highest value.

For Heidegger – unlike Nietzsche, Sartre or Camus – value-thinking is itself nihilism. This is because values are posited, or chosen, by a subject. As such, they could equally be un-posited, or un-chosen. In positing values there is an implicit recognition that what is valued has no *intrinsic* or *objective* value, but only the value the subject chooses to give it. Therefore, in a sense, to value something is to *de*value it. In Heidegger's own words: "precisely through the characterization of something as 'a value' what is so valued is robbed of its worth. That is to say, by the assessment of something as a value what is valued is admitted only as an object for man's estimation" (1993: 251). Furthermore, every valuing is a subjectivizing. It implies a subject who values, who constitutes the ground for value. According to Heidegger, then, Nietzsche understands

Being in terms of value-positing, subjectivizing will to power. This will to power is the culmination of metaphysics and nihilism, because in positing Being as a value it reveals only beings, and in taking itself to be the overcoming of nihilism and metaphysics, it is the ultimate entanglement in nihilism, because it is the ultimate forgetting of Being.

Furthermore, the metaphysics of subjectivity represents the world – that is, everything that is not subject – as *object*. And given its value-positing quality, Nietzsche's subjecticity denies the intrinsic value of anything objective. The objective world is presented to the subject as what lies before it for its own use, for its valuation, for its preservation and enhancement. Heidegger calls the quality that the objective world has for the value-positing subject *Bestand*, a term that is sometimes translated as "constant reserve", "standing reserve" or "resource", and which he famously names as the essence of technology (Heidegger 1977). When things are viewed in this way (which Heidegger calls *Ge-Stell*, "enframing") beings appear as resources to be used by the subject. Heidegger writes:

> The uprising of man into subjectivity transforms that which is into object … The doing away of that which *is* in itself i.e. the killing of God, is accomplished in the making secure of the constant reserve by means of which man makes secure for himself material, bodily, psychic, and spiritual resources, and this for the sake of his own security, which wills dominion over whatever is – as the potentially objective – in order to correspond to the Being of whatever is, to the will to power.
>
> (*Ibid.*: 107)

According to Heidegger, the will to power is manifest in this way in the historical epoch known as modernity, in which the technological and scientific disclosure of beings has gained a monopoly. Heidegger's reading of the essence of technology links his interpretations of Nietzsche's will to power, the *Übermensch* and value-thinking, such that Nietzsche appears as the ultimate thinker of subjectivity, who advocates a wilful domination of the world, which is in turn reduced to a collection of manipulable objects.

Heidegger's critical reading of Nietzsche paved the way for a wider rejection of existentialism, which was seen to incorporate those same issues Heidegger critiques: value-thinking, subjecticity, the will and the metaphysics of essence/existence. (It is notable that Heidegger criticizes Sartre's existentialism on many of these same points; see his

"Letter on Humanism" [in Heidegger 1993].) In France, this critique influenced a younger generation of philosophers, called "poststructuralists", for whom Nietzsche was also an important point of reference. We take up their readings of Nietzsche in the next chapter. Kaufmann was certainly correct when he wrote, "It seems safe to predict that interest in Nietzsche will outlast the fashionable concern with existentialism" (1976: 102). Summing up Nietzsche's relation to this movement in modern thought, he writes: "Nietzsche is timeless, like Plato and Shakespeare. When I speak about 'Nietzsche and Existentialism', I see existentialism as one of the many timely phenomena, one of the many fashions with which Nietzsche has been linked for a while" (*ibid.*: 38).

Summary

Life-philosophy

Life-philosophy turns "life" into a foundational and all-encompassing principle, and understands this principle as something fundamentally irrational.

Nietzsche was an essential reference and inspiration for life-philosophy: he introduced life as an ultimate criterion for all judgements and values; he often associates that which is life-enhancing with the irrational; he introduced the normative antithesis between the healthy and the sick or decadent; and the will to power can be understood as a dynamic and irrational metaphysics of life.

Value-theory

While the German value-theorists were more influenced by philosophers such as Kant and Hegel in their approach, the impetus for their project of finding a new footing for values was largely given by Nietzsche's call for a "revaluation of all values".

Existentialism

"Existentialism" is a term that groups a diverse range of thinkers who generally have many of the following views and concerns in common:

- the existing individual, standing alone in the face of a meaningless universe;

- the objective meaninglessness of the world; the absurdity of human life;
- the unique way that human beings exist, because they are aware of and troubled by their existence;
- a focus on the subject, but in the full range of its existence (the irrational as well as the rational);
- a focus on, and a defence of the significance of, the individual;
- human freedom and agency;
- an ethics based around the categories of authenticity and inauthenticity;
- a suspicion towards philosophical system-building;
- a focus on personal inner experience as a mode of access to truth; and
- a more literary approach to philosophical style.

Jaspers' Nietzsche

Jaspers rejects the idea that there is anything of positive value in Nietzsche's philosophical doctrines, and instead focuses on his "philosophical activity". This activity has value because the many contradictions in Nietzsche's works can make us acutely aware of the limits of rational thought, and enable an experience of transcendence, through which we can gain greater insight into our own existence.

French existentialism

- Sartre: Sartre's relation to Nietzsche is uncertain, but both are united in a concern with nihilism and the problem of value, and in emphasizing the role of creativity in their responses to the question of existential meaning.
- Camus: Camus is both deeply influenced by Nietzsche, and explicitly critical of him. His response to the problem of suicide in *The Myth of Sisyphus* resonates with Nietzsche's *amor fati*, but in *The Rebel* he criticizes Nietzsche's absolute affirmation of existence because it cannot condemn murder.

Kaufmann's Nietzsche

Kaufmann was largely responsible, in the English-speaking world, for rehabilitating Nietzsche's image as an important philosopher from the Nazi "contamination" after the Second World War. He was also largely responsible for positioning Nietzsche as an existentialist. Among other points, Kaufmann sees Nietzsche as an existentialist because of his opposition to traditional philosophy in so far as it is overly rational, systematic, dispassionate and remote from life, and because of his overriding concern with nihilism and the apparent meaninglessness of human existence. However, he also notes significant differences between Nietzsche and other existentialists, and maintains that there is much more to Nietzsche's philosophy than those themes that can be characterized as existentialist.

Heidegger's Nietzsche

Nietzsche became a central concern for Heidegger in the early 1930s, just as he was turning away from his "existentialist period". For Heidegger, Nietzsche is the last metaphysician, and the zenith of metaphysics, precisely because he believes he has overcome it. Heidegger characterizes Nietzsche as a metaphysical thinker because:

- his philosophy is a reversal of Platonism, and retains metaphysical categories;
- will to power = essence; eternal return = existence;
- value-thinking is a subjectivization, and traps thought in the philosophy of the subject;
- the will to power is a will to dominate the earth, and implies enframing (the essence of technology).

two

Nietzscheanism and poststructuralism

Every concept comes into being by making equivalent that which is non-equivalent. Just as it is certain that no leaf is ever exactly the same as any other leaf, it is equally certain that the concept "leaf" is formed by dropping these individual differences arbitrarily, by forgetting those features which differentiate one thing from another ... Whereas every metaphor standing for a sensuous perception is individual and unique and is therefore always able to escape classification, the great edifice of concepts exhibits the rigid regularity of a Roman *columbarium*, while logic breathes out that air of severity and coolness which is peculiar to mathematics. ... [C]oncepts ... are only the left-over *residue of a metaphor* ...   (TL I)

Nietzsche has the rare distinction of being associated not only with existentialism, but with its most important successor movement in twentieth-century continental philosophy, poststructuralism. Existentialism and phenomenology had declined significantly in popularity in France by the 1960s, owing in large part to its displacement by a revolutionary new movement sweeping the humanities: structuralism. By the late 1960s, however, a group of thinkers who came to be known in the English-speaking world as "poststructuralists" critically engaged structuralism (while also accepting some of its insights). Prominent among such thinkers were Gilles Deleuze, Jacques Derrida, Michel Foucault, Luce Irigaray and Jean-François Lyotard. Nietzsche was an important influence on all of these thinkers, many of whom were instrumental in what has come to be known as the "Nietzsche revival" in France of the 1960s and 1970s. These poststructuralist interpretations of Nietzsche were extremely influential internationally in the latter half of the twentieth century, and continue to shape interpretations and debates surrounding Nietzsche today. This rather loose grouping has come to be collectively referred to as "French Nietzscheanism" or "the New Nietzsche", and has been associated with postmodernism and versions of feminism as well as with poststructuralism.

This chapter begins with an introductory outline of poststructuralism and a summary explanation of *why* Nietzsche was important for the poststructuralists. Given the irreducible complexity of historical events, institutional politics and the itineraries and agendas of individual thinkers, it is often difficult to pinpoint exactly why a particular thinker or school of thought "takes off" at a particular time and in a particular place. There is no doubt about the collective fervour of French Nietzscheanism (see Kuzma 2009), but identifying its causes, motivations, and real significance is not an easy matter. Alan D. Schrift, for example, suggests that the most important factor in the Nietzsche revival was the appearance of Nietzsche on the *agrégation* – the compulsory examination for secondary school teachers in France – in 1958 (Schrift 2005: x). Two important conferences on Nietzsche's work are also frequently cited as crystallizing his importance in the French context: one at Royaumont in 1964, and one at Cerisy-la-Salle in 1972 (the latter, titled "Nietzsche aujourd'hui", or "Nietzsche Today", also spawning an important collection of essays). Nevertheless, whatever the institutional context, there are significant *philosophical* reasons we are able to pinpoint for why Nietzsche was extremely useful for this generation of French thinkers.

The interpretation of Nietzsche developed by the poststructuralists owes a great debt to two earlier French interpreters, Georges Bataille and Pierre Klossowski. Following the general introduction to poststructuralism below, a section is devoted to their Nietzsche interpretations. The chapter then outlines the main theoretical points of three of the most prominent poststructuralist Nietzscheans: Deleuze, Foucault and Derrida. In the 1980s there was a backlash against Nietzscheanism in France, and the chapter concludes with a look at this French "anti-Nietzscheanism".

Nietzsche in the poststructuralist context

Poststructuralism can be seen as a critical reaction to a number of dominant movements in French intelligentsia in the 1960s, and the poststructuralist recourse to Nietzsche is explained by the fact that they found in his work powerful correctives to each of these themes. In other words, Nietzsche seemed to suggest solutions to many of the major problems besetting this generation of French thinkers. These problems are various, but may be summarized by the following four intellectual currents.

KEY POINT *Nietzsche's value for the poststructuralists*
Nietzsche provides resources for a critical response to:
- structuralism (meaning as reducible to synchronic linguistic and semiotic structures;
- Cartesian rationalism and the philosophy of the subject (including existential phenomenology);
- Hegelianism (philosophy as systematicity, recuperation, totalization);
- Marxism (a revolutionary and utopian politics on the level of parties and institutions).

Associated with these currents are themes such as humanism, rationalism and the philosophy of history, all of which express particular views about the nature of human beings and the nature of meaning and significance in the world. I shall consider each of these four currents in turn, indicating in a very general way how Nietzsche's work enables a challenge and critical response to them. In this introductory section I shall give most attention to structuralism, since it is arguably this theme that best allows an appreciation of the specific nature of poststructuralism. In the rest of the chapter, many of these themes and ideas will be considered again from the unique point of view of individual poststructuralist Nietzscheans.

Structuralism

It would seem appropriate to begin with the movement from which the term poststructuralism is derived: structuralism. Poststructuralism can be considered both an acceptance and extension of many of the principles of structuralism, and a critique of and counter-movement against it. Some of the key theorists associated with structuralism can also be identified with poststructuralism because of the way their later works developed correctives to the limitations of structuralism proper. Prominent structuralists and their fields include Ferdinand de Saussure (linguistics), Roman Jakobson (linguistics), Claude Lévi-Strauss (anthropology), Jacques Lacan (psychoanalysis), Roland Barthes (literary theory) and Foucault (philosophy/history of ideas). The last three of these are also often identified as poststructuralists.

Structuralism is the name given to a method of analysis that dominated the humanities in France during the 1960s. The advocates of structuralism perceived themselves to be undertaking a revolution in the humanities, applying a *scientific and objective method* of analysis to systems of human meanings. Structuralism is a theory of meaning that understands meaning as given to individual things by the structures they form a part of. Structuralism takes its lead from the structural linguistics developed by Saussure (1857–1913) and applies structural methods to the analysis of a wide variety of social phenomenon and systems of meaning in the world of human life: all those areas that are traditionally the object of study of the humanities (literature, anthropology, psychology, etc.).

KEY POINT

In general, a *structure* is understood as a set of formal elements and the reciprocal relations between these elements, and meaning is understood as being given by those relations.

Structuralism as a theory of meaning is contrasted to the more "traditional" view that meaning is formed freely in the minds of individuals, then communicated to others through language. Instead, it asserts that meanings themselves are a function of extra-individual structures such as language. Structuralism posits that meaning is a function of deep, conditioning, sometimes unconscious, structures that underlie human cultures and which make particular expressions of meaning possible. Structuralism is therefore often understood as supporting a deterministic worldview and undermining the idea of free will, since human beings and their world are understood as being determined by conditions that lie beneath their conscious awareness and control.

Following Saussure's linguistics, structuralism rejects a *diachronic* approach (studying phenomena through their evolution over time) in favour of a *synchronic* one (taking a "time-slice"; looking at relations between things at a particular time). For example, the cultural meaning a particular object, such as a car, is considered according to its relation to other objects in that culture at that point in history, rather than looking at the history of its development.

A point Barthes emphasizes in his illuminating essay "The Structuralist Activity" (1972) is that structures explain or make intelligible the phenomena they represent. As such, structuralism may be seen as an endeavour to extend rational understanding to apparently irrational areas such as myth, ideology and the unconscious. For example, Lévi-Strauss argues that so-called "primitive" peoples are just as rational as modern Westerners because their myths follow rationally consistent structures, and Lacan argues that the unconscious – considered by Freud to be a locus of irrationality – is structured like a language.

The distinctive feature of structures studied in the humanities (as opposed to the natural sciences, which often employ a kind of structural approach) is that the elements of structures are understood as *signs*. This follows Saussure, who suggested that linguistics is only one branch of the general science of *semiology*, which studies the role of signs as part of social life (Saussure 1986: 15).

> **KEY POINT**
> A *sign* is something that stands for something else. For example, a yellowed leaf may be interpreted as a sign of autumn. In a structure, signs refer to other signs in complex networks of meaning.

The sign is composed of two discrete yet co-dependent elements, the *signifier* and the *signified* (Saussure famously says they are like two sides of the same piece of paper, which would be the sign). The signifier is a *sound-image*, that is, both the sound of the spoken world and its visual appearance when written down. The signified is the *concept* to which the signifier refers. Saussure says that the relationship between the signifier and the signified is arbitrary, meaning that, for instance, any particular concept could in principle have any particular word attached to it (and concepts do in fact have different words attached to them in different languages).

If signifiers are arbitrary, then how do they gain their semantic meaning? Saussure's answer is: by virtue of *difference*. He writes: "[A] state of the board in chess corresponds exactly to a state of the language. The value of the chess pieces depends on their position upon the chess board just as in the languages each term has its value through its contrast with all the other terms" (1986: 88). Signifiers differ from each other: for example cat, mat, hat and so on. Signifieds also differ from each other in a similar way. Terms from these two systems of differences are arbitrarily linked to form signs. It is worth noting that this is a very different view of semantic meaning than had been popular up to that point; previously semantic value had generally been understood in terms of *identity*; a word gains its semantic meaning by virtue of that *extra-linguistic entity* that it *identifies* (refers to, or is a signifier of). Signifiers have meaning only *relative* to all the other terms in the language of which they are a part, by *differing* from them. Another related and important idea of Saussure's is that *there are no pre-existing concepts, prior to, and independent of, language*. This point is of decisive importance for twentieth-century continental philosophy; it introduces the influential idea that language, and the social use of signs, is central to our understanding of reality.

From structuralism to poststructuralism

The following points indicate the main ways in which the poststructuralists challenged structuralism, and how Nietzsche's philosophy proved a useful resource in such challenges. It should be borne in mind, however, that this is a schematic generalization, and any individual poststructuralist's thought will not necessarily agree with all the following points. It should also be borne in mind that poststructuralists were called such because they continued to accept some of the central innovations of structuralism – in particular, the view that meaning is extra-individual rather than a product of an individual human consciousness – and hence should be understood as arguing for a *radically modified* version of structuralism, rather than rejecting it outright. As a final point, it is worth noting that, as indicated above, structuralism was introduced as a methodology appropriate to the humanities *tout court*. Part of the impetus of poststructuralism can be understood as a desire to defend the specificity of *philosophical* thought from this hegemonic methodology, and Nietzsche was useful in this precisely in so far as he demonstrated philosophical challenges to a number of doctrines of this methodology.

- *Genesis, not synchrony.* Poststructuralism retains the view that cultural meanings are to be explained in terms of structures, but rejects the ahistorical, synchronic method of the structuralists. Instead, poststructuralism seeks to explain the *genesis* of structures: not just how systems of meaning work, but how and why those systems arise. Poststructuralists tend to see structuralism as inherently conservative because it implicitly endorses the values of an existing order, and gives no vantage point from which those values might be critiqued. Nietzsche's work on genealogy is particularly useful here in showing how the values of the present can be interrogated from a historical perspective. Conservative ideologies often present the values and traditions that they defend as eternal, universal, pure givens. Genealogy shows not only that things have not always been as we often erroneously assume them to have been, but also that present values are contaminated by ignoble origins (e.g. the origins of the notions of good and evil in *ressentiment*; see GM, first essay).

- *Dynamism, not stasis.* Furthermore, poststructuralism rejects the structuralist view that rational systems of meaning can be self-sufficient and internally consistent, and poststructuralist thinkers characteristically posit some kind of "dynamic force" that is essential to the genesis and constitution of structures, yet at the same time tends to disrupt or unsettle them, causing them to change and produce something new. These dynamic forces precede and exceed rationality and linguistic signification, and are variously indicated by such things as the body, the unconscious, libidinal energy, affects and so on. This suggests that structures are plastic, and less rigid or static than structuralists suppose. Nietzsche is useful here in his positing of a dynamic conception of meaning: he criticizes the "Egyptianism" (TI "Reason" 1) of philosophers who mummify meaning into dead, rigid concepts, and suggests that meaning begins with fluid and ambiguous forces such as the will to power, perceptions and the unconscious instincts of the body, and proceeds towards static concepts through complex and falsifying processes of translation and historical habituation. (See also the epigraph at the beginning of this chapter for an example of Nietzsche arguing such a point.)
- *Surface play, not depth.* Many poststructuralists are suspicious of the idea that structures are "deep" and underlie surface phenomena, rejecting this view as a quasi-religious mystification. Instead, poststructuralists see meaning in structures as constituted by a playful movement of meaning among signs that refer to other signs. This rejection of depth draws on Nietzsche's critique of religion: because the world is unintelligible in itself, religions posit a "true world" beyond the world of our senses. In a similar way, structuralists tried to give a rational explanation of the supposedly

irrational – the unconscious, the myths of "primitive" peoples, the sensuous seductions of art, the apparently frivolous productions of culture, such as fashion – by positing them as symptoms of deeper, underlying structures that were fundamentally rational and could be understood rationally. In rejecting deep structures, the poststructuralists follow Nietzsche in rejecting a supposed "true world" as the source of meaning, and instead affirm meaning as entirely the product of the immanent world of appearances.

In addition to these critical responses to structuralism, poststructuralism engages in important ways with the more specifically philosophical traditions that dominated France in the middle of the twentieth century. Once again, Nietzsche was an integral source of inspiration in responding to these traditions. The main points of these engagements follow.

Cartesianism, or the philosophy of the subject

The poststructuralist generation of philosophers sought to radically displace the philosophy of the subject, which may be seen as a persistent legacy of René Descartes (1596–1650) in the French tradition. Descartes posited the subject – the "I think" of "I think, therefore I am" (*cogito, ergo sum*) – as the first and only secure ground of all knowledge (Descartes 1954). Existential phenomenology had begun to displace the centrality of the subject for philosophy but, for the poststructuralists, this displacement had not gone nearly far enough. For example, Sartre had argued in *The Transcendence of the Ego* (Sartre 1960) that the subject is not a stable and continuous self-identity as Descartes and his predecessors had supposed, but reasserted his own Cartesianism in "Existentialism is a Humanism", claiming that philosophy can have no other beginning point than in the Cartesian *cogito* if it is to have any foundation (Sartre 1975: 360–61). In general, the poststructuralists see the subject not as a stable ground that would be suitable for first philosophy, but as a contingent product of more primary factors, whether historical, cultural, political, linguistic or ontological. On the other hand, however, while structuralism seemed at times to entirely efface the subject from the landscape of theory, the poststructuralists are concerned to bring the subject back into play, as decentred, and as something that needs to be explained, rather than as a principle of explanation.

Nietzsche is useful for the poststructuralist critique of the subject because of his own penetrating questioning of this philosophical concept. Nietzsche critiques the subject by questioning the value and

primacy of consciousness in the human organism as a whole, by asserting the epistemic priority of the body over the mind (directly *contra*
Descartes), by questioning the self-identity of the subject (he presents
the self as multiple and fragmented), and by suggesting that the idea of
the subject might itself be a fiction (there is no "doer" behind the deed;
GM I, 13).

An idea that is related to, but differs from, the philosophy of the subject is *humanism*. While this term has a number of meanings, the sense
in which it is a concern for poststructuralists is as the idea that human
beings are the origin and master of meaning in the world. Humanism in
this sense is related to the philosophy of the subject in so far as Descartes
shifted the seat of certainty from God to the human being (in their own
subjective consciousness). In general, poststructuralism retains the antihumanism of structuralism and the belief that meaning is a function
of extra-subjective systems rather than being rooted in the intentions
of conscious subjects. Humanism also portrays the human being as an
ultimate principle of explanation, perhaps the most extreme version of
which is the "anthropic principle" popular among some contemporary
scientists, which saves the meaningfulness of human life in the contemporary cosmological vision by proposing that the cosmos itself was
geared towards producing the human being as its apogee. Nietzsche
critiques humanism by pointing to the illegitimacy of assuming that a
creature in one particular point of its evolution (the human being as it
exists now) is the apogee of a vast cosmological process. Moreover, he
undermines humanism by pointing to all the limitations of the human
being, and pointing towards the *Übermensch* as a goal towards which we
should strive, and for the sake of which the human should be sacrificed.

Hegelianism

From roughly 1930 on, G. W. F. Hegel was a dominant reference point
in French philosophy. French Hegelianism was inaugurated primarily
by Jean Wahl's 1929 book *Le Malheur de la conscience dans la philosophie de Hegel* (The unhappiness of consciousness in Hegel's philosophy)
(Wahl 1951), and by Alexandre Kojève's famous lecture series at the
École Pratique des Haute Études from 1933 to 1939. Alexandre Koyré
and Jean Hyppolite also played a decisive role in this movement. From
the first, French Hegelianism was not "pure" Hegel, but was mixed
with existentialist, Heideggerian and Marxist concerns. The image of
Hegel that emerged from Kojève in particular came to be seen by the
poststructuralists as a foil for their own concerns, and Nietzsche was

seen as providing inspiration for an "anti-Hegelian" philosophy (or, perhaps more accurately, a "post-Hegelian" philosophy, since the relation of poststructuralists to Hegelianism is somewhat akin to their relation to structuralism; it consists in a critical transformation rather than an outright rejection).

As Robert Sinnerbrink explains in *Understanding Hegelianism* (2007: 127), the French critical reaction to Hegel can be understood as revolving around the related themes of the tension between *reason* and its *"other"*, and the *dialectical* movement of thought that seeks to reconcile all differences, understood as oppositions, into a unified whole. Hegel is an idealist, who understands all of reality in terms of a historical and logical movement of thought aimed towards a final reconciliation of all differences. Famously for Hegel, "all that is rational is real, and all that is real is rational" (1952: 10; trans. mod.), and the French tended to see the differences reconciled in the Hegelian unity as the "others" of reason – desire, emotion, the body, the mad, the feminine, the poor, the weak and so on – and to see the Hegelian dialectic's concern with "totality" as sliding towards political "totalitarianism" (Sinnerbrink 2007: 127). A third point that it is crucial to mention here is that in proposing that the dialectic unfolds concretely in history and moves towards a final goal, Hegelianism sees *history as meaningful*, and – according to poststructuralist critiques – gives undue justification to atrocities because they can be seen as grist in the mill of the dialectic (that is, evil is justified by a supposed higher good).

Poststructuralists react against Hegelian rationalism, dialectic and history. Nietzsche proves useful in each case. Against Hegelian rationalism, Nietzsche radically questions the value of reason itself, and valorizes its "others", such as the body, the instincts and the emotions. Against the dialectic, Nietzsche questions the epistemic primacy of the oppositions on which it is based. Moreover, Deleuze in particular finds a "logic of difference" in Nietzsche that contravenes the logic of opposition in Hegel, and affirms difference in itself rather than subordinating differences to a principle of identity. Finally, poststructuralists defend the singularity and contingency of historical events against the view that they can be given determinate meaning in any coherent narrative of history. For Foucault in particular, Nietzsche's reflections on historicism and his genealogical studies contribute to an alternative conception of history that points to the reality and significance of the "remainders" of mainstream historical narratives, which identify only "great" dates, events and individuals along a line of historical progression.

Poststructuralism is often called a *philosophy of difference*. We can summarize the above three points by saying that poststructuralism defends difference against its negation in a Hegelian philosophy of identity. The Hegelian philosophy conceives of thought as able to totalize and unify itself in an elaborate system. Against this, poststructuralism asserts the necessarily aporetic nature of any system that attempts to be totalizing, and affirms the singularity and the value of differences in themselves.

Marxism

Finally, the poststructuralist appropriation of Nietzsche also involves a strategic deployment with and against the Marxism prevalent in France in the 1960s. Since Chapter 3 is devoted to politics, we shall hold off from a discussion of this element of poststructuralist Nietzscheanism until then. In that chapter, these issues will be discussed in relation to Klossowski's discovery, with Nietzsche, of a new meaning of the political, which was an inspiration to the poststructuralists.

Precursors: Bataille and Klossowski

Bataille: the will to chance

Georges Bataille (1897–1962) was a librarian and writer who became a significant influence in French letters and on the poststructuralists in particular. He was associated with André Breton and the surrealists, and founded a number of influential journals, including *Acéphale*, *Counter-Attack* and *Critique*. Bataille's philosophy is one of excess and transgression, and his writings pursue an obsession with eroticism, obscenity, waste and death, all of which are deployed in relation to original notions of politics and community, of mysticism and religion. Nietzsche is a central reference in Bataille's writings, and his work may be cited as the origin of what we now think of as "the French Nietzsche". In an autobiographical sketch he writes that he "Is convinced, from 1914 on, that his concern in this world is with writing and, in particular, with the formulation of a paradoxical philosophy. Reading of Nietzsche in 1923 is decisive" (Bataille 1989: 217–18). While Bataille's own works and reading of Nietzsche are fragmentary, changing and deliberately paradoxical, we may summarize his influence on poststructuralist Nietzscheanism around three main points: (i) a defence of Nietzsche against the Nazi appropriation of his thought; (ii) pitting

Nietzsche against Hegel; and (iii) an emphasis on the irrational and paradoxical in Nietzsche.

First, during the 1930s, when Nietzsche's name in Europe was widely associated with German National Socialism (see Chapter 3 for more on this association), Bataille mounted an important defence of Nietzsche in his journal *Acéphale*. Some of the most important points of this defence are summarized in an appendix to his major text devoted to Nietzsche, *On Nietzsche* (2004), completed in 1944 and first published in 1945. These points all show that there are radical and irreconcilable differences between Nietzsche's philosophy and Nazi ideology. This defence paved the way in France for Nietzsche to be considered seriously as a philosopher (in contrast to other countries such as England, where the Nazi contagion persisted in eclipsing Nietzsche's validity for a much longer time).

KEY POINT *Bataille's defence of Nietzsche against Nazism*
- Nietzsche's philosophy is based in admiration for ancient Greek culture, and the primacy of cultural values remains central for him. By contrast, in the Third Reich, an impoverished culture centres on military power as the only goal.
- Nietzsche glorifies Dionysian values, that is, intoxication and enthusiasm. By contrast, Nazi racism admits only military values.
- Nietzsche denounced the vulgarity of the Germans and asserted the need for new values. Nazism preserves old values rooted in the German "fatherland".
- In contrast to Nazi ideology, Nietzsche often expressed his disgust with anti-Semitism (see Bataille 2004: 163–4).

Second, Bataille interpreted Nietzsche as a kind of anti-Hegel, an interpretation that profoundly influenced poststructuralists such as Deleuze and Derrida, and established the importance of Nietzsche for a generation of French thinkers seeking a way beyond Hegelianism. Bataille's own thought can be considered to have two sides, each pitted against the other: "Nietzsche" and "Hegel/Marx" (Stoekl 1979: 64). The Hegel/Marx side displays a concern with totality and unity, with totalizing and systematizing all experience into an absolute vision of the world. This drive to totality inspires Bataille to – for example – attempt to integrate the erotic dimension of experience into our intellectual and theoretical understanding of human life; to eroticize and corporealize theory itself, admitting into it what it usually suppresses and excludes (Bataille 1988: 21–4). Yet, this attempt at totalization *ruins* the totality or the closed system itself, since it shows that it is not possible to incorporate in a higher synthesis that which is opposed to rationality. Thus, Bataille pits Nietzsche against Hegel in so far as Nietzsche, for him, represents the untotalizable, anti-systematic, fragmentary embrace of excess epitomized by the figure of Dionysus, against the Hegelian principle that all oppositions and negativities can be appropriated in a higher, totalized, rational synthesis.

Bataille theorizes this Nietzsche–Hegel/Marx relation through what he calls "general economy". General economy is opposed to "restricted economy", where the latter refers to the financial markets of goods and monetary exchange, governed by the principles of scarcity and utility. The driving principle of a restricted economy (and here, Bataille includes the approaches of most "traditional" economists) is a maximization of efficiency and an increase in profit and growth. Moreover, we may see restricted economy working in the Hegelian dialectic in so far as it functions to sublate and conserve any differences, subsuming them within a system that functions without producing any excess. By contrast, Bataille's general economy includes all of culture and the natural world: all systems in so far as they can be considered as taking part in exchanges of energy. Bataille argues that in the general economy, there is always an *excess* of production of energy in a system, that is, a system produces more energy than is used in the process of production itself. A privileged example here, for Bataille, is the sun's excessive production of solar energy, but he argues that the same is true of human cultural systems. Excess energies need to be expended, and Bataille sees such expenditure in human culture in phenomena such as sacrifice, orgies, intoxication and war (in fact, he argues that unless such excess energy is expended in less destructive ways such as eroticism, wars are inevitable). Nietzsche's Dionysian principle of excess is here a great inspiration on Bataille, as are his late, unpublished notes on the role of excess in political change (a point taken up by Klossowski, and discussed in Chapter 3).

Third, the principle of excess applies to reason itself, and Bataille finds in Nietzsche a defence of those forces that have been traditionally considered irrational – the body, the unconscious, instinct – as well as a *performance* in his writings of that which exceeds reason. The Hegelian ideal of reason perfectly expressed in a systematic philosophical treatise finds an ideal counter in Nietzsche's aphoristic, fragmentary and often seemingly contradictory and paradoxical writings. In contrast to many interpreters, Bataille's approach to Nietzsche is not to try to systematize, rationalize, and then to either criticize or defend his philosophy, as though it contains within its fragmentary form a total system just waiting to be constituted and assessed by the astute interpreter. Rather, Bataille actually *accentuates* the fragmentary nature of Nietzsche's writings, picking up on and intensifying their potential to subvert systematicity. *On Nietzsche* is itself a very fragmented book, consisting of some short theoretical sections, some appendixes on a variety of topics, and a long selection from Bataille's personal diaries. Moreover, the reading of Nietzsche here is extremely selective, turning some points in Nietzsche's texts against other, better known doctrines. Of particular significance is Bataille's rejection in this text of the will to power in favour of the "will to chance". For Bataille, power implies a goal, and an understanding of time in terms of past and future, an understanding that allows for a plan through which a goal might be achieved. Picking up on fragments where Nietzsche rejects the idea of a goal, however, Bataille prefers to present Nietzsche as a philosopher whose gambit was to try to live without goals, affirming the present instant and the vagaries of chance. As we shall see, each of the above points had a profound impact on later French Nietzscheanism.

Klossowski: the vicious circle

Pierre Klossowski (1905–2001) was a scholar, translator, novelist, artist and actor who began studying Nietzsche under Bataille's influence, and whose work was pivotal in the "Nietzsche revival" in France in the 1960s and 1970s. Other prominent French thinkers of his generation were lavish in their praise of Klossowski: for example, Maurice Blanchot called Klossowski's essay "Nietzsche, Polytheism and Parody" ([1957] 2007) "one of the most important writings on Nietzsche in French" (quoted in James 2007: 210) and Deleuze praised it for having "renewed the interpretation of Nietzsche" (Smith 2005b: vii). Foucault proclaimed Klossowski's major book on Nietzsche, *Nietzsche and the Vicious Circle* ([1969] 2005) to be "The greatest book of philosophy I have ever read, on a par with Nietzsche himself" (Smith 2005b: vii). As such praise indicates, Klossowski's Nietzsche interpretation was a major influence on the work of many philosophers whose work came to be categorized as poststructuralist and postmodernist. Drawing almost exclusively on late unpublished fragments from Nietzsche's notebooks, Klossowski developed a highly distinctive reading of Nietzsche, which revolves around three related points: Nietzsche's political thought, the importance of the body and the radical dissolution of the main categories of philosophy (reality, knowledge and the subject). Each of these points is elaborated through Klossowski's central concern, the meaning of the eternal return. Klossowski's reading of Nietzsche's political thought will be treated in Chapter 3; here we shall deal with the other two points.

Klossowski was himself a highly original thinker, and he applies several of his own unique concepts to his Nietzsche interpretation: the *impulse*, the *phantasm*, the *simulacrum* and the *code of everyday signs*. The *impulse* summarizes various terms used by Nietzsche, including "drive", "instinct" and "affect". Impulses have a degree or magnitude (intensity), which rises and falls, and a quality (tonality), such as aggressiveness or anguish. Impulses are in a constant state of fluctuation, and in themselves are meaningless, without any aim or goal. Nietzsche's vision of the world as will to power and nothing besides (LN 38[12]) may be understood in Klossowski's terms as the fluctuation of impulses. At the most fundamental level, human bodies are also composed of these impulses. The relations between impulses give rise to what Klossowski calls *phantasms*: "obsessional images" that are themselves incommunicable and inexpressible, and which constitute the singular, incommunicable depth of each individual's "soul" (in Klossowski's sense, the soul represents the mysterious depths of our being, but is not something that stands metaphysically apart from the body). Phantasms are given intelligible expression in *simulacra*: simulations or "false copies". Because phantasms are themselves inexpressible, simulacra can only be "mistranslations", since they take the form of something communicable and expressible.

According to Klossowski's reading of Nietzsche, consciousness, language and the categories of intelligible thought are all mistranslations of the body's impulses in the service of communication. This mistranslation takes place through the regularization and stabilization of the fluctuating impulses of the body. Klossowski calls the system of regularized impulses the *code of everyday signs*. In a move that radically reverses the philosophical tradition's privileging of the mind over the body, Klossowski emphasizes, like few other interpreters, Nietzsche's "taking the side" of his body and nervous system against his brain and his mind. Klossowski draws attention to the way Nietzsche used his own bouts of severe ill health to philosophical advantage by using them as opportunities to observe the relationship between the body's impulses and conscious thought. Nietzsche presents the body in its fundamental state as a fluctuation of impulses as the "truth" of our nature, and conscious thought, language and the concepts and categories of philosophy as inversions and falsifications of the impulses. Klossowski places this radical revaluation at the heart of Nietzsche's thought, writing that "a kind of *fault line* ran through Nietzsche's entire mental effort: what if the *act of thinking*, in the end, were nothing but a symptom of total impotence?" (Klossowski 2005: 59). On the basis of his own physiological states, Nietzsche developed four criteria for evaluating all human culture: *decadence* (or sickliness), *vigour*, *gregariousness* and the *singular case*. The first two criteria negatively value sickliness and positively value health, while the second two negatively value gregarious conformity ("herd morality") as a symptom of weakness, and positively value individuality and uniqueness ("unexchangeability") as an expression of strength.

According to Klossowski, the eternal return was primarily a *lived experience* for Nietzsche. As such, it had the quality of a phantasm, and all the various attempts he made at expressing it (as existential thought, as scientific principle, etc.) were simulacra that could never capture its full significance. Klossowski identifies the eternal return as a *circulus vitiosus deus* – "divine vicious circle" – a term used in medieval philosophy to indicate a paradoxical argument. As this term suggests, he focuses on the way it undermines the traditional categories of Western metaphysics through a series of paradoxes. Klossowski asserts that the eternal return can only be a parody of a doctrine because, rather than establishing reality and knowledge, it undermines their very possibility. The thought of eternal return affirms the world as a series of singular instants. Each instant is affirmed as and for itself, with no meaning or goal other than to return to itself through the eternal return. As such, reality affirmed in this way eludes any possibility of being understood in terms of conceptual categories – for example, a historical narrative – that would make existence meaningful. Our meaningful conceptual categories depend on logical laws of thought such as the principles of identity and of non-contradiction, and on exclusions and selections. In affirming everything as necessary, the eternal return affirms the singularity and opacity of every instant, making the content of the doctrine of eternal return itself ungraspable and incommunicable. Thus, Klossowski presents the eternal return as paradoxical with regard to both reality and knowledge: it is a view of reality that undermines our traditional and habitual notion of reality as structured and intelligible, and it is a doctrine that undermines the supposed truth of any intelligible and communicable doctrine (see Klossowski 2007).

Finally, and perhaps most influentially of all for the poststructuralists, Klossowski argues that the eternal return undermines our sense of a unified self and the philosophical concept associated with it, the subject. The experience of the eternal return, he suggests, implies that we cycle through all of our past "selves", as well as all our future selves, in the cycle of returning to our current self. Our current sense of a unified and self-identical self is dependent on forgetting – or only selectively remembering certain aspects of – our past selves. Since we change so radically over time, many aspects of our past selves cannot be incorporated into our current self-identity, so the process of remembering (or "anamnesis", as Klossowski calls it) "overflows" our sense of self-identity. The paradox here is that the eternal return is a lived experience that undermines that which has been thought necessary in order to *have* an experience: the identity of the "experiencer" (see Klossowski 2005: ch. 3, "The Experience of the Eternal Return", 43–57). By undermining reality, knowledge and the subject, the experience of the eternal return returns us to the fluctuation of impulses at the fundamental level of nature and the body. Klossowski's reading of Nietzsche has been particularly influential on poststructuralism in offering a challenge to the Cartesian and existential-phenomenological philosophy of the subject; in offering an alternative to the structuralist analysis of meaning in terms of intelligible signs; in radically and positively revaluing the body and the affects; and in questioning the nature and value of "truth", "knowledge" and "reality".

Deleuze: the return of the different

Gilles Deleuze (1925–95) was one of the most prominent and influential thinkers of the poststructuralist generation, and is regarded by many today as one of the most important philosophers of the twentieth century. Deleuze's 1962 study, *Nietzsche and Philosophy* (Deleuze 1983), was a major influence on the development of poststructuralism and, along with Bataille and Klossowski, Deleuze can be considered instrumental in the rise of French Nietzscheanism. Deleuze continued the defence of Nietzsche against Nazi interpreters by offering unique interpretations of key doctrines such as the will to power and the eternal return, which present an image of Nietzsche radically different from the Nazi one. Moreover, Deleuze also took up and extended Bataille's pitting of Nietzsche against Hegel, and this helps to explain the success of *Nietzsche and Philosophy*: it showed, in a far more detailed and systematic way than did Bataille's work, a way for Deleuze's generation to escape the Hegelianism that had dominated the French philosophical scene.

Unlike many interpreters (and in direct contrast to Bataille, for example), Deleuze portrays Nietzsche as a systematic philosopher who creates precise new terms for precise new concepts (Deleuze 1983: 52). Deleuze's own orientation as a philosopher is primarily ontological: he is centrally concerned with "being", or the nature of reality. His reading of Nietzsche emphasizes this ontological dimension, and central to his reading are active and reactive forces, the will to power and the eternal return, all considered as precise ontological concepts. Nietzsche himself introduces the concepts of the active and the reactive primarily as feelings and psychological types in *On the Genealogy of Morals* (GM), where he undertakes a critique of the values and forms of life that have dominated Western civilization. Through these psychological types, Nietzsche analyses the history of Western civilization as a decline in which the slave morality of the reactive types has progressively become dominant over the master morality of the active types through the institutions of religion, law and culture. Nietzsche calls this process of decline "nihilism". Deleuze argues that in so far as nihilism is in essence a denial of life, what nihilism denies is the dynamic nature of existence as *becoming*. Simply put, this is because becoming resonates with growth and change, which are essential principles of life. In his interpretation of Nietzsche he links the affirmation of life with principles that affirm this becoming, such as *difference* and *chance*, and this equation is prevalent throughout his works.

In his systematization of Nietzsche's thought, Deleuze develops the ideas of the active and the reactive as forces, in accord with Nietzsche's speculations about the nature of the physical universe in *The Will to Power* and influenced by his (Deleuze's) own reading of Bergson. Deleuze describes active and reactive forces, along with Nietzsche's concept of the will to power, as basic constituents of reality. All phenomena, including the physical universe and psychical reality, can be interpreted in terms of forces and the will to power that governs them. As primary constituents of reality, forces are brought together by chance, and exist as forces only in relation to other forces. This relation is the essence of force itself: in order to be a force at all, a force must be in a relation with another force. Forces are defined by their power to affect, and to be affected by, other forces. Forces are never equal, and in a relationship between two forces one will have a greater quantity and one a lesser quantity. The difference in quantity between forces has a corresponding difference in quality, and the terms "active" and "reactive" refer to the qualities of forces: forces of a greater quantity have an active quality and forces of a lesser quantity have a reactive quality. Active and reactive forces are in a relation of superiority and inferiority: active forces dominate, take possession of and command reactive forces, which in turn are dominated by, taken possession by, and obey active forces.

Deleuze defines the will to power as the differential and genetic element of forces; it is what produces the differences in forces. Against the common interpretation of the will to power as the desire for power over others, Deleuze insists that it is primarily a creative and giving force. It is only the slavish, reactive type, operating at a low level of power, who understands will to power as the desire for domination. He writes:

> When nihilism triumphs, then and only then does the will to power stop meaning "to create" and start to signify instead "to want power," "to want to dominate" (thus to attribute to oneself or have others attribute to one established values: money, honours, power, and so on). (2001: 76–7)

This interpretation of the will to power as a creative ontological principle is summed up in Deleuze's formula, "Power, as a will to power, is not that which the will wants, but *that which* wants in the will" (*ibid.*: 73). The will to power also has two qualities: negation and affirmation. Negation is the becoming-reactive of forces; affirmation is the becoming-active of forces. Nihilism is interpreted by Deleuze as the triumph of reactive forces through an alliance with the negative quality of the will to power, known as the "will to nothingness".

KEY POINT

For Deleuze, the will to power is primarily a *creative* and *giving* principle, and only appears as a desire for power and domination from a slavish and reactive perspective.

The eternal return plays a central role in Deleuze's interpretation of Nietzsche as an ontological principle of *selection* that allows the overcoming of nihilism. The originality of Deleuze's approach to the eternal return consists in his assertion that it must not be understood as a return of the *same*, but rather as a return of the *different*. What is the same in the eternal return is not *what* returns, but *the fact of returning* itself (i.e. what remains the same is the continual return of the different). Nietzsche's doctrine of eternal return thus has a central place in the philosophy of *difference* and the ontology of *becoming* that Deleuze develops. The eternal return as selective ontology or selective being means that not everything returns. Only difference, and those things affirmative of difference, return. The eternal return affirms difference, dissemblance, disparateness, chance, multiplicity, becoming and active forces. It eliminates all those things that do not affirm difference and which do not enter fully into the process of becoming: identity and negation, the same and the similar, the analogous and the opposed. Moreover, as selective ontology, the eternal return excludes those things that are opposed to being as selection, and which attempt to make being stable and unchanging. The eternal return is given figural expression by Deleuze as a decentred circle that we should think of as a centrifuge, which expels from itself all that does not affirm difference, and which does not enter fully into becoming. The eternal return ultimately overcomes nihilism because it affirms becoming and eliminates that which denies it.

KEY POINT
For Deleuze, the eternal return is not the return of the same, but the return of the different. What remains the same is that *difference returns* (everything is always in a state of change).

Deleuze situates Nietzsche squarely in the context of the history of Western philosophy, seeing Hegel – or at least, the Hegelianism of later interpreters (since it is not clear that Nietzsche had a good first-hand acquaintance with Hegel's own thought) – as Nietzsche's central enemy, and finding in his work principles that are directly contrasted to Hegel's dialectical method of thought. He claims that "Anti-Hegelianism runs through Nietzsche's work as its cutting edge" (1983: 8). Hegelianism proposes that all thought – which, since Hegelianism is a form of idealism, is identical with all reality – takes part in a vast dialectical process, through which ideas are related to each other according to opposition and negation. That is, different ideas are seen as being fundamentally opposed (they negate each other), and this opposing element is seen as the motor that keeps thought alive and moving through history. In the dialectical movement of thought, opposing ideas are always reconciled in a higher synthesis (*Aufhebung*), a single idea in which that which is unique and best about the opposing ideas is preserved. Deleuze defines dialectics as "the art that invites us to recuperate alienated properties", and asks: "if our properties in themselves express a diminished life and a mutilating thought, what is the use of recuperating them or becoming their true subject?" (Deleuze 2001: 70–71). So, as a first main point of criticism, from a Nietzschean perspective dialectic is powerless to undertake the revaluation of values necessary in order to overcome nihilism, because it preserves nihilism, the life-denying evaluation of the world.

Second, in a related way, Deleuze sees Nietzsche's idea of the *Übermensch* as directed against the Hegelian notion of man as the subject of history. While the Hegelian man will conserve all historical values within them at the apogee of human existence, Nietzsche's *Übermensch* will overcome what it has meant to be human and be free for the creation of new values. Deleuze sees the dialectic's preservation of the past as a "heaviness", in contrast to the "lightness" of Nietzsche's *Übermensch*. Third, Nietzsche identifies the dialectical method as belonging to the slave, to the weak individual. He writes: "One chooses dialectics only when one has no other expedient … Dialectics can only be a *last-ditch weapon* in the hands of those who have no other weapon left. One must have to *enforce* one's rights: otherwise one makes no use of it" (TI "Socrates" 6; quoted in Deleuze 1983: 10).

Finally, and most technically, Deleuze contrasts the *opposition and negation* at the centre of the dialectic with the *difference and affirmation* at the centre of Nietzsche's thought. As we have seen, the Hegelian dialectic proceeds by way of opposition and negation, and Deleuze sees this as reactive and nihilistic in a Nietzschean sense. He contrasts the Hegelian logic of opposition with a Nietzschean logic of difference, and associates negation and nihilism with the former, and affirmation and the overcoming of nihilism with the latter. The logic of difference Deleuze finds in Nietzsche is based on Nietzsche's critique of oppositional thinking and his analysis of the master–slave relationship. In various places (for example, BGE 2) Nietzsche criticizes the oppositional thinking characteristic of metaphysics, arguing that antithetical concepts and values are roughly cut from more complex substrata of thinking and feeling (a continuous plane of subtle gradations; or, in Deleuze's terms, difference). Moreover, opposition is a type of thinking characteristic of the slave, who defines himself by opposing and negating the master, and affirms himself only as a secondary by-product of this primary negation. The master, by contrast, affirms himself first, and if the slave is opposed and negated it is only as a secondary by-product of this primary affirmation. From this Deleuze asserts a logic of difference that resonates with affirmation and differs from opposition and negation. This logic of difference finds various forms in all poststructuralist thinkers (such as Derrida's *différance*, for example), and on this point too Deleuze's Nietzsche interpretation can be considered seminal.

Foucault: truth and genealogy

Michel Foucault (1926–84) was one of the key thinkers first associated (uneasily) with structuralism, and then later with poststructuralism. He held the position of Chair of the History of Systems of Thought at the highly prestigious Collège de France, and was arguably the most famous French public intellectual after Sartre. Despite having devoted only two essays explicitly to Nietzsche (Foucault 1977a; 1990), Foucault was deeply influenced by him, and once stated in an interview: "I am simply a Nietzschean" (Foucault 1989: 327). Foucault was influenced by Nietzsche's *historical* perspective on the problems of philosophy, and his own work combined historical study and philosophical reflection in an original and influential way. For Foucault, however, this project of a *historical* interrogation was very much aimed towards an illumination of the *present*. Through a series of highly influential, if controversial, studies, Foucault developed alternative histories of scholarly disciplines, social institutions and practices, such as psychiatry, medicine, economics, the prison and sexuality. Each of these studies was designed to "free the present" from the restraints imposed by supposing certain cultural values, norms and practices to be eternally fixed and unchanging, showing that our views of things have changed radically over time, and thus opening up the possibilities of change in the present.

Foucault's work focuses on three key themes and the relations between them: *knowledge, power* and *subjectivity*. It is common practice for Foucault scholars to break up his *oeuvre* into three distinct "periods", each of which focuses primarily on one of these themes. Foucault draws significantly on Nietzsche in all of his work, some of which has significance for other topics covered in this book. We shall return to Foucault's Nietzsche in our discussion of the "end of man" in Chapter 6. I shall focus here on the deep underlying Nietzscheanism informing all Foucault's work by examining his concerns with the problem of truth and the method of genealogy.

Foucault's work is further divided into at least two distinct methodological phases: in his early works he employs a method he calls "archaeology", while beginning in the early 1970s he develops a method called "genealogy". Foucault's genealogy is quite explicitly inspired by Nietzsche, and we shall focus on it here. However, it is important to note that while archaeology and genealogy differ in important respects, they share many continuities, and Foucault asserted that archaeology was also deeply indebted to Nietzsche (Foucault 1989: 31). Briefly put, the key differences between them are as follows. In his archaeological phase, the main focus of Foucault's interrogation is knowledge. He seeks to identify the *conditions* for the *possibility* of systems of knowledge. Archaeology focuses on studying how knowledge is formed and expressed through uses of language and systems of communication. Genealogy, by contrast, focuses on the problem of power. It examines the material and ideological *means* of communication: the medium *through* and *as* which the communication is disseminated. Thus social institutions (universities, prisons, etc.), disciplines (philosophy, literary studies, etc.) and general social trends (dominant ideologies) are all objects of genealogical analysis. Moreover, genealogy departs from archaeology in the former's focus on the *body* as the locus of historical description. Whereas the main focus of archaeology is on systems of communication, the focus of genealogy is on the human body as it is formed by power relations.

Despite these differences, what unites archaeology and genealogy is a rejection of a particular view of the role of truth in historical discourse, and the attempt to develop an alternative historical sensibility. The deep Nietzschean influence in all Foucault's work may be seen in his approach to this problem of truth. In the early essay "Nietzsche, Freud, Marx" (1990), presented at the Royaumont colloquium on Nietzsche in 1964, Foucault uses Nietzsche's work to support the view that there are no facts independent of interpretation. For Foucault, Nietzsche's theory of interpretation means that ultimately what gets interpreted is only another interpretation, and so there is nothing but interpretations:

> Nietzsche makes himself master of interpretations that have already seized one another. There is no original signified for Nietzsche. Words themselves are nothing other than interpretations; throughout their history, they interpret before being signs, and in the long run they signify only because they are only essential interpretations. ... Therefore it is not because they are primary and enigmatic signs that we are now dedicated [*voués*] to the task of interpretation, but because they are interpretations, because beneath everything they never stop being that which expresses the great texture of violent interpretations. (Foucault 1990: 65)

Foucault concludes this essay by opposing *hermeneutics* – the Nietzschean philosophy of endless interpretations – to *semiology*, which supposes there is a final "truth" to the sign: an original signified (an object or fact independent of interpretation) that may be discovered. Thus Nietzschean hermeneutics contributes to Foucault's poststructuralist method in so far as it rejects the determinacy of the meaning of signs by rigid structures in favour of a much more fluid, historicized practice of interpretation.

> **KEY POINT** *Foucault on semiology and hermeneutics*
> - *Semiology*: tries to find a final "true meaning" of the sign.
> - *Hermeneutics*: accepts that there are only interpretations, without a fixed or final meaning.

In his essay "Nietzsche, Genealogy, History" ([1971] 1977a), Foucault surveys and summarizes Nietzsche's writings on genealogy. While it is relatively brief, an editor notes that "this essay represents Foucault's attempt to explain his relationship to those sources which are fundamental to his development. Its importance, in terms of understanding Foucault's objectives, cannot be exaggerated" (1977a: 139). The essay expands on the problem of truth and develops Foucault's own understanding of genealogy, a methodological approach that both Nietzsche and Foucault see as leading to an "effective history" (*wirkliche Historie*), which is opposed to "traditional history". Foucault characterizes "traditional history" (which is, presumably, the discipline of history as most historians practise it) as relying on certain philosophical assumptions that he glosses with the term "metaphysics". Metaphysics understands things to have an eternal, unchanging essence at their core. This essence is the "truth" of the thing, and in so far as it is unchanging, it stands "outside" history. In addition, things have "accidental properties": those things that are not part of their true essence and are subject to historical change. Metaphysics links the essence of things with their origin. In addition, it tends to see the current state of things as the end point of any historical development. Thus, Foucault sees the traditional, metaphysical approach to history as ignoring "accidents" and searching for the essence of things, supposedly revealed by linking the current state of things with their origins. For example, traditional history searches for the truth of history by pinpointing the great historical figures and events, construing everything else – the supposedly inconsequential everyday lives of the masses, for example – as "accidental". In sum, traditional history searches for "origins"; it tries to tell a unified story of the metaphysically "real"; it tries to tell the *truth* of history.

By contrast, genealogy rejects the metaphysical idea that things have an unchanging essence, and focuses instead on demonstrating how things have changed over time. Instead of the unified and continuous view of history implied by metaphysical truth, genealogy focuses on the arbitrary nature of history, on disjunctions, conflicts, discontinuities, accidents and multiplicities. Foucault explains that the aim of genealogy:

> is to identify the accidents, the minute deviations – or con-versely, the complete reversals – the errors, the false appraisals, and the faulty calculations that gave birth to those things that continue to exist and have value for us; it is to discover that truth or being do not lie at the root of what we know and what we are, but the exteriority of accidents. (1977a: 146)

Things are thus seen as developing from contingent arrangements of forces and chance events: from ruptures and conflicts and accidents. Instead of passing down through a direct line of descent from an origin, through which an unchanging essence is preserved, genealogy shows things arising in history through an eruption of forces, "the leap from the wings to centre stage" (*ibid.*: 149–50). These forces are interpreters, and are themselves interpretations.

KEY POINT *Foucault on genealogy*
Foucault opposes the genealogical method to "traditional history":
- *Traditional history*: searches for the unchanging essence of things in their origins; it tries to tell a unified story of the metaphysically "real"; it tries to tell the truth of history.
- *Genealogy*: rejects essences, and focuses on demonstrating how things have changed over time; it emphasizes the multiple and contingent nature of history, and understands history in terms of interpretations, rather than truth.

Thus, genealogy replaces truth with interpretation, as outlined in "Nietzsche, Freud, Marx". The aim of genealogy is not, then, to examine invariable objects, but to interpret interpretations. Foucault writes:

> If interpretation were the slow exposure of the meaning hidden in an origin, then only metaphysics could interpret the devel-opment of humanity. But if interpretation is the violent or surreptitious appropriation of a system of rules, which in itself has no essential meaning, in order to impose a direction, to

bend it to a new will, to force its participation in a different game, and to subject it to secondary rules, then the development of humanity is a series of interpretations. The role of genealogy is to record its history. (*Ibid.*: 151–2)

In a way, then, Nietzsche and Foucault have *inverted* traditional history; instead of providing an interpretation of history, the task of genealogy is to provide a history of interpretations. As genealogy opposes the idea of a "true" history, however, it involves an explicit awareness that any history it produces will itself be no more than an interpretation – *one* interpretation of many possible. As Foucault sees it, however, this is sufficient for genealogy to function as a critique, because it undermines the metaphysical notion of invariant essences. Any metaphysical dogma about the nature of something will be critiqued by showing that it is not incontrovertibly linked to an essence at its origin, but can be seen as having changed radically over time. In Nietzsche's *Genealogy of Morals*, morality is the main object of such critique. Foucault takes up the genealogical method in two major studies: of punishment (in *Discipline and Punish*; 1977b) and of sexuality (in *The Will to Knowledge*; 1978). Each of these genealogies also acts as a critique, showing that things have been, and may be, otherwise than they are with respect to the object in question.

Foucault has interpreted and popularized Nietzsche's genealogy as a particular kind of philosophical methodology that may be applied to almost any object of analysis. It is worth noting, however, that Foucault's own interpretation of genealogy has been questioned by some Nietzsche scholars. For example, Leiter (2002: 166–73) has argued, *contra* Foucault, that for Nietzsche the objects of genealogical analysis must remain invariant, while what varies historically is only their value. Whatever the case may be with Nietzsche, Foucault seemed quite happy to accept that the use to which he put Nietzsche's texts involved some interpretive violence:

> For myself, I prefer to utilize the writers I like. The only valid tribute to thought such as Nietzsche's is precisely to use it, to deform it, to make it groan and protest. And if commentators then say that I am being faithful or unfaithful to Nietzsche, that is of absolutely no interest. (Quoted in Schrift 1995: 33)

Regardless of whether or not Foucault's genealogy is Nietzsche's genealogy, it is undeniably a *Nietzschean* genealogy.

Derrida: Nietzsche's styles

Jacques Derrida (1930–2004) is most famous for his invention of the branch of poststructuralist thought known as "deconstruction". Deconstruction was widely taken up in the anglophone humanities, particularly in literature departments, and by the end of the 1980s Derrida was perhaps the best-known living philosopher in the world. In some later writings, such as "Otobiographies" (in Derrida 1986) and *The Politics of Friendship* (1997), Derrida takes up Nietzsche in relation to political questions, such as his culpability for his appropriation by Nazi ideologues. But we shall focus here, first, on Derrida's early writings, in which he develops the idea of deconstruction, and in which references to Nietzsche are frequent, if intermittent. Second, we shall consider Derrida's reading of Nietzsche in relation to Heidegger's interpretation in his best-known work on Nietzsche, *Spurs: Nietzsche's Styles* (1979).

Despite its popularity, deconstruction is notoriously difficult to define. This is because it involves a suspicion of essentialism, and to define deconstruction concisely in a phrase of the type "deconstruction is ..." would seem to fall into what deconstructionists see as an essentialist trap. However, if we must briefly outline Derrida's deconstruction – as we must here – the following may be said. Following Heidegger, Derrida sees what he calls the "metaphysics of presence" as a constant theme in Western philosophy. The metaphysics of presence gives a metaphysical, epistemic and even moral privilege to the present instant (here, now), and constructs conceptual hierarchies in which terms thought to embody presence are privileged, and terms thought to embody absence are denigrated. These hierarchies typically take the form of binary oppositions, in which two terms are opposed, and one is privileged over the other. Derrida's project involves deconstructing these hierarchies: deconstruction is not a destruction so much as a problematizing, with a view to freeing thought so that it might think differently than the structures of the tradition of Western metaphysics have allowed. Simplifying greatly, deconstruction involves a two-step process of inversion and displacement (see box overleaf).

One of Derrida's most famous examples of deconstruction is that of the speech/writing opposition (Derrida 1998). Derrida shows that speech has traditionally been privileged over writing as that form of expression which is supposedly more "present" to meaning. He then employs Saussure's structural linguistics to show that writing is, in fact, in closer accord with the conditions of meaningful expression, so might well be privileged over speech (the inversion). Then he displaces the opposition between speech and writing with concepts such as "arche-writing", "the trace" and "*différance*", which apply to all systems of meaningful expression (so, to both speech and writing) and which displace the metaphysics of presence by suggesting that differing, deferring and absence – not presence – are the conditions of meaning. (This example also shows why Derrida's deconstruction is poststructuralist: it incorporates much structuralist theory, but displaces it, opening it up to questions of the genesis and transformation of meaning.)

The importance of Nietzsche to Derrida's deconstruction is well put by Schrift:

> Nietzsche often appears in the Derridean text as an alternative to the nostalgic longing for full presence that Derrida locates at the core of Western metaphysics. In fact, "Nietzsche" comes to serve a talismanic function as a proper name for the very possibility of thinking otherwise, a shorthand marker for the *other* of logocentrism.   (Schrift 1995: 10)

Schrift goes on to specify Derrida's debt to Nietzsche as centring on the critique of oppositional thinking, which, as we have already seen, is a theme in Nietzsche's thought (see the section on Deleuze above), and which is central to deconstruction. Schrift argues that there is a "proto-deconstruction" in Nietzsche's thought: that he not only denounces oppositional thinking as a metaphysical prejudice in general terms, but also employs the double procedure of deconstruction, inversion and displacement. An example is Nietzsche's critique of the truth/falsity opposition. Nietzsche famously questions the traditional privileging of truth over untruth in the Western philosophical tradition by first inverting it, asserting that untruth in fact might be more conducive to the life of human beings than truth (because, for example, it makes life an easier burden to bear than the stark reality of existence). However, he aims not to simply assert the superiority of lies over truth, but to displace the very epistemic and moral grounds of this opposition by reading both truth and untruth in terms of their value for *life*. This then allows a much more mobile relation to truth and untruth according to their service to life in particular cases. He writes: "The falseness of a judgement is to us not necessarily an objection to a judgement … The question is to what extent it is life-advancing, life-preserving, species-preserving, perhaps even species-breeding" (BGE 4). Similarly, Nietzsche's movement beyond good and evil – despite the occasional provocative references to himself as an "immoralist" – does not simply invert the good/evil hierarchy, but displaces these terms in the interests of a revaluation of all values (Schrift 1995: 21–4).

One of the key motifs of poststructuralism, as succinctly stated by Lyotard, is that "there is a dimension of *force* that escapes the logic of the signifier" (Lyotard 1993: 64). Derrida develops this notion of force through his (non-)concept of "*différance*" (he insists it is not a concept in the traditional philosophical sense because it cannot be pinned down according to stable sets of oppositions), and Nietzsche is one of the key figures he cites as inspiration for this notion. *Différance* indicates the general conditions of possibility for anything to be meaningful. It has affinities with structuralist "difference", but is more fluid than the difference that operates between the rigid structures of oppositional terms in structuralist theory. *Différance* is first of all opposed to the idea that things have meaning by virtue of having a fixed or stable identity. Derrida begins his brief discussion of Nietzsche in his programmatic essay "Differance" (in Derrida 1973) by illustrating this point with Nietzsche's concept of force, citing Deleuze to make his point. For Nietzsche, forces have no identity in themselves; forces (as we have seen) are forces only by virtue of the way they relate to, and *differ* from, other forces. On this point, we must be careful to note that, for Derrida, force must not be thought in any way that would allow it to become a metaphysics of presence (as it arguably sometimes is in philosophy and perhaps also science). Indeed, the point of invoking force is, for him, that "force itself is never present; it is only a play of different quantities" (*ibid.*: 148). Derrida then explains how these differential forces give rise to systems of meaning that *appear* to be stable systems of oppositional terms:

> We could thus take up all the coupled oppositions on which philosophy is constructed, and from which our language lives, not in order to see opposition vanish but to see the emergence of a

necessity such that one of the terms appears as the difference of the other, the other as "differed" within the systematic ordering of the same (e.g., the intelligible as differing from the sensible, as sensible differed; the concept as differed-differing intuition, life as differing-differed matter; mind as differed-differing life; culture as differed-differing nature. (*Ibid.*: 148-9)

This Nietzschean image of meaning as constituted by differential forces differs from both traditional philosophy and structuralism in rejecting the idea that oppositional concepts are fixed and hierarchical, and substitutes for this a fluid play of forces. Structuralism, Derrida argues, is haunted by a "transcendental signified", a supposed ultimate term that would found the entire system of meaning in a privileged point of presence, a "lost origin" of all meaning. In contrast to this negative and nostalgic play of differences in structuralist theory, Derrida valorizes Nietzsche's positive affirmation of a play of forces that each have their own interpretive perspective, and are free from a nostalgia for "full presence":

> Turned towards the lost or impossible presence of the absent origin, this structuralist thematic of broken immediacy is therefore the saddened, *negative*, nostalgic, guilty, Rousseauistic side of the thinking of play whose other side would be the Nietzschean *affirmation*, that is the joyous affirmation of the play of the world and of the innocence of becoming, the affirmation of a world of signs without fault, without truth, and without origin which is offered to an active interpretation.
> (Derrida 1978: 292)

Nietzsche thus appears as a central inspiration for Derrida's deconstruction, and is given intermittent and passing acknowledgement in Derrida's early texts. A key theme that orients Derrida's more extended discussions of Nietzsche, however, is a nuanced engagement with Heidegger's Nietzsche interpretation. This is a central theme of *Spurs*, a text originally presented at the 1972 Cerisy-la-Salle colloquium on Nietzsche. Here Derrida presents a surprising interweaving of the themes of "woman" and "style" in Nietzsche's writings, asserting that, in fact, they refer to the same problematic. Heidegger neglects both these themes in his voluminous texts on Nietzsche, and Derrida finds this neglect significant. Heidegger reads Nietzsche as the last metaphysician (see Chapter 1), and in this sense insists on a unitary meaning, and a single truth, of Nietzsche's texts. Against this, Derrida is concerned to problematize the supposition that Nietzsche's texts can be pinned down to any single, truthful interpretation. For Derrida the twin tropes of woman and style function to this end. Woman is presented, in Nietzsche's texts, as unconcerned with truth; she is associated with mere surface appearances, with seduction and illusion. Derrida underscores this by writing that "There is no such thing as a woman, as a truth in itself of woman in itself" (1979: 101). The question of woman indicates for him the problematic of truth itself in Nietzsche's texts, and the supposed truth *of* those texts. (This theme was taken further by Sarah Kofman; see Chapter 4.)

The theme of style further undermines the supposed unity of meaning and of truth in Nietzsche's texts. Derrida highlights the plurality of Nietzsche's writing styles, as well as the often paradoxical and even contradictory propositions we can find in his writings. He uses this issue of style to undermine Heidegger's characterization of Nietzsche as the last metaphysician. While Heidegger asserts that Nietzsche overturns Platonism and remains trapped in metaphysics, as we have already seen, Derrida recognizes that Nietzsche's thought goes further and displaces the metaphysical oppositions of the philosophical tradition. Moreover, it is in his very play of styles that Nietzsche's texts resist being reduced to the metaphysical tradition, since they cannot be pinned down to a single position or truth that might be subordinated to the structural possibilities of that tradition. Summing up these two interrelated themes, Derrida writes:

> [T]here is no such thing either as the truth of Nietzsche, or of Nietzsche's text. In fact, in *Jenseits* [i.e. BGE], it is in a paragraph on women that one reads "these are only – *my* truths" (*meine Wahrheiten sind*). The very fact that "meine Wahrheiten" is so underlined, that they are multiple, variegated, contradictory even, can only imply that these are not *truths*. Indeed there is no such thing as a truth in itself. But only a surfeit of it. Even if it should be for me, about me, truth is plural.   (1979: 103)

Derrida illustrates this lack of a single true meaning of Nietzsche's texts by concluding *Spurs* with a discussion of a phrase found in Nietzsche's papers, written in quotation marks: "I have forgotten my umbrella". Derrida suggests that it might be a citation, something overheard, a note for later expansion, or possibly not even written by Nietzsche himself. There is no way of knowing for sure, Derrida insists, the meaning of this phrase. While this seems an extreme example, Derrida argues that all Nietzsche's texts have this undecidability of meaning (*ibid.*: 123–43).

It is worth concluding this section with a corrective to a common misunderstanding of Derrida: he is *not* arguing that, since there is no single, true interpretation of a text, any and all interpretations are equally plausible, or that there are an infinite number of possible interpretations. Derrida insists that interpretations are constrained by their context, so plausible interpretations are limited, and some interpretations are more plausible than others. His claim is just that interpretations are never absolutely decidable: that there will always be more than one plausible interpretation possible. The key issue here is that interpretations are not constrained by the idea of a single truth to which they refer (as the metaphysics of presence would have it), but by a relatively flexible structure (the context), which allows various possibilities of meaning and makes claims to a single "true" interpretation undecidable. For Derrida, it is this undecidability of interpretation that is eminently displayed by Nietzsche's texts. Derrida's focus on interpretive undecidability and the significance of Nietzsche's plural writing styles was highly influential on other Nietzsche interpreters, such as Kofman (1993) and Alexander Nehamas (1985), and the deconstructive strand of Nietzscheanism inaugurated by Derrida is an important dimension of poststructuralist Nietzscheanism.

French anti-Nietzscheanism

While Nietzscheanism was prominent in the French philosophical scene in the 1960s and 1970s, by the 1980s a backlash was under way. A younger generation of philosophers sought to distance themselves from the "master thinkers" of the 1960s, such as Foucault, Derrida, Deleuze and Lacan, that is, from poststructuralism. One of the principal ways in which they did this was to pick up on and critique the Nietzscheanism of this generation, recognizing that while other philosophical influences (Freud and Marx in particular) were important for the poststructuralists, none were so important as Nietzsche. A key text unambiguously marking this French anti-Nietzscheanism is *Why We Are Not Nietzscheans* (Ferry & Renaut 1997), which includes essays by Vincent Descombes, Alain Boyer, André Comte-Sponville, Robert Legros, Philippe Raynaud, and Pierre-André Taguieff, as well as the editors. The thinkers included in that book are all, broadly speaking, defenders of liberalism, democracy and human rights, and much of the thrust of the attack on Nietzscheanism is political as well as strictly-speaking philosophical. (Notably, Luc Ferry has been very actively involved in French politics; he served as Minister for Education from 2002 to 2004.) Ferry and Alain Renaut have been particularly outspoken and polemical in their criticisms of poststructuralist Nietzscheanism, and we shall take their views here as representative of French anti-Nietzscheanism.

In their preface to *Why We Are Not Nietzscheans*, Ferry and Renaut immediately announce that "To think with Nietzsche against Nietzsche" might well be another title for the book (*ibid.*: vii). They accept the importance and the lessons of Nietzsche in some respects: "Naturally, the scales have fallen from our eyes: no one today believes in Absolute Knowledge, in the meaning of history, or in the transparency of the Subject. That is precisely why it is together with Nietzsche that we have to think against Nietzsche" (*ibid.*: vii–viii). It is more against post-structuralist Nietzscheanism than against Nietzsche himself that their arguments are directed, although those aspects of Nietzsche they see as inspiration for the poststructuralists come under attack with direct references to Nietzsche's texts. In their co-authored article for their edited collection, "What Must First Be Proved is Worth Little", Ferry and Renaut situate Nietzsche as a neo-traditionalist who rejects argumentation, discussion and thus the democratic use of reason, as adequate bases for society. They see him as searching for "something analogous" to tradition, since he clearly does not believe we can simply return to the pre-modern way of life of the Greeks or Romans.

Drawing on various sections of *Twilight of the Idols*, they suggest that what Nietzsche believed went wrong in the ancient world and led to the failings of modernity was Socrates' introduction of the dialectical method of discussion and argumentation, which undermined traditional, unquestioning belief in the force of authority. They read him as identifying the brute assertion of authority with active forces of life-affirmation, and dialectical argumentation with reactive forces of life-diminution. Thus, they characterize Nietzsche as an authoritarian philosopher opposed to the democratic exercise of argumentative reason. After noting that Nietzsche's critiques of democracy are well known, they quip that this leaves them "somewhat whimsically perplexed as to how they did not prevent a generation of our philosophers – that of the 1960s – from professing Nietzscheanism" (*ibid.*: 97). Summing up these lines of argument, they conclude that Nietzsche's rejection of argumentation can only mean the return of authority. They imply that this is something the poststructuralists failed to see or take seriously, but that their own generation cannot forget (*ibid.*: 106).

KEY POINT *Ferry and Renaut: Nietzsche as anti-democratic*
Ferry and Renaut see Nietzsche as opposed to the democratic use of reason, as exemplified by his criticisms of Socratic dialectical discussion and argumentation. They see him as instead supporting a social model based on unquestioning acceptance of tradition and authority.

Here and in other works (see esp. Ferry & Renaut 1990), Ferry and Renaut criticize Nietzsche and poststructuralist Nietzscheanism on a variety of other subjects, such as the critique of the subject, the critique of science and the critique of modernity. This brief outline of their position on Nietzscheanism *vis-à-vis* argument and authority, however, serves to indicate the general tenor of their criticisms: they see Nietzscheanism as undermining *responsibility* in relation both to the demands of reason established by the philosophical tradition, and to the demands of justice established by the liberal democratic tradition. Thus, they see poststructuralist Nietzscheans as both philosophically and politically irresponsible.

I do not wish to end this chapter by implying that the French anti-Nietzscheans have had the last word. Schrift has presented a far more sympathetic reading of French Nietzscheanism in his book *Nietzsche's French Legacy* (as, I hope, I have also done here), and has raised serious doubts about the accuracy of many of the French anti-Nietzscheans' characterizations of French Nietzscheanism (e.g. Ferry and Renaut claim that the poststructuralists want to entirely liquidate "the subject", but this is clearly not their position; rather, it is to "decentre" the subject). Moreover, Schrift notes that Nietzsche has been subject to many rises and falls in popularity, and recent French anti-Nietzscheanism in no way reflects a real end to Nietzscheanism, either in France or the rest of the world. There is no space to discuss these issues in detail here, and interested readers are referred to Schrift's fine book for further reading (Schrift 1995: 120–26). However, some of the political questions raised by the French anti-Nietzscheans' criticisms will be taken up in the next chapter.

Summary of key points

The value of Nietzsche for the poststructuralists

Nietzsche provides resources for a critical response to:

- structuralism (meaning as reducible to synchronic linguistic and semiotic structures):
  - genesis, not synchrony;
  - dynamism, not stasis;
  - surface play, not depth.
- Cartesianism, or the philosophy of the subject (including existential phenomenology);
  - critique of humanism
- Hegelianism (philosophy as systematicity, recuperation, totalization):
  - dialectic;
  - reason and its "other";
  - history as meaningful.
- Marxism (a revolutionary and utopian politics on the level of parties and institutions).

Bataille's Nietzsche

Bataille defends Nietzsche against the Nazi appropriation of his thought, pits Nietzsche against Hegel, and places an emphasis on the irrational and paradoxical in Nietzsche.

Klossowski's Nietzsche

Klossowski places a central focus on the eternal return, interpreted as "the vicious circle". He also explores Nietzsche's sickness, in a way that has radical implications for the relationship between thought and the body (giving the body greater value than thought). Klossowski interprets Nietzsche's philosophy as undermining the traditional philosophical notions of reality, truth, and the subject.

Deleuze's Nietzsche

Deleuze develops a systematic, philosophical reading of Nietzsche focusing on a metaphysics based on the principle of difference. He presents Hegelianism as Nietzsche's central target of critique. For

Deleuze, the will to power is a metaphysics of differential forces, and only in a deficient mode as a desire for domination. Moreover, for him the eternal return is the return of the different (not the same).

Foucault's Nietzsche

Foucault presents Nietzsche as proposing a hermeneutics (there are only interpretations), and opposing semiology (a final, fixed meaning). Foucault develops Nietzsche's genealogy as a method opposed to "traditional" history: where traditional history seeks to tell a unified narrative of the "true" meaning of history, based around the supposed unchanging essence of things, genealogy acts critically by telling alternative histories that accentuate how things have changed, undermining the notion of essence and demonstrating that things might have been otherwise than they are.

Derrida's Nietzsche

For Derrida, Nietzsche is a key figure who challenges "the metaphysics of presence". Nietzsche is a forerunner to deconstruction in his employment of the double strategy of inversion and displacement of hierarchical binary oppositions. In his reading of Nietzsche, Derrida explores the displacement of the idea of a fixed, true meaning of a text through the issues of woman and style in Nietzsche's writings.

French anti-Nietzscheanism

French thinkers such as Ferry and Renaut see Nietzsche as an irrational, neo-conservative thinker who rejects the democratic use of reason and seeks to replace Enlightenment values with an unquestioning acceptance of tradition and authority.

three

Nietzscheanism and politics

It is only beginning with me that the earth knows *great politics*.
(EH "Destiny" 1)

From the earliest receptions of Nietzsche in the late nineteenth and early twentieth centuries, he was embraced enthusiastically by representatives of both the extreme right and extreme left of the political spectrum, in the belief that his philosophy had significance for their own politics. Moreover, this interest in the purported political dimension of Nietzsche's thought was signalled by Nietzsche's first significant popularizer, Georg Brandes. During his lectures on Nietzsche in 1888, he focused on the political dimension of Nietzsche's critique of culture, and ascribed to Nietzsche a political philosophy he described as "aristocratic radicalism" (a term Nietzsche himself approved) (Leiter 2010). Throughout the first part of the twentieth century, Nietzsche's work was often embraced in relation to the politics of cultural renewal. This culminated with the darkest chapter in the history of Nietzscheanism, with which any consideration of Nietzscheanism and politics must come to terms: his appropriation by the Nazi Party, and the sullying of his name with the marks of nationalism and racism of the very worst extremes. After the end of the Second World War, Nietzsche interpreters typically sought to redeem him from the Nazi association by painting him as in reality an *unpolitical* thinker. However, matters have now changed. Interest in the political dimension of Nietzsche's thought was substantially renewed by Tracy B. Strong's *Friedrich Nietzsche and the Politics of Transfiguration* ([1975] 2000), and Nietzsche's political thought has become one of the burgeoning areas of Nietzsche studies over the past twenty or so years.

In this chapter we shall explore Nietzscheanism and politics through the following issues. First, we shall examine Nietzsche's own political context in order to establish the nature and scope of his likely political interests. Next, we shall engage Nietzsche's Nazi appropriation, considering how his work came to be enlisted in the Nazi cause. We shall then consider some of the main lines of interpretation concerning Nietzsche's own political philosophy that have emerged over the past twenty years. In doing so, we shall review some contested interpretations of his thought in relation to the established political positions of aristocratism, liberalism, socialism and democracy. In the final section of this chapter we shall turn our attention to more unconventional (from the perspective of mainstream political theory) ways of interpreting the political significance of Nietzsche's thought. We shall examine how a new idea of the political emerges in French Nietzscheanism, and the diverse impact of Nietzsche on the tradition of critical theory.

Nietzsche's political context

Nietzsche's own reflections on political issues were undoubtedly shaped by the political context in which he lived, as well as by the texts he read. The most significant fact of this context was the unification of the German states under the leadership of Otto von Bismarck (1815–98). Bismarck was Chancellor of Prussia from 1862 to 1890, a period covering the entirety of Nietzsche's sane adult life. A key event in the unification process was the Franco-Prussian War (1870–71), in which Nietzsche served as a medical orderly. The war was deliberately orchestrated by Bismarck as a vehicle for the unification of Germany, and the resounding victory of the Germans over France successfully achieved this end. The Second German Empire (the Second Reich) was proclaimed in 1871, with King Wilhelm I of Prussia declared Emperor of Germany. The Bismarckian system of government was constitutional and semi-parliamentary, but the general view is that it was in reality a dictatorship cloaked with aspects of a party-political system to give the appearance of a balance of powers. There were three branches of government: the executive (the chancellor and the emperor), the federal council and the parliament. The members of the parliament were democratically elected, and all legislation required their consent. However, the executive had a great deal of power, including control of the military, and the discretion to dissolve the parliament (see Cameron & Dombowsky 2008: 3). It is generally thought that Bismarck's aim was to conserve the authority of the aristocratic land-owning class and feudal-military structures against the threats of democracy and socialism (*ibid.*).

The political and cultural context for Nietzsche's writing was thus a newly unified Germany, with a prevalent mood of nationalism and a military confidence born of the victory over France. Nietzsche's own political views changed over time. In the early 1860s, he was a royalist, and – after being initially critical of Bismarck for his attempt to annex Austria to Prussia through military force in 1866 – he was a strong supporter of Bismarck. Nietzsche's one and only brief period of active involvement with politics came in the summer of 1866, when he campaigned in support of a candidate of the Saxon National Liberals. This party advocated a unified German Empire, along with a free economy, free trade and a constitutional state (Ansell-Pearson 1994: 25). The candidate Nietzsche supported lost, and subsequently Nietzsche expressed a disdain for politics (while continuing to have political opinions). Keith Ansell-Pearson characterizes Nietzsche's political views in the 1870s as centred on the hope of cultural renewal through art (in particular, Wagner's music-dramas, which he understood as the "rebirth of tragedy") rather than party politics, and in this period he was critical of Bismarck's new Germany for its excessive focus on military power and its failure to renew German culture (*ibid.*: 27). In the later 1870s, his sympathies towards Bismarck increased because he saw him as a counter to what he perceived as the threat of socialism. Another event key to understanding Nietzsche's political context is the revolution of 1848 (which took place in both France and Germany), which demonstrated the growing tide of socialist sentiment in Europe. In the 1880s, Nietzsche became more critical of Bismarck's policies, especially German nationalism, politics based on military power (*Machtpolitik*) and anti-Semitism. However, he still seemed to admire Bismarck as embodying a strong type, close to his ideal of the free spirit.

Nietzsche's political views are complex, ambiguous and a matter of lively debate. We shall examine various perspectives on these views in the section on "Nietzsche's political philosophy" below. But simplifying greatly, we may summarize the main points as follows.

KEY POINT *Nietzsche's political views in context*
Apart from a brief period of his support for the National Liberals, Nietzsche was critical of liberalism; he was hostile towards socialism; he turned from supporting nationalism to opposing it; and he was ambivalent about Bismarck's Germany.

Nietzsche's political views placed him out of step with both the mainstream right and mainstream left of his time, and he cannot easily be placed on the political spectrum. As Frank Cameron and Don Dombowsky (2008: 21) comment, Nietzsche's anti-egalitarianism alienated him from the left, while his anti-Christianity and opposition to anti-Semitism alienated him from the right. A main point of contention for understanding Nietzsche's politics is the relationship between *politics* and *culture* in his thought. As Ansell-Pearson (1994: 27) emphasizes, there is a sense in which Nietzsche disdained power-politicking because he saw it as undermining cultural renewal, which was always his primary concern. However, Cameron and Dombowsky insist that these issues cannot be separated for Nietzsche, that "He saw a direct correlation between the transformation of the political order and cultural regeneration" (2008: 2). In fact, both views are present in his writings, and as usual with Nietzsche it is a matter of which view one chooses to emphasize. Let us turn now to the uncomfortable, but essential, question of how Nietzsche's politically complex and ambivalent thought came to be appropriated by the crude ideology of Nazism.

Nietzsche and National Socialism

Ansell-Pearson writes: "It is somewhat paradoxical that a writer who promoted the cause of Europe as opposed to that of Germany, who lambasted all forms of racism in politics, especially anti-Semitism, should be perceived so widely as an ideological founder of Nazism" (1994: 28). Such an appropriation did not happen overnight, but can be understood as the culmination of a line of Nietzsche reception established by Elisabeth Förster-Nietzsche from the first few years after her brother's breakdown, which adapted his work to the cause of German nationalism (and frequently, of anti-Semitism). Elisabeth was deeply involved with the anti-Semitic movement. She married Bernhard Förster, an anti-Semitic activist, and some of Nietzsche's most vitriolic comments about anti-Semitism were probably inspired by this union, of which he profoundly disapproved. In 1887 the couple founded the colony *Nueva Germania* in Paraguay, South America, initially with twelve German families. Their intention was to create a community of pure Aryans. The colony was badly organized and there were many problems. Facing anger from the settlers and mounting debts, Bernhard committed suicide in 1889. Elisabeth returned to Germany in 1893. She founded the Nietzsche Archive and, as we have seen, took control of the editorship of Nietzsche's published works. She also wrote an extensive biography of him. Elisabeth shaped Nietzsche's reputation in line with her own nationalist and racist commitments, and edited out of his writings those passages that conflicted with her interests (including some passages in which her brother criticized her). In the 1930s, when the Nazis came to power, Elisabeth actively supported them, endorsing the idea that Nietzsche's philosophy resonated with their ideology. The Nietzsche Archive received funding from the Nazi government, and Hitler visited the archive twice. (There is an infamous photo of Elisabeth presenting him with Nietzsche's walking stick.)

As much as Elisabeth is culpable for the distortion of Nietzsche's legacy towards the nationalist and anti-Semitic ends that made it attractive to the Nazis, she was not alone. Nietzsche's work was attractive to many representatives of the extreme right in the early decades of the twentieth century, and it received a number of influential interpretations that can be broadly described as "romantic nationalist". First, as discussed in Chapter 1, the *Lebensphilosophie* interpretations of Nietzsche associated the vital force of life with the irrational, and often with the violence of domination and war, as well as with the racial type of the "blond beast". The outbreak of the First World War added fuel to the fire of life-philosophy, and its belligerent side came to be emphasized (Safranski 2003: 328). Nietzsche was often enlisted in Germany as an ideological support for the war, and some French, English and American writers came close to blaming him for the war itself (*ibid.*: 329).

Rudiger Safranski concisely describes Bertram's *Nietzsche*, the most influential book on Nietzsche between the two world wars, as "the creation of a myth suited to uniting a nation under a common banner now that religion had faded" (2003: 331). As he further notes, this idea of creating a nationalist myth has its source in the romantic tradition, and was endorsed by Wagner, as well as the young Nietzsche. In his book, Bertram not only wishes to present Nietzsche as attempting to create such a mythology, but attempts to mythologize Nietzsche himself, to turn him into a figure who can revivify German culture by reflecting in his life the "soul" of Germany. Bertram's interpretation placed Nietzsche firmly within a right-wing tradition (Diethe 2006: xxv), and developed themes that would later be turned to Nazi ideological ends, with Bertram's own encouragement. Safranski illustrates how Bertram's interpretation came to serve the Nazi cause with the image of "knight, death, and devil" he extracts from Nietzsche's work. In *The Birth of Tragedy*, Nietzsche uses Albrecht Dürer's engraving *Knight, Death, and the Devil* (1513–14) to exemplify Schopenhauer's pessimism. Bertram suggests that the same image may be used to characterize the German spirit, where the knight is the pessimistic, but stoical and heroic, figure who accepts the inevitability of death and evil. Under the Third Reich, this image was transformed so that the knight was understood as the racially pure Aryan, and was sometimes depicted as Hitler himself, in artistic propaganda commissioned by the Nietzsche Archive (Safranski 2003: 332).

Nevertheless, it must be noted that Bertram's work is far more complex and subtle than its fate under the Third Reich would suggest. Thomas Mann, a close friend of Bertram's, greatly admired the book, and the recent republication of it in French translation, and its first publication in English translation, are winning it renewed and positive attention. Bertram's book has been admired as itself a literary work of art, which gives valuable insight into artistic and psychological themes in Nietzsche's thought. One of its valuable contributions to Nietzsche scholarship is its study of the works of art and literature Nietzsche himself admired, while another is the attention it draws to elements of Nietzsche's thought, such as "philosophical lineage", masks and justice, which are typically marginalized (see Ansell-Pearson 2009). In his preface to the French translation, noted classical scholar Pierre Hadot opines that "After the appearance of the great works devoted to Nietzsche in the course of the twentieth century, Bertram's book retains all its value and its relevance" (2010: 82).

Other notable Nietzsche interpreters whose views resonated with the ultra-right currents of the times, and thus contributed directly or indirectly to Nietzsche's association with National Socialism, include Ernst Jünger and Oswald Spengler. Jünger's popular books such *Storm of Steel* and *The Worker* enlisted Nietzsche for the celebration of an aestheticized form of warfare understood as a life-affirming, masculine, creative activity (Aschheim 1992: 158). Spengler's widely read book *The Decline of the West* ([1918] 1932) drew on Nietzsche's view of history and of the nihilism of the current age to argue that we live in a time of decline. Spengler characterized the culture of the contemporary West as "Faustian", indicating a constant striving after goals that elude fulfilment. He was critical of democracy, seeing it as an inappropriate form of government for the times, and instead advocated a dictatorship. (Spengler's work was initially embraced by the National Socialists, but he fell out of favour because he criticized them for their crude biological racism, and publically quarrelled with their principal ideologist Alfred Rosenberg.)

Baeumler's *Nietzsche, der Philosoph und Politiker* (1932) presented what has come to be known as the "official" Nazi interpretation of Nietzsche.

Baeumler focuses on Nietzsche's concept of the will to power, and uses it to develop a "Heraclitean" worldview of forces in a continuous flux of becoming, before drawing out the political implications of this metaphysical interpretation. Baeumler accentuates the dimension of *power* in Nietzsche's thought, and understands the will to power as consisting of forces in constant struggle for dominion over one another. He denies the possibility of any Hegelian synthesis, suggesting that any apparent synthesis will simply be the triumph of one side that has co-opted certain traits of the other (Safranski 2003: 336). Baeumler rejects any "stable being" implied by the repetition of the eternal return, arguing that the will to power implies constant conflict without any stability, and justifying his interpretation with the argument that Nietzsche's experience of the eternal return took place before his developed theory of the will to power, which then superseded it.

Baeumler argues that all knowledge claims, as well as moral and cultural values, are simply expressions of the power which underlies them. He endorses a kind of relativism of power, in which "might makes right". Politically, Baeumler's Nietzsche endorses the inevitability of war and the importance of nationalism and racism, but on grounds that are self-consciously contingent and relativist. One has no choice over what body or what country one is born into, but since life is inevitably conflict, with winners and losers, we ought to support the side we happen to find ourselves on through the accident of birth and do all in our power to ensure that our own side triumphs against the "others". Baeumler endorses the superiority of the Nordic race, and its warring against other races, but on grounds that are knowingly relativist. (This possible association between violence and relativism is perhaps sometimes forgotten by "postmodern" relativists, who suppose a direct support for tolerance in relativism.) While Baeumler's interpretation of Nietzsche is rightly to be regarded with scepticism because of its unsavoury associations, it is not entirely without is merits. Safranski suggests that his study "reconstructed a series of compelling links between the philosopher's ideas in a precise and philosophically astute manner" (2003: 335), while Gianni Vattimo (2001: 176) notes that it began a new phase in Nietzsche interpretation because of its emphasis on the way Nietzsche deployed the will to power against the western metaphysical tradition.

The ideological prominence Nietzsche was given by the Third Reich caused widespread condemnation of his work in the "Allied" countries during and after the Second World War. In America, for example, Crane Brinton's study *Nietzsche* (1941), which argued that Nietzsche's philosophy served as direct inspiration for Nazism, became the accepted interpretation in the 1940s (Ratner-Rosenhagen 2006: 255). During the 1950s and 1960s, however, a host of interpreters – such as Kaufmann in America and Deleuze in France – worked to "save" Nietzsche from the Nazis. Today, it is almost universally acknowledged that the Nazis were only able to co-opt Nietzsche for their cause by severely editing and grossly distorting his work. During the Third Reich, the popular editions of Nietzsche's writings that circulated contained only those statements of his that would seem to support the Nazi cause, and his anti-German Nationalist and *anti*-anti-Semitic sentiments were censured. As the National Socialist philosopher Ernst Krieck admitted: "All in all, Nietzsche was an opponent of socialism, an opponent of nationalism, and an opponent of racial thinking. Apart from these three bents of mind, he might have made an outstanding Nazi" (quoted in Safranski 2003: 340).

Nevertheless, questions of Nietzsche's culpability for the ends to which the Nazis put his work remain, and philosophers such as Derrida have insisted that while we must, of course, insist that Nietzsche was not a proto-Nazi, we must nevertheless acknowledge that there are perspectives in his work that lent support to some of the Nazi's crimes. Some of these perspectives will become evident as we explore Nietzsche's political philosophy below.

Nietzsche's political philosophy

Taking a broad summary view, the recent works on Nietzsche's political philosophy have established three main competing lines of interpretation:

- Nietzsche as unpolitical;
- Nietzsche as aristocratic radical; and
- Nietzsche's philosophy as consistent with liberal democracy.

The first of these continues the view established by Kaufmann, popular roughly from the 1950s to the 1980s, that Nietzsche had no political philosophy of his own, and was in fact uninterested in politics. The second interpretation is based on Nietzsche's most explicit political statements (as well as his endorsement of this description of his thought by Brandes), and seeks to elaborate, systematize and often criticize an elitist politics of exploitation found in his writings. The third interpretation of Nietzsche seeks to appropriate his thought for more liberal and/

or democratic ends, and is often predicated on the assertion that there is a disconnection between his philosophy and his politics. We shall briefly consider the first interpretation (to which there may be some truth, but which is nevertheless uninteresting), before exploring various dimensions of the second two, more complex, strands of interpretation under the headings of aristocratism, liberalism, socialism and democracy. There has been so much written on Nietzsche's political philosophy over the past several decades that we cannot hope to give anything like a comprehensive survey, and must content ourselves with some of the most notable positions in the literature. (For further works on this topic, see the Further Reading.)

Nietzsche as unpolitical

Is Nietzsche really a political philosopher? Does he have anything to offer to political philosophy? These are issues of some controversy among Nietzsche scholars. As noted above, Kaufmann's immensely influential portrait of Nietzsche was one of an unpolitical thinker. Kaufmann identifies, as the "leitmotif of Nietzsche's life and thought ... the anti-political individual who seeks self-perfection far from the modern world" (1974: 418). Kaufmann's Nietzsche is a steadfast individualist, contemptuous of the masses and of politics as a herd-phenomenon on which an authentic individual is better to turn his back. This interpretation has the obvious advantage of distancing Nietzsche from his Nazi usurpers: if Nietzsche had no politics, he clearly could not have endorsed the politics of the German National Socialists. Thus Kaufmann's interpretation had a certain expediency in the post-war period. However, this view also has its contemporary advocates.

One of the most recent statements of the "unpolitical" case is made by Leiter (2010). After noting that "Nietzsche's political philosophy" has been one of the most popular themes in recent scholarship, he denies that Nietzsche is a political philosopher or has anything to offer political philosophy. His argument is that Nietzsche does not discuss the themes that have predominated in Western political philosophy from Plato to John Rawls. He has no developed criticisms or positive theories of the state, law or social institutions. Leiter concedes that Nietzsche occasionally expresses *opinions* about politics in his writings, as he expresses opinions about a vast array of things. But he denies that these opinions add up to anything like a developed or systematic political philosophy. Moreover, he asserts that the political interpretations of Nietzsche are usually based around a handful of statements in his writings that are incorrectly interpreted because they are taken out of context: a contextual reading reveals that they are not intended to make substantive political claims. (As an example, Leiter cites sections 56–7 of *The Anti-Christ*, which have often been read as endorsing the elitist politics of the *Laws of Manu*, but which, he contends, are aimed only at furthering the critique of Christianity.) Leiter further concedes that Nietzsche's views – for example, about morality – have some political *implications*, but insists that this is not enough to justify positioning him as a political philosopher. Leiter writes: "The canon of political philosophers is composed of thinkers (like Hobbes, Locke, and Rousseau) who have philosophical views about political questions – the state, liberty, law, justice, etc. – not thinkers whose views about *other* topics merely had 'implications' for politics" (2010).

Notably, however, Leiter does not acknowledge some of the works that not only refer to a wide range of textual evidence of Nietzsche's political views, but which develop plausible accounts of the political dimension of all Nietzsche's thought (e.g. Ansell-Pearson 1994). Let us conclude our brief consideration of the "unpolitical" interpretation of Nietzsche by noting one point of contention between Leiter's and Ansell-Pearson's interpretations, which shows the scope of what is at stake in such interpretive choices. Like Kaufmann, Leiter contends that Nietzsche was interested in the individual, not the political. In contrast, however, Ansell-Pearson contends that Nietzsche's interest in the individual can be properly understood only in a political light. According to him, Nietzsche's understanding of the individual is often wrongly conflated with the liberal conception of the individual: the individual understood as an atomistic, private individual, with a minimal ethical obligation to the state, society and culture.

Ansell-Pearson contends that Nietzsche criticized liberalism precisely because it produces this kind of individual, who is concerned only with his or her own personal development and gain. The problem is that liberalism erodes the shared culture that gives meaning and value to life. It is only from within this cultural context that individuals with proper cultural depth can be forged, and individuals need to have an ethical relation to the state so that their own creative, interpretive efforts in turn contribute to culture as a whole. Thus, on Ansell-Pearson's view, Nietzsche's concern with the political theme of the relation of the individual to the state is key to understanding much of his philosophy; he is concerned with the cultivation of the citizen on the ancient Greek model, *not* the cultivation of the modern liberal individual as is often supposed (see *ibid.*: 87). What this brief consideration shows is that the interpretive choice of whether or not Nietzsche has a political philosophy is not simply a peripheral issue, but can have a significant impact on how we interpret Nietzsche's philosophy as a whole. Moreover, those who contend that Nietzsche was a political thinker – to whom we now turn – often also claim that Nietzsche's thought contributes to our wider understanding of political philosophy, and the political problems of modernity in particular, with which we frequently still contend.

Aristocratism

Nietzsche's politics has often been thought of as aristocratic and elitist. His endorsement of Brandes's characterization of his philosophy as "aristocratic radicalism" lends support to this interpretation, as do some significant passages in his writings. One of the most significant interpretations of Nietzsche along these lines is Bruce Detwiler's *Nietzsche and the Politics of Aristocratic Radicalism* (1990). Noting the unusual nature of Nietzsche's political position, he comments that "While aristocratic conservatives and egalitarian radicals have been plentiful in recent times, it is difficult to think of another modern of Nietzsche's stature whose political orientation is both as aristocratic and as radical as his" (1990: 189).

KEY POINT *Aristocratic radicalism*
Nietzsche's politics is aristocratic in that he endorses an elitist, class-based society, but radical in that he advocates a *new* aristocratic social arrangement, rather than conserving existing arrangements.

Nietzsche does not provide anything like a blueprint, a body of legislation or implementation procedures for the kind of aristocratic society he advocates, but he describes it in broad outline:

> Caste-order, *order of rank*, is just a formula for the supreme law of life itself, splitting off into three types is necessary for the preservation of society, to make the higher and highest types possible, – *unequal* rights are the condition for any rights at all. – A right is a privilege. Everyone finds his privilege in his own type of being. ... A high culture is a pyramid: it needs a broad base, its first presupposition is a strongly and healthily consolidated mediocrity. (A 57)

The above passage takes as its basis the Hindu document on caste the *Laws of Manu* (and, as we noted above, Nietzsche's actual endorsement of the political views expressed here is disputed). However, the "three types" of caste mentioned here also appear in Plato's ideal form of society outlined in the *Republic*, by which Nietzsche is also influenced. For Plato, the bottom caste, of which there are most numerous members, are menial workers. The "middle class" is composed of state functionaries and soldiers. The least numerous upper class is composed of "philosopher-kings". As Ansell-Pearson (1994: 76) notes, Nietzsche's preferred political structure closely follows Plato's, except that his philosophers are conceived on the model of artists rather than of Socratic men of knowledge .

Nietzsche argues that inequality and exploitation are essential, and a class or caste-based society is necessary, for the flourishing of "higher individuals". His argument, in short, is that higher individuals require leisure for their creative activities, and this leisure is possible only in a society in which the majority devote themselves to the labour necessary for the material sustenance of all. A concise statement of this view appears in *Human, All Too Human*: "A higher culture can come into existence only where there are two different castes in society: that of the workers and that of the idle, of those capable of true leisure; or, expressed more vigorously: the caste compelled to work and the caste that works if it wants to" (HAH 439).

In a word, Nietzsche endorses a form of *exploitation* of one class by another. He acknowledges that exploitation is an evil, but sees it as a *necessary* evil. He sees the position of the aristocratic masters as one not so much of privilege but of obligation and burden. To command is a difficult task, and requires self-discipline; command of others first requires command of the self. Moreover, Nietzsche acknowledges the burden of guilt the masters are likely to be threatened with because of the exploitation they subject the masses too, and advocates the discharge of this burden of guilt in creative acts. The obligation to the exploited masses must be met by the masters through their diligence in pursuing the creative activities that the labouring masses facilitate. Nietzsche writes: "Let us not underestimate the privileges of the *mediocre*. Life becomes increasingly difficult the *higher* up you go, – it gets colder, there are more responsibilities" (A 57). (In this sense, Nietzsche's aristocratism has an ethical dimension lacking in contemporary liberalism, in which the individual is regarded as free to pursue their own ends independent of any positive obligation to the community or to those they may exploit.)

Nietzsche grounds the "right" to exploitation not simply in pragmatic concerns about elevating the exceptional individual, but in the naturalistic explanation of life processes as essentially exploitative. In *Beyond Good and Evil*, he writes:

> [T]hese days, people everywhere are lost in rapturous enthusiasms, even in scientific disguise, about a future state of society where "the exploitative character" will fall away: – to my ears, that sounds as if someone is promising to invent a life that dispenses with all organic functions. "Exploitation" does not belong to a corrupted or imperfect, primitive society: it belongs to the *essence* of being alive, and because life *is* precisely will to power. (BGE 259)

Moreover, Nietzsche argues that the exploited will be *happy* with their exploitation, because their role in society will correspond with their natural talents and abilities. He writes:

> To be a public utility, a wheel, a function, – you need to be destined for this by nature: it is *not* society but rather the type of *happiness* that the vast majority of people cannot rise above that make them intelligent machines. For the mediocre, mediocrity is a happiness; mastery of one thing, specialisation as a natural instinct. (A 57)

As Daniel W. Conway (1997b: 36) points out, all members of society are thought by Nietzsche to benefit in some way by the production of higher types, and the activities of these exceptional individuals. In the broadest sense, Nietzsche argues that the existence of the mediocre is justified by the existence of the exceptions. He argues that the most meaningful sense of life is to be achieved, by most persons, in the service of higher types. More concretely, for Nietzsche, there is no intrinsic, given meaning or value of life, and the higher types are given the role of creating such a meaning. In fact, the order of rank is established by Nietzsche around not physical, economic or political strength, but *creative* strength, where that is understood as the strength honestly to face the horrors of existence and creatively to forge a meaningful interpretation out of it, whether this be through art, philosophy or some other means. When Nietzsche speaks of "great politics" in the quote appearing at the beginning of this chapter, he is referring to the combination of political process and philosophical reflection: great politics consists in the legislation of values created by philosopher-artists.

As Klossowski emphasizes (see "The politics of the French Nietzsche", below), Nietzsche's aristocratic "masters" are far from the political and economic upper class of contemporary capitalist societies: as we have just seen, they are philosopher-artists who create and legislate values. One might well think that Nietzsche's aristocratism is open to finding a paradoxical justification in the existential value it provides to the masses of humankind: but Nietzsche does not take this path. For him, the higher types justify their own existence, as well as the existence of the mediocre masses (Conway 1997b). In some of Nietzsche's most disturbing passages – generally found only in his unpublished notes – he speaks of the right of the higher types to use the masses in experiments (he does not specify what type) that may result in massive loss of life. Nietzsche's "aristocratic radicalism" might, then, be understood in a second sense, as a radical value ascribed to the aristocratic class that justifies the extreme exploitation of "lesser" types. Detwiler summarizes the originality of Nietzsche's radically aristocratic political stance: "Among modern philosophers Nietzsche stands virtually alone in his insistence that the goal of society should be the promotion and enhancement of the highest type even at the expense of what has traditionally been thought to be the good of all or of the greatest number" (1990: 189).

Socialism

Nietzsche consistently opposed socialism throughout his writings, even during the "middle period" when he took a more negative view of exploitation and a more positive view of democracy (see below). Nietzsche's primary objection to socialism would seem to be that it demands justice, forbids exploitation and wants to abolish the class-based aristocratic society that he believes provides the only fruitful conditions for the production of higher types. In *The Anti-Christ*, he writes:

> Who do I hate most among the rabble today? The socialist rabble, the Chandala-apostles who undermine workers' instincts and pleasures, their feelings of modesty about their little existences, – who make them jealous, who teach them revenge … Injustice is never a matter of unequal rights, it is a matter of claiming "*equal*" rights. (A 57)

Thus, Nietzsche saw socialism as a threat to the artistocratic society he advocated. In the early unpublished essay "The Greek State", he acknowledges that the demand for social justice is a legitimate one, but it is nevertheless a danger to the greater good of a meaningful culture (which he believes can be based only on inequality). He writes of his fear of "the cry of pity tearing down the walls of culture" with the result that "the urge for justice, for equal sharing of the pain, would swamp all other ideas" ("The Greek State", in Ansell-Pearson & Large 2006: 90).

In addition to this general concern, as Ansell-Pearson analyses it, Nietzsche has four further, more specific objections to socialism.

KEY POINT *Nietzsche's objections to socialism*
- Socialism is dangerous because it is based on a naive morality of natural goodness.
- Abolishing private property is a serious and unwarranted attack on the liberty of the private person.
- Socialism threatens an excess of state power (despotism and terrorism).
- Socialism attempts an economic management of culture in which culture is devalued and a purely utilitarian logic governs (Ansell-Pearson 1994: 91–3, 40).

First, Nietzsche believes socialism is predicated on a theory of human nature as naturally good, a theory associated with the French Enlightenment philosopher Jean-Jacques Rousseau (1712–78). For Nietzsche, human nature contains vanity and egoism, as well as competitive and even cruel impulses (as he argues in the early unpublished essay "Homer's Contest" [in Ansell-Pearson & Large 2006]). While socialists argue that such impulses are simply the products of unjust social arrangements, which, when removed, will reveal true human goodness, Nietzsche believes that these impulses are not only natural, but necessary to a healthy culture. Second, Nietzsche rejects the aim – associated with some forms of socialism, notably communism – to abolish private property and make all property a matter of collective ownership. He argues that the communal ownership of property cannot provide the kind of motivation to individuals that the prospect of private ownership can.

Third, and perhaps most significantly, Nietzsche argues that a socialist society can only be imposed and maintained by the state exercising a great deal of coercive power over individuals. Socialism will require a despotic politics, and even a state terrorism, to bend individuals to its ends. Nietzsche writes:

> [Socialism] desires an abundance of state power such as only despotism has ever had; indeed it outbids all the despotisms of the past inasmuch as it expressly aspires to the annihilation of the individual, who appears to it like an unauthorised luxury of nature destined to be improved into a useful *organ of the community* ... it requires a more complete subservience of the citizen to the absolute state than has ever existed before ... Socialism can serve to teach, in a truly brutal and impressive fashion, what danger there lies in all accumulations of state power, and to that extent to implant mistrust of the state itself. (HAH 473)

Nietzsche's concern is not only that such a socialist state would not allow the freedom necessary for the flourishing of strong individuals. As he indicates at the end of this quotation, he is concerned that the despotism of the state will turn people against the state itself. In Nietzsche's view the state is necessary, and citizens should feel a sense of duty and obligation towards the state. One of the dangers of the despotic state, then, is that it will encourage resentment of the state in individuals and prevent the right kind of citizenship.

Fourth, Nietzsche believes that socialism will not overcome the problems he sees with liberalism (see below), but will reiterate the same problems. For him, both socialism and liberalism erode an organic sense of community based in a culture with shared concerns and bounded by a horizon of shared understanding concerning what is significant in life. Socialism will replace such a healthy, meaningful culture with a bureaucratic, rational calculation of the highest good of all based on the notion of justice. For Nietzsche, justice is a real concern and a real problem, but he unflinchingly asserts the superiority of a culture imbued with value and significance as a far more important concern. He asserts what for him is the "hard truth" that the condition of such a culture is social inequality and even slavery.

Liberalism

Ansell-Pearson (1994: 9) notes that Nietzsche's philosophy is often thought to be compatible with liberal individualism because of his emphasis on the freedom and self-realization of the individual, a value upheld against the collective life of "the herd" and against political parties and structures. However, as Ansell-Pearson argues, this is not the case. As indicated above, apart from Nietzsche's brief support for the National Liberal party candidate in the 1866 elections, he took a consistently critical approach towards liberalism. Nevertheless, some sophisticated readings of Nietzsche have tried to appropriate his thought for a liberal political theory. After outlining Nietzsche's critique of liberalism *via* Ansell-Pearson, we shall examine William E. Connolly's work as one prominent attempt to make Nietzsche compatible with, and useful for, liberalism.

Ansell-Pearson summarizes the three main points of Nietzsche's objections to liberalism as follows.

KEY POINT *Nietzsche's objections to liberalism*
- The noble ideals of European liberalism have been corrupted by nationalism.
- When viewed historically, the development of philosophical liberalism has to be seen as inseparable from economic liberalism (*laissez-faire* capitalism).
- Liberalism rests on an abstract and ahistorical conception of the individual self and its realization (Ansell-Pearson 1994: 10).

A useful way to approach an understanding of these critiques in more detail is to appreciate how Nietzsche can valorize *the individual* while nevertheless condemning liberalism (which is typically understood as the defence of the freedom and rights of the individual). As intimated earlier in our comparison of Leiter and Ansell-Pearson, Nietzsche believes that liberalism encourages the production of a "lower type" of individual, and undermines the conditions necessary for the production of the "higher type" of individual he values. For Nietzsche, this "higher type" of individual requires the fertile soil of a vibrant culture in which to grow, and the worth of such an individual resides in large part in his or her ability to make a contribution to culture through the active creation and legislation of values. As Ansell-Pearson phrases it, it is important to Nietzsche that the individual have an *ethical* relation to the state: an obligation and capacity to contribute to public life and culture. It is only through such a relation to public life that Nietzsche's claim that the higher types (the "free spirits", "nobles" or *Übermenschen*) justify the existence of humankind makes sense. Paradoxically, perhaps, while for Nietzsche the existence of human beings can be justified only by its highest specimens, the value of those specimens lies at least in part in their ability to legislate meaning and value for "the masses".

Nietzsche's central objection to liberalism is that it promotes a *private* conception of the individual, defined negatively in relation to the state and culture in terms of the individual's *rights*. Rights protect the private freedom of the individual from the demands of the state, and undermine the notion of the individual's ethical obligation to the state or to culture. The overall effect of modern liberalism, for Nietzsche, is an *atomization* of society into private individuals, which undermines the collective life of culture, necessary for a sense of meaning and value in life, and for the flourishing of any and all individuals. This general critique takes into account the three main points listed above. Nationalism corrupts any positive conception of liberalism which might be possible because it tries to replace the genuine culture of a people with a sense of national unification, enforced through power-politics and militarism (see Nietzsche's criticisms of Bismarckian nationalism outlined above). Economic liberalism (*laissez-faire* capitalism) contributes to the atomization of society by placing excessive value on the property rights of individuals, and mediating social relations through abstract economic transactions in which the only values operative are economic values. Furthermore, for Nietzsche, modern liberalism rests on an abstract and ahistorical conception of the individual, which must be challenged in order to reveal real hierarchical differences, which he believes are necessary for a healthy culture (see "Aristocratism", above). Ansell-Pearson concludes that Nietzsche's individualism is to be understood as an artistocratic, not a liberal, individualism (*ibid.*: 11).

Connolly presents a nuanced appropriation of Nietzsche's thought for liberal political theory in his *Political Theory and Modernity* (1993). While Connolly concedes that Nietzsche does not have a political theory as such, he argues that a Nietzschean perspective on political thinkers such as Hobbes, Rousseau and Hegel is highly instructive in helping us understand political theory in the context of modernity. Moreover, Connolly argues that Nietzsche's thinking lends itself to a corrective to traditional liberal theory, and to support of what he calls a "radicalized liberalism" (*ibid.*: 174). Connolly suggests that modern political theory can be understood in terms of the experience of nihilism in modernity. He understands modernity as characterized by a drive to master and order the world, as compensation for the nihilistic loss of faith in a transcendent order. The price for warding off nihilism after the death of God, Connolly argues, is the eradication of "otherness" through the attempt to create a perfectly ordered self and perfectly ordered world.

He writes: "The modern quest to ward off the experience of nihilism becomes the drive to force everyone and everything into slots provided by a highly ordered system and to pretend the result is self-realisation, the achievement of reason, the attainment of the common good" (*ibid.*: 13–14). The cost of this drive is the "normalization" of individuals, which erodes their freedoms.

According to Connolly, traditional liberalism is blind to the way in which normalization erodes freedom, because it understands the individual as already constituted in a natural way, rather than seeing the individual as constituted by social forces and relations of power. For him, Nietzsche acts as a useful corrective to liberal theory because he advocates an affirmation of the world as contingent as the best way to confront nihilism, and thus offers us an alternative perspective to that of the modern striving for mastery. Moreover, Connolly offers an interpretation of a "Nietzschean ethics" that subverts normalization and allows "space for difference to be" (*ibid.*: 161). The ground for this ethic lies in the inbuilt resistance to things implied by the ontology of the will to power; given that everything is understood by Nietzsche as composed of fundamentally conflictual relations of force in ever-changing configurations, the project of mastery is an illusory goal (*ibid.*). Moreover, Nietzsche's perspectivism implies that every force that seeks mastery is merely one force among others, with no legitimate claim to totality or supremacy. While Connolly admits that this ethic of "letting difference be" is only one side of Nietzsche's thought, and that the will to mastery is also evident in his work, he asserts that the ethics of difference is a more promising stance to explore in our contemporary context (*ibid.*).

Summarizing his radical liberalism and its debt to Nietzsche, Connolly writes:

> Perhaps a reconstituted, radicalized liberalism is needed today; one which reaches into the subject itself rather than taking it as a starting point for reflection; … one which restrains the drive to comprehend and cure various forms of otherness by confronting first the way its own contestable standards of normality and realization help to constitute these phenomena.
>
> (*Ibid.*: 174)

Connolly's appropriation of Nietzsche for the liberal cause is certainly not a reading of Nietzsche *as* a liberal. He suggests that this perspective stands Nietzsche on his head (as Marx said of Hegel), and stands to Nietzsche in a relation of antagonistic indebtedness (*ibid.*: 175).

Democracy

Nietzsche was critical of democracy in the early and late phases of his work, but defended it in some of the writings in his middle period. Moreover, a number of contemporary Nietzsche interpreters have attempted – as the title of one such interpretation puts it – "a Nietzschean defence of democracy" (Hatab 1995). Generally, these interpreters propose that there is a disconnection between Nietzsche's politics and his philosophy, and that elements of his philosophy can be used in support of a democratic political theory.

From the descriptions above of Nietzsche's support of aristocratism and opposition to socialism and liberalism, it should already be apparent why Nietzsche is critical of democracy in his earlier and later thought. He opposes the principle of egalitarianism, which is often invoked to support democracy, since he believes in the natural inequality of human beings, and believes that society needs to be structured in a way that reflects these inequalities in order to allow higher types to flourish. He argues for the necessity of exploitation, and even slavery, which a democratic distribution of power would threaten to undermine by giving the exploited classes a part in political process. Perhaps most significantly, Nietzsche opposes the levelling effects that government by "public opinion" would have on politics and culture as a whole.

In *Human, All Too Human* and *The Wanderer and His Shadow*, however, Nietzsche takes a more positive view of democracy. In this middle period, he seems to believe that democracy is not necessarily a threat to a strong culture, and concedes the rights of the masses to determine their own existence and government. He writes:

> [I]f the purpose of all politic really is to make life endurable for as many as possible, then these as-many-as-possible are entitled to determine what they understand by an endurable life; if they trust to their intellect also to discover the right means of attaining this goal, what good is there in doubting it?
>
> (HAH 438)

However, he is careful to note that politics and culture need to remain to some extent divided spheres, so that the "populism" that governs democratic politics is not allowed to extend to culture, and thus to restrict higher types from flourishing.

In *The Wanderer and His Shadow*, Nietzsche argues that democracy is the best protection of culture against the dangers of socialism and nationalism. It will protect against these by ensuring a greater distribution of wealth and power, and thus enable a more stable and secure society in which people will not be tempted by the potentially destructive extremes of socialism and nationalism (Ansell-Pearson 1994: 90). Perhaps surprisingly, Nietzsche now even argues against exploitation for similar reasons. He writes:

> The *exploitation* of the worker was, it has now been realised, a piece of stupidity, an exhausting of the soil at the expense of the future, an imperilling of society. Now we already have almost a state of war: and the cost of keeping the peace, of concluding treaties and acquiring trust, will henceforth in any event be very great, because the folly of the exploiters was very great and of long duration. (WS 286)

Those who support a separation between Nietzsche's politics and his philosophical "perspectivism" that can be recuperated in a more politically positive vein include Alan White in *Within Nietzsche's Labyrinth* (1990); David Owen in *Nietzsche, Politics, and Modernity* (1995); and Conway in *Nietzsche and the Political* (1997b). However, we shall take Lawrence Hatab (1995) as a representative example here.

Hatab describes his project as challenging Nietzsche's politics on Nietzsche's own terms, and he contends that "whatever political views Nietzsche did entertain, he should have preferred democracy to any other political arrangement – and this in the spirit of his own thinking" (*ibid*.: 3). While fully acknowledging Nietzsche's significant criticisms of democracy, Hatab seeks to "deconstruct" Nietzsche's political thinking by showing that there are significant themes in his own writings that undermine his opposition to democracy, and which in fact can be mobilized for a philosophical defence of democracy. The three main themes he focuses on are listed in the box overleaf.

On the first point, Hatab suggests that the Greek idea of the *agon*, or contest, which Nietzsche advocates, might provide a basis for democracy alternative to the idea of equality. Hatab suggests that the idea of equality, based on the identity of persons, is out of step with postmodern thinking about *difference* as the basis for justice, and argues that Nietzsche's idea of agonism can thus provide an alternative, and preferable, basis for a democratic society.

Second, Hatab argues that Nietzsche's perspectivism makes an opening for democracy because the denial of an absolute or uniform truth leaves us with a plurality of perspectives in contest and debate. In the political arena, when decisions need to be made on the context of this plurality of perspectives, democratic processes (the vote of the majority) would seem to be expedient. On the third point, Hatab notes that "Aristocracies and authoritarian regimes have historically defended their right to dominance and unchecked power by way of confident knowledge claims about the nature and order of things" (*ibid.*: 70). Given Nietzsche's wide-ranging suspicion and scepticism towards any confident truth-claims, Hatab argues that his thought ought to lead more naturally to an *undermining* of aristocratic and hierarchical political systems than to their defence. Such scepticism towards any claims that would justify a powerful elite, Hatab argues, should lead to the pluralism and openness of a democratic system. With these themes, democracy is redescribed as an ungrounded, continual contest, without equality being necessary. For Hatab, this project of appropriating Nietzsche for a democratic politics has value not just as a work of Nietzsche interpretation, but as a philosophical defence of democracy in a postmodern milieu (*ibid.*: 4).

The "popular, progressive" political reading of Nietzsche championed by Hatab, Connolly and the other authors mentioned above, has been challenged by Fredrick Appel in his *Nietzsche contra Democracy* (1999). (And we have also seen Nietzsche charged as anti-democratic by Ferry and Renaut in Chapter 2.) Against any reading that would claim to reconcile Nietzsche with liberal or democratic ideals, Appel argues that Nietzsche's work "is best understood as an uncompromising repudiation of both the ethic of benevolence and the notion of the equality of persons in the name of a radically aristocratic commitment to human excellence" (*ibid.*: 2). Appel reiterates in uncompromising terms many of the aspects of Nietzsche's "aristocratic radicalism" outlined above. More than this, however, he argues for "the all-encompassing nature of Nietzsche's elitist predilections" (*ibid.*: 6), asserting that the "order of rank" applies not only to Nietzsche's most overtly expressed political opinions, but conditions his epistemology, metaphysics and philosophy generally. He critiques Nietzsche's idea of agonism as an adequate basis for a democratic politics, arguing that there is nothing in it that would proscribe violence and cruelty. He asserts that the best use of Nietzsche for democratic theorists is to stimulate them to defend the egalitarian values he holds in contempt (*ibid.*: 7–8).

Appel asks a perspicacious question of those who try to democratize Nietzsche, a question that it is apposite to reiterate at the close of this section because it brings the value of Nietzsche's political philosophy, and its study, into relief. He asks: why bother going to the great trouble of "democratizing" Nietzsche when we can learn just as much from other political philosophers who explicitly defend democracy? A possible answer to this question is suggested by Detwiler, according to whom Nietzsche is a highly original political thinker who questions many of the founding assumptions – unquestioned by other thinkers – of modern political philosophy. For Detwiler – who to some extent shares Appel's abhorrence of Nietzsche's political convictions – we can learn much from Nietzsche's questioning of such assumptions, despite the conclusions which he himself drew (Detwiler 1990: 6, 196).

A "reconversion of politics"

> Enough: the time is coming when politics will have a different meaning. (WP 960)

We saw above that interpreters such as Leiter argue that Nietzsche was "unpolitical" on the grounds that his works do not express in a developed and systematic way the canonical themes of political philosophy. However, even if Leiter's argument is correct, the absence of "mainstream" political philosophy in Nietzsche's works does not necessarily mean it is without political significance. Beyond the tradition of Western political philosophy, there are other possible meanings of "the political". In its broadest sense, the political – from the ancient Greek word *polis* – simply refers to public things, or the collective "being together" of people. For many interpreters, Nietzsche offers important political insights in this wider sense, and his value as a political philosopher may even be seen as contributing to an alternative, or expanded, sense of what may be meant by "the political". In the rest of this chapter, I shall examine the way in which some influential interpreters have employed Nietzsche's thought for a "reconversion of politics".

The politics of the French Nietzsche

Nietzsche's political thought was appropriated by the French leftist intellectuals to inspire a new approach to politics in the wake of a disillusionment with (mainstream) Marxism, and of the new possibilities suggested by the events of May '68. This involved a move away from the politics of governments and institutions towards a politics of conspiracy and strategy; from macropolitics to micropolitics; from traditional political representation to the cultural politics of minorities. Thus, the politics of the French Nietzscheans opened up a line of political significance in Nietzsche far removed from the dire consequences of what the Nazis took from him.

Among the many productive contentions of Klossowski's reading of Nietzsche (discussed in Chapter 2) is an interpretation of the political meaning of his thought. Klossowski insists on a new meaning of the political in Nietzsche: "Nietzsche's position draws us away, in any case, from all that which has up to the present been called 'political action'; it requires the creation of a new comportment with regards to conflict and strategising" (2009: 42). Klossowski sees Nietzsche as uncannily prophetic of political developments in the twentieth century, and develops an interpretation of Nietzsche's own political thought as revolving around the notion of "conspiracy" (*complot*). Klossowski's political interpretation was taken up and extended by other French Nietzscheans, such as Deleuze and Lyotard, but we shall concentrate on Klossowski's reading of Nietzsche's politics here.

Unsurprisingly, Klossowski's treatment of Nietzsche's politics revolves around the categories of master and slave. Klossowski contends that the slaves of the contemporary world are all those who work at menial tasks without knowing the overall *goal* for which they work. The masters, on the other hand, are those who are able to exploit the labour of the masses towards their own ends. The slave "caste" is associated with what Klossowski calls the "gregarious", a term indicating herd morality (see Chapter 2), while the masters are those rare individuals ("singular cases", in Klossowski's terminology) who are able to create and legislate values. However, the problem for contemporary politics is that the weak have prevailed over the strong; the slaves have instituted a cultural order that suppresses potential masters. Nietzsche's political task is to reverse this situation and restore the masters to their proper place. For Nietzsche, the slaves have dominated through a complex alliance of Christianity and morality, which creates an ideal of community in which individuals all belong to the same, mediocre level. Nietzsche sees contemporary science, and Darwinism in particular, as complicit in slave morality, in so far as it aims towards, and attempts to justify, the preservation of the species as a collection of mediocre individuals.

Now, Nietzsche introduces an important distinction between *false* and *true* masters, which prevents any possibility of identifying his ideal political system directly with the class exploitation of capitalism that Marx critiques. The false masters are in fact Marx's bourgeois exploiters, the "industrialists, military men, bankers, business men, bureaucrats, etc." (Klossowski 2005: 121). According to Nietzsche these false masters are unconscious slaves, because the aims they pursue are perfectly confluent with, and actively promote, herd morality. Nietzsche sees the capitalist system as contributing to the levelling of humanity because everything becomes homogenized in universal commodity exchange, and all value judgements become mercantile. The capitalist system itself promotes the loss of any meaningful goal for humanity, because it increasingly focuses on efficient means for the circulation of commodities as an end in itself. In a note that Klossowski sees as particularly prophetic, Nietzsche identifies the "common economic management of the earth" as the high point of social levelling and nihilism. With the advent of globalized economic planning, "mankind will be able to find its best meaning as a machine in the service of this economy" (WP 866; quoted in Klossowski 1997: 122–3).

The true masters, on the other hand, are the strong types who are able to legislate values and the meaning of life, and whom Nietzsche characterizes collectively as a "contemplative" caste. These true masters are able to turn the activities of the false masters, as well as the labouring of the masses that these false masters direct, to their own ends. Nietzsche sees these contemplative individuals as forming a *conspiracy* that aims to overturn the existing order of false masters and herd morality, and to institute what he sees as a "just" political system of exploitation aimed towards higher ends.

How does this conspiracy unfold? The strategy Nietzsche outlines is not to decrease the levelling processes of planetary economic planning, but to contribute to and exacerbate them, with the idea that such levelling will of necessity produce a *counter-movement* with the potential to transform the existing order. (This is the political counterpart to Nietzsche's advocacy of active nihilism as a strategy aimed at pushing nihilism to a point of self-overcoming.) This counter-movement is produced by the system of economic utility itself as the waste and surplus that it cannot use as means: that it cannot incorporate into its efficient functioning. In one posthumous note, Nietzsche speaks of the masters as "surplus men", those who cannot be made useful in the society of economic utility and herd morality:

> [A]lways remember that this enormous effort, this sweat, this dust, this din of the labour of civilization is at the service of those who know how to use it all without participating in this work; that surplus men who are maintained by this universal surplus-labor are necessary, and that these men of surplus constitute the meaning and apology of all this fermentation!
>
> (Quoted in Klossowski 2005: 121)

Nietzsche provides no details about exactly what activities the conspiracy of "surplus men" would engage themselves in. However, two notable points can be discerned from this concept of conspiracy: first, as already noted, Nietzsche presents it as only a *transitional stage* in his politics, aimed towards the institution of a new social order in which the "hidden masters" will publicly take control in directing the course of humanity; and second – seemingly contrary to this first point – the notion of conspiracy in this Nietzschean sense suggests a new model of community on its own terms.

In the discussion following Klossowski's paper at the celebrated 1972 Cerisy-la-Salle conference on Nietzsche, Deleuze clearly summarizes the difference between community as traditionally conceived ("society"), and the new notion of community posed by Klossowski's work on Nietzsche:

> What we call a society is a community of regularities, or more precisely, a certain selective process which retains select singularities and regularises them. … But a *conspiracy* – this would be a community of singularities of another type, which would not be regularised, but which would enter into new connections, and in this sense, would be revolutionary.
>
> (Quoted in Klossowski 2009: 46–7)

Moreover, the possibility suggested by Nietzsche is that links between singularities in a "conspiratorial" community would have the eternal return as their criteria. What this amounts to is an attempt to conceive of communities – groups and whole societies – beyond the notion of identity. Just as the lived experience of the eternal return dissolves the identity of individuals (again, see Chapter 2), so too conspiracy implies community beyond identity.

As Joseph D. Kuzma notes, in gesturing towards this new model of community, Klossowski's Nietzsche interpretation can be seen as a precursor to later French political thought, such as Jean-Luc Nancy's *The Inoperative Community* ([1982] 1991) and Maurice Blanchot's *The Unavowable Community* ([1988] 2006) (Kuzma 2009: 32).

Klossowski also links his reconstruction of Nietzsche's politics with the "anti-psychiatric" concerns taken up by poststructuralists such as Deleuze, Foucault and Félix Guattari. Klossowski suggests an identification of the Nietzschean "singular case" with those individuals identified by psychiatry as "pathological cases" in need of constraint and normalization, and suggests that "the pathological case will feel more and more comfortable if he lives, and imposes himself, by subverting the institutional investigations which brand him pathological" (Klossowski 2009: 42). Moreover, the influence of Klossowski's treatment of Nietzsche's political themes can be seen in the notion, present in the thought of many poststructuralists, that any attempt to constitute a homogenous, totalized social order will inevitably produce a disruptive backlash. This theme is evident – to take just one example – in Jean Baudrillard's controversial essay on the terrorist attacks of 11 September 2001, in which he argues that the attacks constituted an inevitable counter-movement to the attempted American global hegemony (Baudrillard 2003).

Klossowski thus presents an interpretation of Nietzsche's politics as prophetic of the age of globalized capitalism. This politics involves an "esoteric" conspiracy conducted by true masters against the "external" conspiracy of bourgeois morality and economic utility. What is at stake in this conflict of conspiracies is summarized by Klossowski under the sign of the eternal return (characterized by him as a "vicious circle"). The capitalist system presents a gross caricature of the eternal return in so far as it reduces human life to the service of the circulation of commodities, without end or goal (just as the eternal return presents the world as a continual circulation of moments, which have no other goal than to return to themselves through endless repetition). However, the "true" meaning of eternal return is precisely what challenges the capitalist system by revealing what cannot be translated into economic value and is thus only recognized as waste or surplus in the system of com-modity exchange. What resists economic value is the *lived experience* of the eternal return, which reveals the unintelligible, unexchangeable depths of the soul (see Chapter 2). This is, then, the reason that the true masters – whose most significant mark is that they have been able to understand and incorporate the idea of the eternal return – are "surplus men", and are able to work for a meaning and a goal beyond economic utility. This political meaning of the eternal return was also taken up by other French Nietzscheans, for example Lyotard (1978).

Many have been quite surprised and puzzled that the French left intelligensia took Nietzsche – ostensibly an extreme right-wing thinker – as a major source of political inspiration in the 1960s and 1970s. On the face of it, Nietzsche's politics would appear to be diametrically opposed to Marx's: while Marx strove to overcome class exploitation, Nietzsche defended a version of it and wanted to implement it. However, Klossowski's analysis shows that Nietzsche's critique of bourgeois and industrial culture is parallel to Marx's, and this has allowed French Nietzscheans with Marxist orientations to appropriate Nietzsche for their own political agendas. Moreover, Nietzsche helped the French poststructuralists, who had become disillusioned with mainstream Marxism, to turn the very meaning of "the political" in a new direction.

Nietzsche and critical theory

A further significant impact of Nietzsche's works on attempts to rethink the political is evident in the tradition called "critical theory". This term encompasses a variety of Marxist interdisciplinary approaches to society and politics. Nietzsche is an important reference for several prominent critical theorists, but for widely diverging reasons. For Georg Lukács (1885–1971), Nietzsche is a dangerous irrationalist. In *The Destruction of Reason* ([1952] 1980), Lukács presents Nietzsche as the founder of irrationalism in what he calls "the imperialist period". He sees Nietzsche as motivated by a fear that the imperial or ruling class of his time was in danger of losing its power, which he hoped to shore up through the creation of a new, irrational mythology (Vattimo 2001: 189). The tenor of Lukács's critique of Nietzsche is captured in the following comment on his stylistic choice of the aphorism: "The inner rottenness, hollow-ness and mendacity of the whole system wrapped itself in this motley and formally disconnected ragbag of ideas" (Lukács 1980: 395). One of the main effects of Lukás's reading was to deter Marxists from reading Nietzsche.

Similarly, for Jürgen Habermas (b. 1929), Nietzsche marks a lamentable turn to "postmodernism", associated with French thinkers such as Bataille, Derrida and Foucault, and understood by him as the abandonment of critical reason (Habermas 1987). While Habermas acknowledges some of the negative effects of particular modes of reason identified by Nietzsche, he believes that Nietzsche and the postmodernists "throw the baby out with the bathwater" by rejecting reason in its entirety. For both Lukács and Habermas, it is not Nietzsche's explicit political views that are objectionable, as much as his attacks on reason itself. For them, critical theory should defend reason as the only possible basis for the emancipation of society, and they see Nietzsche primarily as an opponent of this project. We shall focus here, however, on the more positive image of Nietzsche present in the critical theory of Theodor W. Adorno and Max Horkheimer. For them, Nietzsche has great value as one of the most important philosophical critics of the Enlightenment.

Horkheimer and Adorno were the principal early members of the Institute for Social Research (*Institut für Sozialforschung*) or, as it has become known, the Frankfurt School. This institute, founded in 1923, is the origin of what has come to be called critical theory, and the members of the institute remain most closely associated with this term. The Frankfurt School researchers developed a "critical" theory that was not meant to be a value-free method of studying society without changing it (as was "traditional" sociological theory), but a method of study that incorporated a basis for critique and prescription for change.

Dialectic of Enlightenment ([1944] 1997), co-authored by Adorno and Horkheimer and first published in 1944, is often recognized as the principal text of the early Frankfurt School. The book heavily criticizes the state of the contemporary world, and links its problems with the legacy of the Enlightenment. In the introduction to *Dialectic of Enlightenment* they explain that the task they undertake in the book is "nothing less than the discovery of why mankind, instead of entering into a truly human condition, is sinking into a new kind of barbarism" (1997: xi).

While Adorno and Horkheimer are "wholly convinced … that social freedom is inseparable from enlightened thought" (*ibid.*: xiii), they believe that the Enlightenment project has self-destructed in modernity. Furthermore, they believe that the seed for this self-destruction is contained within "enlightened thought" itself. Adorno and Horkheimer characterize the problems of modernity in a number of ways, the most significant of which is the problem of *domination*.

While developments in science and technology have resulted in a certain degree of *material* emancipation (i.e. higher living standards, etc.), Adorno and Horkheimer argue that we have become "psychically", "spiritually" or "mentally" dominated by the very apparatus that makes this material emancipation possible. According to them, the key mistake in the project has been the *domination of nature*, which they see as synonymous with the *disenchantment* of nature. They write that "Men pay for the increase of their power with alienation from that over which they exercise their power" (*ibid.*: 9). Thus, while we have learned to control the world, we are no longer at home in it. The Enlightenment project, while liberating us materially, has crippled us spiritually. Modernity has not made our lives more meaningful. On the contrary, it has *robbed* our lives of meaning.

Adorno and Horkheimer claim that a certain kind of thinking – and its historical manifestation – is the culprit of this unfortunate outcome. This is "identity thinking": the tendency to make one thing *equivalent* to another – to measure, to calculate and to subsume under mathematical laws. It is this form of reasoning that has become autonomous; separated from reasoning about "ends", that is, what is good for society, identity thinking has developed through science, technology, and bureaucracy in a way that has transformed the social world into a place in which we feel alienated and oppressed.

KEY POINT *Dialectic of Enlightenment*
The dialectic is between two aspects of reason:
- a harmonious coordination of pure and practical reason (what we think and what we do), to produce social emancipation (freedom);
- calculation; identity thinking; instrumental rationality (domination).
For Adorno and Horkheimer, contemporary society is ideological or based on a "lie" because we believe the first kind of reason has set us free, whereas in fact the second kind of reason has dominated us.

Adorno and Horkheimer reference Nietzsche throughout the text, and claim that "Nietzsche was one of the few after Hegel who recognised the dialectic of enlightenment" (*ibid.*: 44). More profoundly than such explicit references, however, many scholars have noted the deep influence of Nietzsche on Adorno's thought in particular, and on *Dialectic of Enlightenment* as a whole. Gillian Rose, for example, argues that "the notion of a 'dialectic of enlightenment' is an interpretation of Nietzsche" (1978: 26). Nietzsche is central to the thesis of the book because of the link he draws between reason and domination (in contrast to the Enlightenment thinkers, who saw in reason nothing but emancipation). From his earliest writings, Nietzsche pointed out how the ascendancy of reason could produce a decline in meaningful culture, and it is this idea that Adorno and Horkheimer pick up on as a "dialectic".

Moreover, *Dialectic of Enlightenment* presents a theory of ideology as all pervasive. In contrast to the traditional Marxist theory of ideology, there is no class that has access to the "truth" of the social situation. Rose cites Nietzsche's theory of will to power as an influence on this theory of ideology. For Nietzsche, all knowledge claims are expressions of the desire for power, and "false" in the sense that they do not result from a dispassionate search for truth (*ibid.*: 20). Thus, all knowledge is ideological in the sense that it is thoroughly embroiled in power relations.

However, Nietzsche also points the way towards a kind of ideology critique through his genealogical method and his criticisms of identity thinking. For Adorno in particular (and this is manifest in writings other than *Dialectic of Enlightenment*; see e.g. Adorno 1978), Nietzsche has value as a trenchant critic of bourgeois morality and of traditional philosophical assumptions. In both cases, Nietzsche wants to show that the world is one of constant change, or *becoming*. From this perspective, all claims to universal validity – to posit something as an essential and unchanging fact about human nature, for example – appears suspect. Adorno has strong sympathies with Nietzsche's project for a "revaluation of values", through which existing values that are generally taken as universally valid can be shown to be a contingent product of social and historical formations (the difference being that for Adorno, the aim of such a revaluation is far more Marxist in intent).

The critique of identity thinking that underlies *Dialectic of Enlightenment* also has an important Nietzschean influence. As we have seen in the chapter on poststructuralism, Nietzsche critiques the kind of thought based on identity and opposition, in favour of a recognition of subtle gradations and differences that underlie any supposed identities. Nietzsche's refusal of identity thinking as a "hypostasis of the mind" is praised by Adorno as a "liberating act, a true turning point of Western thought" (quoted in Rose 1978: 22). One of the problematic issues these kinds of critiques face is the question of their own foundation. That is, if everything is somehow "false", isn't the critical perspective itself false? If everything is ideological, aren't the ideas expressed in *Dialectic of Enlightenment* themselves ideological? This question of methodology is a further notable point of Nietzsche's influence on *Dialectic of Enlightenment* and on Adorno's version of critical theory in particular. Adorno sees in Nietzsche an attempt at "antifoundational" thinking enacted through an ironic style. Instead of referring to supposed "facts" to found critique, the critique takes place through a quasi-literary style of writing that presents ideas only to undermine them, without promising to replace them with other truths. *Dialectic of Enlightenment* is itself written in an unusual style for a book of social theory, eschewing sociological data in the form of statistics and dispassionate analysis, and instead imaginatively engaging with literary texts such as those of Homer and the Marquis de Sade in order to present an ironically self-undermining "counter-myth" to the contemporary myth of the Enlightenment and modernity. Not just the explicit content, but also the style of this key text of critical theory, owes much to Nietzsche, in so far as it is polemical, literary and, at times, fragmentary. In contrast to other critical theorists, such as Lukács and Habermas, Adorno and Horkheimer see Nietzsche as one of the most important philosophical critics of modernity. While he lacked a social theory as such, and his own political views were radically out of step with Marxist aims and values, they nevertheless see much in his work which can be mobilized for such aims.

Summary of key points

Nietzsche's political context

The key political event of Nietzsche's lifetime was the unification of Germany under Bismarck. Bismarck's state was a sham democracy hiding a dictatorship. He favoured an aristocratic elite and repressed socialist unrest. Nietzsche admired Bismarck as a strong character and viewed him at times as a necessary protection against socialism, but often criticized him for focusing on military power rather than cultural renewal.

Nietzsche and National Socialism

Nietzsche's appropriation by the Nazis was made possible by a line of "romantic nationalist" interpretations of his work, beginning with that of his sister Elisabeth Förster-Nietzsche. Nietzsche's works had to be edited to be made palatable by the Nazis, since he stridently opposed German nationalism and anti-Semitism.

Nietzsche's political philosophy

- *Nietzsche as unpolitical*: Interpreters such as Kaufmann have argued that Nietzsche was generally uninterested in politics, and more interested in the individual. After the Second World War, this interpretation helped distance Nietzsche from his Nazi appropriation. The view continues to have contemporary defenders, such as Leiter.

- *Aristocratism*: Nietzsche approved of the characterization of his philosophy as "aristocratic radicalism". He argues for the necessity of social inequality and exploitation because he believes it is the only way a culture can produce "higher types". These higher types (the "aristocracy") are in turn necessary for creating a healthy and meaningful culture through their creative activities.

- *Socialism*: Nietzsche opposes socialism for a variety of reasons, the primary one being that it threatens the aristocratism he supports. He also argues that it is based on a naive philosophy of human moral goodness; that private property is necessary to motivate people; that socialism gives excessive power over the individual to the state; and that it implements a destructive economic management of culture.

- *Liberalism*: Nietzsche is critical of liberalism because he believes it produces atomized individuals without grounding in, or obligation to, a collective culture. However, Connolly argues that Nietzsche's philosophy is useful to a contemporary rethinking of liberalism because he critiques the tendency to domination of nature in modern liberalism, and his work is suggestive of a liberal ethics based on respect for differences.

- *Democracy*: Apart from some writings in his middle period, Nietzsche is generally critical of democracy because he sees it as based on equality, and as a threat to social hierarchy. Hatab has argued that Nietzsche *should* have embraced democracy, and sees a theory of democracy based on *agonism* rather than equality emerge from Nietzsche's writings. However, Appel has argued against the "progressive" readings of Nietzsche's thought as somehow consistent with liberalism or democracy, underlining his uncompromising aristocratism.

The politics of the French Nietzsche

Many of the French Nietzscheans were influenced by Klossowski's reading to develop a new understanding of "the political". The "masters" of today are in fact those who cannot be made useful within the capitalist system, and who engage in a conspiracy against this system. Klossowski's notion of a political "conspiracy" (i) aims to institute a new social order; and (ii) itself acts as a new model of community. Klossowski enabled both a turning of Nietzsche towards Marxist ends, and a turning away from mainstream Marxist political theory.

Nietzsche and critical theory

Nietzsche has inspired starkly contrasting views among critical theorists. For Lukács and Habermas, Nietzsche has had a strongly negative impact on the cause of social emancipation because of his attacks on rationality. For Adorno and Horkheimer, Nietzsche is one of the most insightful critics of modernity and bourgeois morality, whose works can be put to good use by critical social theory.

four

Nietzscheanism and feminism

This chapter explores the seemingly unlikely, but in fact significant, place Nietzsche has held in feminist thought. It begins by highlighting the deep ambiguity of this place: on the one hand Nietzsche is widely regarded as an outrageous misogynist because of some of his published statements on women; on the other, many prominent feminist theorists have found resources in his work for combating the patriarchal philosophical tradition. The chapter considers both aspects of Nietzsche's relation to feminism, but concentrates on the latter. It looks at the nature and extent of Nietzsche's perceived misogyny, and his dismissal by some feminists on this ground. It then examines the various attempts to "rehabilitate" Nietzsche for use by feminist theory. In fact the value of Nietzsche for feminism was recognized relatively early, by German feminists in the late nineteenth and early twentieth centuries. After acknowledging this early influence, the chapter focuses on more recent and influential feminist interpretations of Nietzsche. It introduces Kofman's argument that there is no single, essentialist view of "woman" in Nietzsche's texts, but different types of women, including life-affirmative ones. It examines Irigaray's influential reading of Nietzsche in *Marine Lover*, which both reveals Nietzsche's deep complicity with patriarchal tradition and opens up his work towards feminist concerns. The chapter then explores one example of Nietzsche studies in contemporary anglophone feminism in the work of Kelly Oliver. Overall, beyond Nietzsche's manifest misogyny, this chapter focuses attention on the way that Nietzsche's revaluation of aspects of life that have traditionally been associated with the feminine, such as the body and affect, as well as his radical critiques of the nature of human identity, have made Nietzsche's texts a rich resource for feminist philosophy. As we shall see, however, many feminists remain critical of Nietzsche for not going nearly far enough in this direction.

Nietzsche on women

Any consideration of Nietzsche's place in feminism must acknowledge the challenge posed by Nietzsche's notoriously misogynistic comments about women. The following list provides a sample of such comments:

- "You go to women? Do not forget the whip!" (Z: 1 "Of Little Women Old and Young")
- "Oh, what dangerous, insidious, subterranean little beasts of prey they are! And so pleasant into the bargain! … – Woman is incomparably more evil than man, cleverer too; goodness in woman is a form of *degeneration* …" (EH "Books" 5).
- "Did anyone hear my answer to the question of how to *cure* – 'redeem' – a woman? Give her a baby. Women need children, the man is only ever the means: thus spoke Zarathustra" (EH "Books" 5).
- "A woman wants to be a mother, and if she does not want this, even though she can, she almost belongs in prison as a general rule" (Unpublished note from 1885, quoted in Diethe 2006: 302–3).
- "When a woman has scholarly inclinations, there is usually something wrong with her sexuality" (BGE 144).
- "'Emancipation of women' – that is the intrinsic hatred of *failed* women, which is to say infertile women, against those who have turned out well" (EH "Books" 5).
- "[T]he danger to the artist, to the genius … lies with women: adoring females are their ruin. Hardly anybody has enough character not to be ruined – 'redeemed', when he feels he is being treated like a god: – he immediately *condescends* to the level of a woman. – A man is a coward in the face of all eternal-feminine: women know this. – In many cases of female love and perhaps in the most famous in particular, love is just a subtler *parasitism*, a nesting in a foreign soul, and occasionally even in foreign flesh – and oh! always at the expense of the 'host'!" (CW 3).

One strategy that has been used to meet Nietzsche's misogyny is to argue that such comments can be isolated and ignored. This strategy was advocated by, for example, Kaufmann (Oliver & Pearsall 1998b: 1). However, it can well be argued that Nietzsche's sexism pervades his philosophy at a much deeper level than that of the explicit statements he makes about women: the metaphoric language structuring Nietzsche's value judgements seems thoroughly gender biased. Oliver, who has examined his gender-loaded metaphors, writes:

> Nietzsche identifies with the eternal *manly* truth and looks forward to the day when all of mankind is manly ... Nietzsche orders us to become "hard!" ... For Nietzsche impotence is the real enemy of life ... It is no wonder that he chooses the god of fertility, Dionysus, whose symbols are blood-red wine and the tumescent phallus, to represent life's force. And repeatedly, degenerate life is figured in terms of castration, emasculation, effeminacy, and impotence. (Oliver 1995: 141)

In *The Anti-Christ*, for example, Christians are referred to as a "cowardly, feminine, saccharine group", while the Romans Nietzsche accuses the Christians of corrupting are described as having "masculine-noble natures" (A 58). In short, Nietzsche often seems to use "masculine" as a virtual synonym for "noble", and "feminine" for "slave". Nietzsche thus repeats the value judgements, plentiful throughout the history of philosophy, that the masculine qualities are to be admired and advocated and the feminine qualities to be feared and scorned.

Moreover, it is clear from his numerous statements to this effect that Nietzsche opposed the women's liberation movement, in its infancy at the time, but already with many strong advocates. He opposed higher education for women, women's careers and women's writing, and reasserted the conservative view that women should remain in the home, fulfilling the social roles traditionally ascribed to them: wife and mother. As Diethe notes, it is important to understand *why* Nietzsche consistently opposed feminism. (It is not at all a simple, unthinking conservatism, which of course we should never expect from Nietzsche.) As she explains it, it is because the culture he most admired was that of Hellenistic Greece. In that society, women accepted their social roles as cloistered wives and mothers (Diethe 2006: 89). As discussed in the previous chapter, there is an important sense in which, for Nietzsche, a healthy culture depends on social ranks and hierarchies; it is thus possible to see his opposition to women's liberation as a modality of his general opposition to breaking down social structures of rank and exploitation. If, as Nietzsche often argued, the menial labour of the masses was necessary to produce the fertile soil from which the occasional "higher type" could grow, then it seems that he thought all women should remain in the realm of the labouring masses.

In contrast to Nietzsche's misogynistic statements and written opposition to liberated women stand the facts regarding his general treatment of women, and the company of which women he chose. In practice, he seems to have enjoyed the company of well-educated women, such as Lou Andreas-Salomé and Meta von Salis-Marschlins (*ibid.*: 302). At Sils Maria, he was sometimes visited by female PhD students from Zurich University (*ibid.*), and he in fact voted for women to be admitted for degrees at Basel University, despite his published opposition to women's higher education. Moreover, Diethe notes that apart from his own sometimes antagonistic relations with his mother and sister, Nietzsche generally treated women with great respect. As she puts it, "the man of dynamite (as he described himself to his Jewish friend Helen Zimmern) was nothing if not a gentleman" (*ibid.*). Nietzsche's female acquaintances were of course familiar with his notorious comments. Malwida von Meysenbug considered his early sexist comments to be the result of his lack of experience with women, and thought it a passing phase he would outgrow (unfortunately this did not turn out to be the case). Zimmern, an English translator of Nietzsche as well as a personal friend, commented of his relations with her that "Certainly he did not use the famous whip" (quoted in Wininger 1998: 238).

As some feminists have pointed out, more positive assessments of women can also be found in Nietzsche's texts. For example, even though we have noted the use of sexist metaphors in *The Anti-Christ*, we also find in that text criticisms of Christianity for debasing women, and praise for the Laws of Manu (a Hindu text) for a more positive conception of women. Nietzsche writes:

> All the things that Christianity treated with its unfathomable meanness, procreation, for instance, woman, marriage, are treated here [i.e. in the Laws of Manu] with seriousness, with respect, with love and trust … I do not know any book that says as many kind and delicate things to females as the law book of Manu; these old men and saints have a way of minding their manners in front of women that has perhaps never been surpassed. "The mouth of a woman", it says at one point, "the breasts of a girl, the prayer of a child, the smoke of a sacrifice

are always pure.' Another passage: "there is absolutely nothing more pure than the light of the sun, the shadow of a cow, air, water, fire, and the breath of a girl". A final passage – perhaps a holy lie too -: "all bodily orifices above the navel are pure, all the ones below are impure. Only in girls is the whole body pure."   (A 56)

An important argument further detailing how a positive conception of women is also to be found in Nietzsche, made by Kofman, is discussed below.

Women on Nietzsche

Despite Nietzsche's misogynistic statements and opposition to women's liberation, many feminists have found Nietzsche's work a powerful resource for pursuing their ends. Kathleen J. Wininger usefully explains the value many feminists have seen in Nietzsche in terms of the inspiration and instructiveness of his work with regard to personal and social transformation:

> A great deal of his philosophy contains models that are meant to help understand changes. ... The idea that values and truths change, intellectual fashions change, and that these ideas are culturally embedded have often appealed to women. The appeal is especially great to women who have as their own agenda social and intellectual transformation.   (1998: 237)

These "models for change" do not concern social institutions and social roles so much as *philosophical concepts*. In approaching feminist philosophy, it is essential to appreciate that feminists criticize the philosophical tradition not just because it has generally excluded women (which it has; lists of the canonical figures in the history of Western philosophy typically do not include *any* women), but also because, it is claimed, the basic categories of this tradition are thoroughly infused with gender bias. This is quite evident, for example, in Plato's philosophy. Plato sets up a basic division between the *intelligible* and the *sensible*, where the intelligible has a higher value than the sensible. Plato associates the intelligible with the "true world" of the Forms and the activity of philosophical thought. For him, we are in fact "souls" trapped in bodies, and the proper task of the philosopher is to free himself from the body through philosophical activity. The sensible, on the other hand, is associated with the world of appearances, with the body, and with sensuous enjoyment. Significantly, Plato associates the intelligible with the masculine, and the sensible with the feminine. In his philosophy, only men are considered capable of philosophy; women are considered too "bodily" and sensuous. The main point, however, is that Plato's *metaphysical* and *epistemological* categories are aligned with these gender biases.

Plato is only one example. Feminist philosophers have argued that gender biases infuse the history of Western thought on such a deep level that they often go unnoticed. However, studies of key texts in the Western tradition often reveal these biases in the form of gendered metaphors. A particularly striking, and disturbing, example is Francis Bacon's 1620 book *New Science* (*Novum Organum*), a key text in the development of the modern scientific worldview. Steven Best and Douglas Kellner note that Bacon makes use of frequent, often violent, sexual metaphors: "Nature is portrayed as a female to be captured by the male mind, tortured through mechanical inventions, 'bound into service,' put into 'constraint,' and made a 'slave' to rational knowledge, which will 'penetrate' its hidden secrets" (Best & Kellner 1997: 200).

Contemporary feminist philosophy admits of many variations. While some simply seek to include more women in the dialogue of philosophy as it has traditionally been practised, those who have found Nietzsche a useful reference have generally engaged philosophy at the level of conceptual gender bias, and seen Nietzsche as both complicit with this gender bias in certain ways, but as powerfully subverting it in others. (We have already noted above that Nietzsche often uses gender-biased metaphors.) Moreover, to single out a particular point of interest, as Diethe (2006: 89) notes, the German term *Übermensch* is not gendered, and this has allowed some feminists to take his work as inspiration for the project of creating a super*woman*: a new kind of woman not bound by the constraints that patriarchal culture places on her. These positive potentials of Nietzsche's work have been taken up by feminists from the time when Nietzsche's name was first becoming known in Germany and across Europe. In recent decades, there has been a strong revival of interest in Nietzsche among feminist theorists.

Early Nietzschean feminism

Early Nietzschean feminism can be considered a minor but significant aspect of the broader, mainstream feminism that was in its infancy in the last decades of the nineteenth century. In Germany, the mainstream feminist movement was represented by the General German Women's Association (Allgemeiner Deutscher Frauenverein) founded in 1865 by Louise Otto-Peters. Nietzschean feminism itself came in a number of varieties, from the less to the more radical, and – like other political Nietzscheanisms – attracted adherents from both extremes (left and right) of the political spectrum. Simplifying greatly, the main strands of early Nietzschean feminism may be schematized as follows.

- *Bourgeoise liberal.* These Nietzschean feminists advocated greater rights and improved conditions for women, including access to higher education, and campaigned against the patriarchy of the existing order. However, they supported existing social institutions, including marriage, and the role of women as homemakers.
- *New Morality (Neue Ethik).* A movement associated with the League for the Protection of Mothers, established in 1905. They considered the authentic path to female self-actualization to lie in motherhood, but they shocked their mainstream feminist sisters by advocating free love and childbirth out of wedlock.
- *Bohemian.* Radical bohemian Nietzscheans also advocated and often practised free love, viewing the Dionysian as a principle of sexual freedom. Unlike the advocates of the "New Morality", however, they developed radical ideas on the freedom of women from social institutions such as the family, and traditional roles such as wife and mother.

Some of the key Nietzschean feminists in this early period are as follows. Their ideas can be categorized, to varying degrees, in terms of the three broad headings above. Some were leaders of movements, while other Nietzschean feminists were independent thinkers whose ideas cut across any neat divisions.

Lily Braun (1865–1916)

Braun was born of an aristocratic family, but embraced a radical social-democratic position. Initially seeing in Nietzsche only the potential for individual and general human emancipation, she later embraced a Nietzschean understanding of female liberation as "a heroic Nietzschean act of self-creation culminating in the formation of a superwoman" (Aschheim 1992: 88). In line with her socialism, Braun saw the super-woman as a kind of collective subject, to be realized in solidarity with other women, rather than as a project of individual self-actualization.

The ideal of the superwoman itself was understood to coincide with "the release of women's creative powers in all spheres of life, especially those traditionally blocked to them" (*ibid.*). For Braun, this liberation of creative powers also meant women's sexual liberation.

Helene Stöcker (1869–1943)

Stöcker was a leading figure in the New Morality movement, and one of the most prominent feminists in Germany in the late nineteenth and early twentieth centuries. Until 1900, Stöcker was a relatively conservative bourgeois feminist. Then, inspired by Nietzsche, she began to attack traditional sexual norms and advocated the "New Morality", which called for an end to the double standard regarding sex outside marriage. Stöcker saw in women's sexual liberation "the joyous creation of new forms and new feelings for new people" (quoted in Aschheim 1992: 89). Stöcker took over leadership of the League for the Protection of Mothers soon after its inception. The league lobbied to legalize abortion; promoted free love, provided contraception, set up hostels for unmarried mothers, and advocated state recognition of informal marriages (*ibid.*: 90).

Stöcker and the other members of the New Morality (by 1912 the League could boast 4000 members [*ibid.*]) embraced a kind of erotic Nietzscheanism, which saw the Dionysian as a principle of sexual freedom, for women as well as men. They saw women as having a unique, feminine nature that needed to be realized, and associated this nature with pregnancy and motherhood. They tended to quote Nietzsche's statements "everything about a woman has only one solution, namely pregnancy" and "the aim is always the child" (*ibid.*: 91). Unlike some other feminists, who wanted to liberate women from these roles, the New Morality venerated motherhood as tied to a kind of feminine essence, and sought to liberate it from the patriarchal and oppressive social institution of marriage. But by tying woman to motherhood, some feminists criticized the New Morality for reinforcing the patriarchal oppression of women. For example, one contemporary wrote: "In truth, Nietzscheanism in the female world signifies a renunciation of the demands of the 'radical egalitarians.' It establishes anew the [centrality of] the biological role and also, in transfigured form reaffirms male domination" (Marie Hecht, quoted in *ibid.*).

Hedwig Dohm (1831–1919)

Dohm was a German-Jewish feminist writer. She sometimes criticized Nietzsche on feminist grounds, and criticized Lou Andreas-Salomé (whose views on women's liberation were close to Nietzsche's own, despite the fact that she herself was a highly educated writer and practicing psychoanalyst). Yet Dohm considered Nietzsche to have provided useful resources to help women to throw off the shackles of conventional religious morality, and she wrote a number of novels with Nietzschean heroines who attempt a liberated self-realization, including one with the Nietzsche-inspired title *Become Who You Are* (1894) (Diethe 2006: 65–6).

Mary Wigman (1886–1973)

Wigman was a German dancer, considered one of the most important figures in both German expressionism and in twentieth-century dance generally. She was an enthusiastic reader of Nietzsche, and her dance took important inspiration from Nietzschean ideas. It incorporated radical movements designed to free the body from the traditional strictures of stylized dance, and was sometimes accompanied by drumming and even recitations from *Zarathustra* (Aschheim 1992: 61). Wigman was strongly influenced by Rudolf Laban (1879–1958), himself a Nietzschean dancer who believed that dance had the potential to regenerate life as a whole (*ibid.*: 60). Wigman's dance was often interpreted as a freeing of women's bodies from patriarchal expectations of what they should be and how they should move, and was therefore considered a powerful feminist artistic statement.

Isadora Duncan (1877–1927)

Another dancer, often considered the inventor of modern dance, Duncan was born in the United States of America, but was most successful in Europe. After reading Nietzsche in Berlin in 1902, she wrote that "The seduction of Nietzsche's philosophy ravished my being" (quoted in Aschheim 1992: 61). Duncan professed a Nietzschean idea of the superwoman as a dancer, writing in her lecture "The Dance of the Future": "Oh, she is coming, the dancer of the future: more glorious than any woman who has yet been: more beautiful than the Egyptian, than the Greek, than the early Italian, than all women of past centuries – the highest intelligence in the freest body!" (quoted in *ibid.*).

From this brief sampling we can see that Nietzsche was an important inspiration in what is frequently called "first-wave" feminism (which spans the period from approximately the 1860s to the 1920s) in Europe. In general, Nietzsche was hailed as providing models for radical change that could be applied to feminist cultural politics despite his own stated views on women. Some feminists embraced the erotic Nietzscheanism of Dionysian sexual liberation, some valorized women as having a separate feminine essence associated with motherhood, and some sought to extend women's intellectual and creative powers into the spheres of higher education, careers and authorship, traditionally reserved for men. Nietzsche was also taken as an inspiration by some key representatives of "second-wave" feminism (roughly the period of the 1960s and 1970s), especially in France. There, the Nietzsche revival associated with poststructuralism (discussed in Chapter 2) made an impact on feminist representatives of this movement. The French feminists of this generation typically learned from, but also sought to supersede, the "existentialist" feminism of Beauvoir, which had made a powerful impact in the 1940s and 1950s. Below we examine two of the most influential of the French Nietzschean feminists, Kofman and Irigaray.

Kofman: Baubô, a female Dionysus

Sarah Kofman (1934–94) was a French philosopher who contributed, among other things, important studies on feminist issues in relation to the works of Freud and Nietzsche. Her doctoral thesis was supervised by Deleuze, and she was significantly influenced by Derrida. (See Chapter 2 for a discussion of Derrida's work on woman and style in Nietzsche, which was particularly influential for Kofman, as well as for other Nietzschean feminists.) Her several books on Nietzsche include the influential *Nietzsche and Metaphor* (Kofman 1993) and a two-volume study of Nietzsche's autobiography *Ecce Homo*. We shall focus here, however, on her groundbreaking and influential article "Baubô: Theological Perversion and Fetishism" (Kofman 1998), written in 1973. This article questions Nietzsche's status as a supposed misogynist, and complexifies the status of women in his works, opening up further possibilities for feminist interpretations of Nietzsche.

Against the simple idea of Nietzsche as a misogynist, Kofman argues that there is no single, essentialist idea of "woman-in-herself" in Nietzsche's texts. Rather, she analyses "Nietzsche's many heterogenous texts on woman" (Kofman 1998: 46), arguing that multiple figures of woman are evident, and that they are differently valued. Importantly, Kofman notes that, for Nietzsche, some women are given a higher value – in Nietzsche's terms, they are interpreted as more life-affirmative – than some men (*ibid.*: 40). "Baubô" is the name of a minor goddess from Greek mythology who Nietzsche mentions, and who Kofman interprets as a feminine counterpart to Dionysus in order to underscore the positive valuation of women that can be found in Nietzsche. But the place of women in Nietzsche's texts is a complex one, and Kofman draws on her deep knowledge of Freudian psychoanalysis to develop a typology of women in Nietzsche according to the categories of "theological perversion" and "fetishism" on the one hand, and on the figure of Baubô, on the other. She thus distinguishes two main types of woman in Nietzsche: the nihilistic and the affirmative.

The first image of woman she discerns corresponds with Nietzsche's supposed misogyny. She notes that the figure of an *old woman* is often present in Nietzsche's texts as an accomplice to the belief in God. Furthermore, Kofman notes that when Nietzsche attacks the feminists and the "liberated women" of his age, he construes them as *infertile women*. These images of woman are analysed by Kofman according to the concepts of theological perversion and fetishism, concepts that may be found in both Freud and Nietzsche.

KEY POINT

"Theological perversion" is the nihilistic reversal of values associated with the ascetic ideal; it consists in the belief in a "true world" and the consequent devaluation of "this world". It is perverse because it prefers those values that are life denying over those values that are life affirmative.

The widespread presence of theological perversion in Western culture represents, for Nietzsche, a triumph of the weak over the strong. Nietzsche then associates this capacity for the weak to triumph with the feminine power of *cunning seduction*. As Kofman explains Nietzsche on this point, "the weak act like *women*: they try to seduce, they charm, by misrepresenting and disguising nihilistic values under gilded trim" (*ibid.*: 26).

This first, nihilistic image of woman is associated with the Greek goddess Circe. This image is found in Nietzsche: "morality has shown itself to be the greatest of all mistresses of seduction … the actual *Circe of philosophers*" (quoted in Kofman 1998: 26). Circe is a goddess of magic and trickery. In Homer's *Odyssey*, she turns Odysseus' crew into pigs by poisoning the food she gives them, and Odysseus is warned by Hermes that she will castrate him if she succeeds in seducing him. Circe is the figure of woman who seduces because she has something to hide. She is woman as mere appearance opposed to reality, and as illusion opposed to truth. With this figure, Nietzsche seemingly repeats the misogyny of the theological tradition, which has understood woman as the bringer of original sin and the origin of evil in the world, responsible for seducing men away from truth. This image of woman depends on an idea of an absolute truth or reality that the seductive woman obscures.

Similarly, "fetishism" is an attempt to hide something by providing a substitute for it. The idea of the fetish is found in both Freud and Nietzsche, and Kofman believes we can draw a legitimate parallel between them. Nietzsche associates fetishism with a primitive form of thinking, which consists in a kind of self-deception. Freud understands fetishism, in one of its manifestations, as "abnegation": the belief, but refusal to admit to oneself, that woman – and in particular, one's mother – is castrated. (Freud thought it common that, seeing our mother naked in early childhood, we explain to ourselves the fact that she does not have a penis by imagining that she has been castrated. This belief can persist at a deep unconscious level in adulthood, and continue to affect our psychological make-up.) The idea of woman as a castrated man is a perverted, unnatural view of woman, because it fails to see her own unique relation to life (that is, in terms of the specific function of her sexual organs). When Nietzsche attacks "liberated women", he sees them as infertile women, and as accomplices to the theological, perverted way of understanding woman as a castrated man. As Kofman interprets him, he claims that such women, instead of bearing children, try to gain their own penis by engaging in politics or writing books. He understands their behaviour as an expression of *ressentiment* against life.

Kofman deploys a "deconstructive" reading of Nietzsche influenced by Derrida in order to show how a more positive image of woman also emerges in Nietzsche's texts. On this reading, the theological, perverse perspective is what sets up oppositions between castration and virility, between appearance and reality, and between truth and illusion. She writes: "The whole idea of castration and its opposite is part of the syndrome of weakness and keeps one from speaking of a truly living and affirmative life, be this masculine or feminine" (Kofman 1998: 39). Life can never itself be reduced to such oppositions, which negate its value, but is rather best affirmed from a position beyond them. The life-affirmative position beyond oppositions is explained by Kofman in terms of Nietzsche's perspectivism and the image of the "camera obscura".

The camera obscura is a precursor to contemporary photography; it is a box that collects light from surroundings and can project an image. Nietzsche uses it as a metaphor for perspectivism, and for its denial. While the camera obscura was often touted as an absolutely accurate representation of reality, what it reproduces is really dependent on the perspective it is able to capture according to its placement in its surroundings. As Kofman presents it, Nietzsche's perspectivism asserts that we have access to things only from certain limited perspectives; an "absolute" perspective, which would allow us to see the final truth of things, is not available to us. The perverse, theological perspective claims to represent reality perfectly, and denies perspectivism. It desires to see nature stripped naked, and, Kofman says, is an affront to woman's modesty. Theological perversion understands woman as Circe; it wants to bypass her seductions and see her naked. In Nietzsche's revaluation, perspectivism reveals that everything is perspectival, but there are better and worse perspectives. First and foremost, the perspective that acknowledges perspectivism is "higher" than the perverse perspective that denies it.

KEY POINT *The significance of Baubô*
- Baubô is a female Dionysus (subverts the assumption that the life-affirmative is unambiguously male in Nietzsche's writings).
- Baubô is life and its eternal return, identified with woman and her reproductive organs.
- Baubô supplements Dionysus with a deconstructive logic: an affirmation of perspectivism that is an affirmation of life.

In contrast to Circe, who denies perspectivism, according to Kofman the acknowledgement of perspectivism is represented by Baubô, the goddess of veils behind veils (woman who hides herself because there is no "truth" to reveal). Nietzsche references her when he writes: "Perhaps truth is a woman who has reasons for not letting us see her reasons? Perhaps her name is, to speak Greek, *Baubo*?" (quoted in Kofman 1998: 42). Baubô is a minor Greek goddess associated with the goddess Demeter who played a part in the religious rites of the cult dedicated to her. Baubô is said to have made Demeter laugh while mourning for Persephone by lifting her skirts and showing her belly. Moreover, in the religious rites Baubô was represented by female genitalia. As such, she is the symbol of female fertility, regeneration and the eternal return of all things (*ibid.*: 45). Baubô is thus life, and highlights the essential role of women in its processes. Baubô is associated with Dionysus, and Kofman interprets her as a female Dionysus. This subverts any assumption that the life-affirmative is unambiguously gendered masculine in Nietzsche's writings. However, Baubô also acts as a supplement to Dionysus. While Dionysus appears naked, Baubô is veiled with skirts. Kofman writes: "The figure of Baubô indicates that a simple logic could never understand that life is neither depth nor surface, that behind the veil, there is another veil, behind a layer of paint, another layer" (*ibid.*: 44). Thus for Kofman, Baubô both positively revalues woman in Nietzsche's texts, and demonstrates the connection between the affirmation of perspectivism and the affirmation of life.

To summarize, Kofman finds both negative and positive images of woman in Nietzsche. These images hinge on the issue of absolute truth versus perspectivism. Circe, the negative image of woman, is a symptom of theological perversion and fetishism: these attitudes deny perspectivism and believe woman hides truth. Baubô, the positive image of woman, values her natural relation to life as child-bearer, and also deconstructs the truth/falsity opposition and affirms perspectivism. Thus Kofman revalues Nietzsche's apparently misogynist statements about woman being "mere appearance" by showing that in fact this is a trope for the affirmation of life, his highest value.

Irigaray: Nietzsche's marine lover

Luce Irigaray (b. 1932) is a Belgian-born French feminist theorist whose interdisciplinary work engages with philosophy, psychoanalysis, linguistics and phenomenology. In 1974, she published *Speculum of the Other Woman* ([1974] 1985), and she has since become one of the most influential of the contemporary French feminists. She has also often been categorized as one of the major poststructuralist thinkers. Her book *Marine Lover of Friedrich Nietzsche* ([1980] 1991) is a unique and significant contribution to feminist interpretations of Nietzsche. As the title suggests, in this book Irigaray positions herself as Nietzsche's lover, which may strike us as surprising. As Frances Oppel asks, "what, after all, is a subtle feminist, who until this point stressed the pleasures of lesbian love-making, doing in a relationship of amorous sexuality with a moustachioed misogynist like Nietzsche?" (1993: 88). In order to understand this unusual book, it needs to be approached with a basic knowledge of Irigaray's overall project.

This project is to analyse the exclusion of women in Western thought (especially in philosophy, psychoanalysis and linguistics). Her basic argument about how women have been excluded is that they have been subordinated to categories such as matter, nature and the body, which effectively means they have no subject position (because such a position is associated with the opposite of these terms, form, culture and mind). Without a "subject position", women have traditionally been excluded from thought, speech, and autonomous action. Moreover, she argues, women have often been understood simply as a derivative and inferior modification of men. This also has an exclusionary effect. For example, she argues that the possibility of a unique and authentic female sexuality has been undermined by the fact that (in psychoanalysis in particular) female sexuality has typically been understood as an inferior modification of male sexuality.

While a good deal of Irigaray's project has been critical, the aim of this project has been to liberate more positive alternatives, to which her works often gesture without giving absolute prescriptions. For example – and this is a crucial point in approaching some of her more textually experimental works – she argues that the linguistic structures of the dominant modes of discourse have a masculine bias, and attempts to develop a "feminine language". Her project is ultimately to develop a "legitimate" female subject and sexuality, but she considers a critique of the masculine biases of the Western tradition as essential preliminary groundwork. Her engagement with Nietzsche displays all these points. It at once critiques his masculine biases and develops points in his thought with positive potential for feminists, while the text itself is written in a "feminine" style that dramatically departs from accepted modes of academic discourse.

KEY POINT *Irigaray's style(s)*

Rather than set out an argument in a direct manner, much of the "point" of Irigaray's *Marine Lover of Friedrich Nietzsche* is in the style itself, which engages a variety of shifting devices: "repetition, polyvocality, allusion, ambiguity and contradiction; a sensuous diction; mimicry, parody and irony; open-endedness: a linguistic duplicity much like Nietzsche's" (Oppel 1993: 92).

Marine Lover of Friedrich Nietzsche takes the form of an extended love letter, addressed to Nietzsche, from an imaginary aquatic lover (a mermaid or sea nymph). This is an unusual approach for a text on one of the great philosophers, but is motivated in relationship to Irigaray's project as follows. First, she chooses to relate to Nietzsche as a lover because this unsettles the traditionally accepted ways of relating to philosophers through their texts, and allows a new, feminized relationship to develop. Typically, philosophers write on other philosophers as apprentices relating to masters, or as critics to adversaries. Such relations might be thought as coded with a masculine gender bias: both the relations between master and apprentice, and the adversarial relation, have been social relations in which both roles have typically been played by men. When women have written on philosophers in such a mode, they have generally copied the same modes of address, thus taking on masculine roles. Irigaray proposes the erotic love relationship as a new possible model for a philosophical, critical, textual relationship, one that follows women's relations to men and opens on to numerous possibilities (for example, and as Irigaray often enacts in her text, the lover can also be an accuser, and love relationships are ones in which inequalities, power relations and, in general, issues of gender politics can be laid bare). Second, Irigaray chooses the element of water as a major theme of her study because it is often associated with the feminine, and is also (Irigaray claims) that element which Nietzsche most feared (Irigaray 1981: 43). The feminine body, it has frequently been noted, has been construed as more "fluid" than the male; it is associated with menstrual blood, amniotic fluid, milk and so on (for an insightful wider discussion of this issue, see Grosz [1994]). In Nietzsche's texts, Irigaray notes, water is often associated with groundlessness and the abyss: the wide open seas we must brave after the death of God. The element of water thus allows Irigaray to relate key themes in Nietzsche's works to the ambivalent status of the feminine in his texts.

On one level, Irigaray engages Nietzsche's great ideas such as the eternal return, the will to power and the *Übermensch*, accusing him of repeating the masculine biases of the Western philosophical tradition. She argues that the eternal return, understood as an economy of the Same, appropriates and synthesizes all otherness, including the otherness of the feminine. Moreover, she writes to Nietzsche (and this quote will also serve as a brief example of her style in *Marine Lover*):

> [Y]ou ask a woman to help you in this operation. To redouble your affirmation. To give yourself back as a unit – subjects and objects of all your ecstasy. To fold all your becoming back into your being. To give you back, in the here and now, everything you have believed, loved, produced, planned, been …
> (Irigaray 1991: 34–5)

Against this idea of the eternal return as a masculine economy of the Same, she defends the irreducibility of differences, in particular sexual difference. Drawing on psychoanalysis, she argues that we can understand the Nietzschean "death of God" as a special opportunity for re-establishing sexual difference on a more authentic footing. She argues that the masculine subject position depends on an exorcism of the feminine, motivated by the (infantile, then unconscious) idea that the female is a castrated male. This exorcism leaves a "hole" in the subject's worldview, a hole that is filled in by the idea of God (here Irigaray draws on Freud's theorization of fetishes as substitutes, discussed in the Kofman section above – so the idea of God appears as a kind of fetish). What the death of God means, on Irigaray's analysis, is that we have lost the ability to invest this fetish with significance, so the "hole" is staring us in the face. The tendency of the male will be to flee again before the feminine, to find a new fetish substitute. But, Irigaray argues, the death of God also provides a unique opportunity for the female to be given back her rights, to take her place in a more authentic economy of sexual difference. In this "new" economy, the female will no longer be condemned to the status of an object, and understood as an exorcised, inferior male. Rather, she will occupy her own unique subject position, and take part in an economy of asymmetrical sexual difference (asymmetrical not in any hierarchical sense, but because male and female will be genuinely different).

As Oppel notes, Irigaray was initially pessimistic about the prospects of success for her project of articulating an authentic subjectivity for women, but this pessimism gave way to cautious optimism in the 1980s (Oppel 1993: 91). Her increasing optimism appears directly related to her readings of more recent philosophers, beginning with Nietzsche, and including Heidegger, Levinas and Derrida (*ibid.*). Philosophers such as these, she believes, are "turning back towards the origins of their culture ... to the point at which male identity constituted itself as patriarchal and phallocratic" (quoted in *ibid.*). These origins are the Presocratic philosophers, in whom Nietzsche and Irigaray share a deep interest. Most crucially for Irigaray's reading of Nietzsche is the question of language and its place in philosophy in relation to sexual difference. Simply put, Irigaray posits a rupture between poetry and philosophy, which has marked most of the philosophical tradition, but which was not present with the Presocratic philosophers. She sees in this rupture the marks of the problematic differentiation of the sexes that has conditioned the history of philosophy: philosophical language has been gendered masculine, while poetry has been gendered feminine and excluded from "serious" discourse. Despite all his complicity with the "phallocratic" tradition, according to Irigaray, Nietzsche harbours a great deal of value for feminism because, both in his themes and his uses of language, he helps to heal the split between philosophy and poetry. In order to understand the feminist uses to which Irigaray believes Nietzsche may be put, then, it is essential to move to a much deeper level of his texts than his explicit pronouncements on women, and to understand the crucial importance of language itself in constructing and sustaining sexual difference.

Oliver: womanizing Nietzsche

Over the past couple of decades, a significant anglophone trend in Nietzschean feminism has emerged through several important monographs and collections of essays, a trend that frequently draws on and responds to European feminist studies of Nietzsche (such as those of Kofman and Irigaray). We shall examine just one example of this trend here, Oliver's *Womanizing Nietzsche* (1995). Oliver's study also serves as an example of a more critical trend in feminist Nietzsche studies, which recognizes the positive contributions of Nietzsche's works to challenging the masculine biases of the Western philosophical tradition, but which at the same time sees Nietzsche as failing to provide genuine possibilities for the "feminine" to enter philosophy.

Oliver's *Womanizing Nietzsche* examines not just Nietzsche's texts, but also (most significantly) those of Derrida, as well as drawing on Freud, Lacan, Irigaray, Kristeva and others. In her words, "The central thesis of *Womanizing Nietzsche* is that while Nietzsche and Derrida, in particular, attempt to open up philosophy to its others – the body, the unconscious, nonmeaning, even the feminine – they close off philosophy to any specifically feminine other" (1995: xi). Oliver thus argues that while some philosophers, notably Nietzsche, have made some progress in attempting to open philosophy to the things it has traditionally excluded, ultimately they have done so in a way that continues to exclude the feminine. While Nietzsche, especially as interpreted by Derrida, seems to open a place for woman in philosophy, Oliver argues that in the Nietzschean text "woman" remains construed as an object, and remains excluded as a possible subject position. Just as with the rest of the history of Western philosophy, for Nietzsche, man is subject and woman is object. Oliver discusses in particular the way that the mother – the maternal "other" – is excluded by Nietzsche.

One example that Oliver discusses is "the body". The body is one of the things that has traditionally been associated with the feminine, and excluded from philosophy (which has privileged the disembodied mind). Oliver notes the way Nietzsche argues for the importance of the body, but argues also that the body he privileges is always a *male* body. She elaborates this through an analysis of Nietzsche's understanding of reading and writing, as presented in the *Genealology of Morals*. She argues that we can distinguish two approaches to reading and writing: one associated with reactivity and slave morality and the other associated with activity and noble morality. The first is a simple or naive reading, associated with traditional philosophical rationality, which searches in the written text for a meaning understood to be a single, true, transcendent referent of that text. By contrast, an active or noble reading is sensuous and bodily; it is indicated by Nietzsche's "genealogy". On Oliver's reading, genealogy combines interpretation and the diagnosis of symptoms. Texts need to be interpreted because they are not assumed to be transparent bearers of meaning. Moreover, texts can be diagnosed for the symptoms they bear in so far as these are symptoms of the *investments* of feeling and desire in the text. Bodily, sensuous feelings and desires are the "other" of the transcendent, conceptual meanings traditionally thought to be the only significant elements of philosophical texts. Oliver argues that "Genealogy is a way of reading that opens on to the other of a text. Yet within Nietzsche's genealogy, that other is not permitted to be feminine" (1995: 20).

Oliver discusses a rather cryptic aphorism from *Thus Spoke Zarathustra*, repeated at the beginning of the third essay of the *Genealogy of Morality*, which Nietzsche tells us is a lesson in reading. This aphorism reads: "Unconcerned, mocking, violent – thus wisdom wants *us*: she is a woman and wants only a warrior" (quoted in *ibid.*: 17). What does this mean, and how can it act as a lesson in reading? Against other interpreters (notably Nehamas), Oliver proposes that we have to take seriously here Nietzsche's suggestion that "wisdom is a woman", who "wants a warrior". Oliver points to the relation between the woman and the warrior, underlining the fact that the woman here is the active lover, the warrior the passive beloved. One way of interpreting this as a lesson for reading is to understand the text as the wise woman, which has the power to actively transform the reader into a "warrior". As Oliver indicates, this suggests a certain violence: "Nietzsche wants a sensuous, violent reading and writing that come from the body" (*ibid.*: 23).

Oliver then argues that this construal of the bodily processes of reading and writing, of writing with one's own blood, as Nietzsche writes elsewhere (Z: 1 "On Reading and Writing"), evokes specifically the *male* body. Thus Nietzsche opens philosophy to its other in the form of the body, but this opening forecloses the possibility that this other be a feminine other because the body is construed as always only a male body. She underlines this point, and gestures towards a more positive possibility, by indicating that, in relation to women's bodies, blood is not necessarily the product of violence: "The image of a woman reading and writing with her own blood promises a creativity that is neither sadistic nor masochistic, that does not require violence toward the reader or self-violence" (*ibid.*: 24).

A further argument Oliver makes in *Womanizing Nietzsche* is that we can gain insight into Nietzsche's misogyny and masculine biases by distinguishing between the feminine and the maternal (that is, between "women in general" and "the mother"), a distinction, she argues, that tends to be conflated in Nietzsche's texts. It then becomes apparent that the attitudes towards the feminine in general in Nietzsche's texts devolve from a problematic relation towards the maternal. To explain this, Oliver draws on Julia Kristeva's psychoanalytic concept of "abjection".

KEY POINT *Abjection*

Abjection is the feeling of horror, disgust or nausea in the face of things that threaten clear distinctions between borders, especially between the self and the other. This feeling can be produced, for example, by bodily wastes such as faeces, blood or vomit, which threaten the border between the inside and the outside of the body, the distinction between what should be considered part of the self, and what not part of the self. Abjection can also be applied to our relation to our mother's body, since before birth our own body was not distinct from that of our mother.

While Oliver does not believe that psychoanalytic theory can legitimately be used to find in texts symptoms of the psychology of Nietzsche the man, she does believe it can be used to interpret the attitudes evident in the texts themselves. After revisiting many of the misogynistic statements regarding women in general in Nietzsche's texts (such as those highlighted in the first part of this chapter), Oliver employs Kristeva's concept of abjection to show that these attitudes stem from a deeper problematic relation with the maternal.

Kristeva argues that the feelings of abjection in relation to the maternal body function differently for the female and for the male child (see Kristeva 1982). Oliver suggests that her account of the male child's abjection can be applied to Nietzsche's writings. The male child feels his identity threatened by the maternal body: "How can he become a man when 'he' was once part of a woman's body?" (Oliver 1995: 138). Kristeva argues that in order successfully to negotiate this crisis, the child needs to "split" the mother into two: the abject mother, associated with the maternal function, and the sublime mother, which can become an object of love for the child. To simplify Kristeva's rather complex argument, making the mother abject allows the boy to split from his mother and become autonomous. If the child does not successfully go through the stage of abjection, he will not properly separate himself from his mother's body; that body will then become a "phobic object" – an object of continued fear and anxiety. Furthermore, if he does not go through this stage successfully and is not able to isolate, and separate himself from, the mother, he will confuse the mother with *all* women. All women will thus become objects of fear and anxiety, as the result of "misplaced abjection". Kristeva argues that the male child needs a loving "imaginary father" in order to successfully pass through the abject phase. Success will mean gaining independence from the mother, being able to love the mother as an independent person, and being able to separate other women from the maternal function.

In light of this concept of abjection, Oliver argues that we find in Nietzsche's texts evidence of precisely the symptoms Kristeva identifies as misplaced abjection. Nietzsche's texts are replete with imaginary fathers who, far from being "loving", are severe and impossibly demanding (such as Julius Caesar or Alexander the Great; EH "Wise" 3). Moreover, as Oliver argues, there is plenty of evidence of anxiety regarding separation from the mother in Nietzsche's writings. The following passage is particularly telling:

> The free spirit will always breathe a sigh of relief when he has finally decided to shake off the maternal care and protection administered by the women around him. What is the harm in the colder draft of air that they had warded off so anxiously? What does one real disadvantage, loss, accident, illness, debt, or folly more or less in his life matter, compared with the bondage of the golden cradle, the peacock-tail fan, and the oppressive feeling of having to be actually grateful because he is waited upon and spoiled like an infant? That is why the milk offered him by the maternal disposition of the women around him can so easily turn to bile.
>
> (HAH 429; quoted in Oliver 1995: 144–5).

The upshot of misplaced abjection is deep ambivalence towards the mother; a simultaneous overidentification with, and feelings of hostility towards, the mother. As Oliver (following Jean Greybeal here) notes, this ambivalence is acutely marked in a passage in the first chapter of *Ecce Homo*, which was suppressed by the editor, Gast, at the time of initial publication (presumably because of the vitriol expressed by Nietzsche against his mother and sister). This chapter begins: "The happiness of my existence, perhaps its uniqueness, lies in its fatefulness; to give it the form of a riddle: as my father I am already dead and as my mother I am still alive and growing old" (EH "Wise" 1). Here we have a strong identification with the mother. But later on, in the suppressed part of the chapter (EH "Wise" 3), Nietzsche expresses deep hostility towards his mother and his sister, calling them "rabble" and a "hell-machine" (cited in Oliver 1995: 140).

Moreover, this hostility is projected onto all women, onto "the feminine" as such, as in the many examples of misogynistic statements we have already seen. Oliver's central claim here is, then, that "Nietzsche's texts abject all women and femininity because he cannot abject the maternal. He misplaces abjection onto women and femininity in general as a defence against his own identification with the maternal body" (*ibid*.: 145). So, Oliver's analysis construes Nietzsche's misogyny as a kind of aberrant psychosexual symptom. But more than this, this analysis leads to an illustration of one more way in which, despite his models of radical change, the feminine is excluded from Nietzsche's logic.

According to Oliver, Nietzsche's misplaced abjection manifests itself in his descriptions of life-affirmative creativity, and conditions his models of freedom, such as the free spirit and the *Übermensch*. This model of creativity denies the maternal role of the mother in so far as creation, for the Nietzschean "higher type", is always a *self*-creation, a kind of giving birth to oneself. The *Übermensch* has no need for a mother. In Nietzsche's texts, the model of the subject as a masculine, self-creating one thus leaves no place for a feminine subject. On Oliver's reading, the positive role that would be accorded to the feminine in Nietzsche (and as Kofman identifies it through the figure of Baubô) – life and creation as childbirth – are subsumed into the masculine, while the maternal itself remains the object of hostility, and this hostility is displaced to *all* women. Once again, Oliver shows how, for all of Nietzsche's apparent gains, the possibility for a genuine subject position for the feminine remains foreclosed in his texts. Asking what it means for women to read these texts, she concludes that Nietzsche's writings are not themselves addressed to women, as potential readers: women remain the *objects* of his discourse (and frequently the objects of criticism, at that).

What we have seen in this chapter is a variety of possible perspectives on the relation of Nietzsche to feminism. While it is understandably tempting to dismiss Nietzsche as a misogynistic opponent of women's liberation, in fact many feminists have found his radical challenges to the patriarchal Western philosophical tradition liberating. However, feminist readings of Nietzsche are frequently nuanced, and often contain criticisms of him more sophisticated than simple accusations of misogyny, in the form of careful examinations of his metaphors and the attitudes implicit in his texts. Such criticisms, like those of Irigaray and Oliver, find that he often excludes the feminine from philosophy even at those points where he begins to make useful openings in the patriarchal tradition. Nietzsche thus appears as an ambivalent figure for feminism, but one whose work many have found useful through his deconstructions of the metaphysical tradition, his critique of "truth" and advocacy of perspectivism, his defence of the bodily and the sensuous, and his call for a radical revaluation of the values of the Western tradition. For feminists, such a revaluation must include a revaluation of the feminine, even if Nietzsche did not see that himself.

Summary of key points

Nietzsche on women

Nietzsche can be considered a misogynist both because of his explicit statements about women and because of the gender-biased metaphors he uses. He expressly opposed the women's liberation movement of his day. This opposition to women's liberation can be understood in terms of his general arguments supporting exploitation and a caste-based society.

Women on Nietzsche

Despite his misogyny, many feminists have found Nietzsche's models for radical change an inspiration for women's liberation. Feminist philosophy views the history of Western philosophy as deeply marked by masculine biases in many of its conceptual categories and the values ascribed to them. Nietzsche is useful in the eyes of many feminists because of the way he questions these traditional categories, and positively values some things traditionally associated with the feminine.

Early Nietzschean feminism

Three main trends in early Nietzschean feminism can be identified:

- bourgeois liberal;
- New Morality; and
- bohemian.

These trends are distinguished by their views on women's sexual liberation, and women's social roles. Some early feminists have adapted Nietzsche's idea of the *Übermensch* to create an ideal of the "superwoman". Important figures in early Nietzschean feminism include Lily Braun, Helene Stöcker, Hedwig Dohm, Mary Wigman and Isadora Duncan.

Kofman's Nietzsche

According to Kofman, there is no single image of woman in Nietzsche's writings, but multiple images. She contrasts the goddess Circe with the goddess Baubô. Circe is the negative image of woman, associated with theological perversion, fetishism and the denial of perspectivism. She seduces man away from the truth. Baubô is the positive image of woman, construed as a female Dionysus and associated with the feminine life-affirmative power of procreation, and with the eternal return of life through this power. She affirms perspectivism through her veils, which hide only further veils.

Irigaray's Nietzsche

Irigaray examines the exclusion of an authentic subject position and sexuality for women in Western thought, and Nietzsche is found to be complicit in such exclusions through ideas such as the eternal return. However, she also sees Nietzsche as contributing to an overturning of the logic of this exclusion by breaking down the divide between academic philosophical discourse (gendered masculine) and poetry (gendered feminine). Her book *Marine Lover of Friedrich Nietzsche* develops both attitudes towards the philosopher, through a "feminine style" of writing.

Oliver's Nietzsche

Oliver argues that while Nietzsche opens the philosophical tradition for new possibilities of thought, he simultaneously excludes women from such new possibilities. For example, while he valorizes the body, it is always a *male* body. Oliver argues that Nietzsche's misogyny can be understood through the concept of abjection, as misplaced feelings of hostility towards the mother. This hostility towards the maternal further excludes the feminine from his affirmative categories such as that of the *Übermenschen*, who are men who have no need of the maternal because they can give birth to themselves.

five

Nietzscheanism and theology

> God is dead! God remains dead! And we have killed him! How
> can we console ourselves, the murderers of all murderers! The
> holiest and mightiest thing the world has ever possessed has
> bled to death under our knives: who will wipe this blood from
> us? With what water could we clean ourselves? What festivals
> of atonement, what holy games will we have to invent for our-
> selves?   (GS 125)

In 1966, a cover of the popular American magazine *Time* presented the
question, in bold red letters against a black background, "Is God Dead?"
The story was not on Nietzsche, but on a movement in theology known
as "death of God", or "radical" theology. Nietzsche's thought, however,
was a central reference for this movement. It may seem the height of
irony that the thinker best known for his proclamation "God is dead",
the author of *The Anti-Christ*, has had a significant influence on theology, which is precisely the study of God. The cover of *Time* in the mid-
1960s was Nietzschean theology's most public moment. But, as Vattimo
has noted, "the idea that Nietzsche could be read as a Christian thinker
[goes] back to the earliest years of his reception" (Vattimo 2001: 184).
Significantly, in her book on Nietzsche, Salomé stated that he retained
a religious attitude in spite of his alleged atheism (cited in Diethe 2006).
Vattimo notes that early theologians interpreted Nietzsche's breakdown
as an unsuccessful attempt to overcome Christianity and then find his
way back to God (2001: 169). More positively, some viewed Nietzsche's
"antichrist" as a new Christ (*ibid.*). After the Second World War there

was a significant revival of interest in Nietzsche in relation to theology, an interest that continues to this day.

In order to understand the possibility, and perhaps paradox, of Nietzsche's adoption by some theological thinkers, it is important to understand the nature of his opposition to theology, and to Christianity in particular. This is examined in the first section below. The rest of the chapter then outlines developments in Nietzschean theology, which may be understood roughly according to the categories of existential theology, radical theology, weak theology and recent developments. As we shall see, these developments in theological appropriations of Nietzschean thought throughout the twentieth and early twenty-first centuries have broadly paralleled wider developments in philosophy and theory, so that earlier Nietzschean theologians such as Karl Barth and Paul Tillich have existentialist sympathies, and weak theology is associated with postmodern and poststructuralist thought. We shall conclude the chapter by noting some recent developments concerning the impact of Nietzsche on theology, including recent Nietzschean theological works, as well as the challenge to Nietzsche's interpretation of Christianity posed by the enthusiasm for St Paul in some recent continental philosophy.

Nietzsche as antichrist

Nietzsche's critical reaction to Christianity and theology in general arises early in his works, but achieves its most detailed and flamboyant articulation in his 1888 book *The Anti-Christ: A Curse on Christianity*. Nietzsche certainly pulls no punches in voicing his hostility towards Christianity, and in the pages of *The Anti-Christ* we find comments such as the following:

- "Christianity has taken the side of everything weak, base, failed, it has made an ideal out of whatever *contradicts* the preservation instincts of a strong life; it has corrupted the reason of even the most spiritual natures by teaching people to see the highest spiritual values as sinful, as deceptive, as *temptations*" (A 5).
- "Anything a theologian thinks is true *must* be false: this is practically a criterion of truth" (A 9).
- "The Christian idea of God – God as a god of the sick, God as Spider, God as spirit – is one of the most corrupt conceptions of God the world has ever seen … God as declared aversion to life,

to nature, to the will to life! God as the formula for every slander against 'the here and now', for every lie about the 'beyond'! God as the deification of nothingness, the canonization of the will to nothingness! ..." (A 18).

- "[Y]ou should put on gloves before taking up the New Testament. The presence of so much uncleanliness almost forces you to" (A 46).
- "Christianity has been the worst thing to happen to humanity so far" (A 51).
- "[O]nly a sick reason can be used as Christian reason, Christianity sides with everything idiotic" (A 52).
- "I call Christianity the one great curse, the one great innermost corruption, the one great instinct of revenge that does not consider any method to be poisonous, secret, subterranean, *petty* enough, – I call it the one immortal blot on humanity" (A 62).
- "I *condemn* Christianity, I indict the Christian church on the most terrible charges an accuser has ever had in his mouth. I consider it the greatest corruption conceivable" (A 62).
- "The priest is the most vicious type of person: he *teaches* anti-nature. Priests are not to be reasoned with, they are to be locked up" (A "Laws against Christianity", first proposition).
- "[T]he words 'God', 'saviour', 'redeemer', 'saint' should be used as terms of abuse, to signify criminals" (A "Laws against Christianity", sixth proposition).

Moreover, Nietzsche states not only his opposition to the religion of Christianity, but to theology in general: "We need to say *whom* we feel opposed to – theologians and everything with theologian blood in its veins – the whole of our philosophy" (A 8). Indeed, Nietzsche often appears so opposed to religion that it may seem difficult to understand how theological thinkers have managed to reconcile themselves in any way with his thought. And, in fact, Nietzsche has often enough been condemned by Christians outright as an "antichrist" (a condemnation that we should acknowledge he did his best to invite).

A closer reading of *The Anti-Christ*, however, reveals a rather different story. As many readers have noted, Nietzsche is most vitriolic about Paul and the tradition of Christianity he inaugurated, while for Jesus Christ himself Nietzsche has many words of praise. Indeed, Nietzsche suggests that "Jesus could be called a 'free spirit', using the phrase somewhat loosely" (A 32). Jesus is included in the short list of historical figures Nietzsche indicated as examples of "higher types" of humanity;

not themselves *Übermenschen*, but prophetic intimations of what they might be. What distinguishes these higher types is their character as strong, active creators and legislators of values. Thus, it is not so much Jesus and the "Jesus cult" (as some scholars term early Christianity), but Pauline Christianity that is the target of Nietzsche's vitriol. In fact, Nietzsche argues that Jesus's "good news" (or "evangel") died on the cross with him, and that from the very first his message began to be corrupted into a "dysangel" ("bad news") by his followers. He glosses this by claiming that "*there have never been any Christians*"(A 39).

How, then, does Nietzsche understand Jesus and his message? For him, Jesus radically overturned the Jewish focus on law, religious *belief* and the doctrine of human sin. Jesus replaces the idea of religion based on a belief in a transcendent God with an abolition of the gulf separating the human and the divine, and a focus on a *way of life* rather than a belief. He writes: "*[o]nly the evangelical practice* leads to God, in fact it *is* 'God' – What the evangel *did away with* was the Judaism of the concepts of 'sin', 'forgiveness of sin', 'faith', 'redemption through faith' – the whole Jewish *church doctrine* was rejected in the 'glad tidings'" (A 33). Instead of the promises of reward and redemption, Jesus offered a way of living *here and now* that promised to make *this* life "the kingdom of heaven". ("The 'kingdom of heaven' is a state of the heart – not something lying 'above the earth' or coming 'after death'" (A 34).) This way of life was based on *love*: as Nietzsche interprets it, love is an emotion that "falsifies" life, but in a way that makes it easier to bear and to affirm (a point he frequently argues in relation to art, for example). So as a first point, for Nietzsche, Jesus rejects a transcendent beyond, and is able to affirm this life here and now. Second, Jesus offered a morality that rejected *ressentiment*, and Nietzsche sees this rejection as the primary meaning of the crucifixion: "the main point, the exemplary character of dying in this way, the freedom, the superiority *over* every feeling of *ressentiment*" (A 40). For Nietzsche, then, Jesus was in a sense a "free spirit", in so far as he rejected two key aspects of nihilism: transcendence and *ressentiment* morality.

Nietzsche argues that Jesus's message began to be corrupted by his earliest followers, and that in effect it has never really been understood. Nietzsche accords the lion's share of the blame for this corruption to Paul, who, as Saul, had persecuted Christians before famously himself converting to Christianity after experiencing a vision on the road to Damascus. Much of the New Testament of the Bible is composed of Paul's letters, and, as such, Pauline Christianity comprises much of what is understood by "Christianity" to this day. According to

Nietzsche, Paul epitomized the opposite type to Jesus, and effectively reversed his message. He calls Paul "the genius in hatred, in the vision of hatred, in the merciless logic of hatred" (A 42). Paul reversed Jesus's message by turning what was a doctrine of happiness here and now into a new faith of deferred redemption, based on a *belief* in Jesus's resurrection. While Jesus shifted the emphasis from a transcendent and deferred blessedness to a blessedness of life here and now, Paul shifted the "kingdom of heaven" once again into the world of the beyond. Moreover, instead of emphasizing a way of life, Paul made the attainment of this "kingdom of heaven" dependent on a *belief*, in what Nietzsche considers the *lie* of the resurrection. But most poisonously for Nietzsche, Paul reintroduced the doctrine of sin, and reconfigured Jesus's message around the need to be redeemed from sin. Moreover, Paul identifies the weak and the downtrodden as the chosen of God, and – according to the analysis of master and slave morality Nietzsche undertakes in *On the Genealogy of Morality* – he understands Paul as choosing a slave morality, based on the instinct of revenge against the strong. For this reason, he argues that "Paul was the greatest of all apostles of revenge" (A 45).

KEY POINT
It is not Jesus and his message that Nietzsche opposes, but what he sees as the later corruption of that message, especially by Paul.

It is Paul, then, and not at all Jesus, whom Nietzsche identifies as originating the Christianity he castigates. As should already be clear by now, Nietzsche's opposition to Christianity is best summarized by his characterization of it as a form of nihilism. He makes this point both poetically and polemically by noting that the words "Christian" and "nihilist" rhyme (in German – *Nihilist* and *Christ* – they do), and do more than just rhyme (A 58). Nietzsche famously calls Christianity "Platonism for 'the People'" (BGE "Preface"), and he understands it as the popular, cultural form of the nihilistic philosophy of Plato (as a matter of historical fact, Christianity was strongly influenced by Platonic philosophy).

In so far as Christianity is perhaps the major form of cultural nihilism to condition Western history for Nietzsche, it is perhaps not surprising that in his characterizations of Christianity we find practically all the main things he condemns. At a high level of generality, and as we have already seen, it combines the metaphysical belief in a "true world" with a slave morality (which Nietzsche calls "the two most vicious errors in existence"; A 10). In more detail, Nietzsche criticizes Christianity on the following further points:

- *False knowledge.* Christianity denies perspectivism, and dogmatically asserts false beliefs as true. "This universally faulty optic is made into a morality, a virtue, a holiness, seeing-*wrong* is given a *good* conscience, – *other* types of optic are not allowed to have value any more now that this one has been sanctified with names like 'God', 'redemption', and 'eternity'" (A 9). (This theological denial of perspectivism has been previously covered in relation to Kofman's discussion of this issue; see Chapter 4.) This dogmatic assertion of truth militates against experimentation (since it asserts that truth is already known; A 57). Moreover, Nietzsche asserts that Christianity is opposed to science and to knowledge as such: "truth" is seen as aligned with faith, and in opposition to knowledge and reality.
- *Anti-naturalism.* For Nietzsche, Christianity promotes the idea that nature is corrupt and evil. He writes: "Once the concept of 'nature' had been invented as a counter to the idea of 'God', 'natural' had to mean 'reprehensible', – that whole fictitious world is rooted in a *hatred* of the natural (- of reality! -)" (A 15). As a related idea, Christianity condemns sensuousness, sexuality and the body. For the Christian, "The body is an object of hatred, hygiene is rejected as sensuousness" (A 21).
- *Opposition to "higher types".* As we have seen elsewhere in this book (see for example the Introduction), Nietzsche understands higher types, or *Übermenschen*, as the highest form of affirmation of life, and the only real solution to nihilism. According to him, "Christianity … has waged a *war to the death* against this *higher* type of person" (A 5). It has done this by taking the side of the weak, promoting the idea of equality, and encouraging feelings of pity. Moreover, Nietzsche sees Christianity as weakening the strong types by instilling in them a bad conscience, teaching that self-assertion and the individual creation of values are sinful.

While Nietzsche's attacks are frequently vitriolic, it must be noted that his analysis of Christianity is also nuanced, and he argues that while it is dominated by negation, it harbours a certain kind of stimulus to life (albeit a sick and impoverished form of life). For example, he notes that "strong *hope* is a much greater stimulus to life than any piece of individual happiness that actually falls our way" (A 23). He also acknowledges that Christianity has inspired many of the greatest cultural achievements in European history. Nevertheless, he believes that it functions to preserve life at a much lower level of will to power than is possible (and is evident, for example, in ancient Greek culture).

As we have now seen, despite Nietzsche's expressed hatred of Christianity, a closer look at his philosophy makes it less surprising that some theologians have found immense value in his work. For what Nietzsche criticizes is primarily a *corrupt* Christianity, and his works offer the suggestion of a "true" Christianity that has never properly been realized. In addition, his deep awareness and analysis of the far-reaching *implications* of secular atheism have led many to see him as a key thinker for understanding the crisis of faith in the contemporary world.

Existential theology

We have seen in Chapter 1 that Nietzsche's reception in the mid-twentieth century was strongly associated with the wider intellectual movement of existentialism. In the early 1970s, John Macquarrie wrote: "In recent decades existentialism has in fact been the type of philosophy most influential with theologians" (1972: 270). It is perhaps not surprising, then, that some of the most prominent theologians to have been influenced by Nietzsche's thought have also frequently been characterized as existentialists. What characterizes a theologian as existentialist? Maurice Friedman provides an indication in his critical reaction to Sartre's claim that all existentialism must begin with the death of God. This is not the case, Friedman suggests, if Sartre just means atheism. But we can agree with Sartre, if we understand by this "the recognition of the crisis that has brought modern man face to face with the absence of a meaningful direction of existence, with the 'absurd,' or with 'the eclipse of God'" (Friedman 1964: 242). Existential theologians are concerned to deal with these issues, but within the purview of a religious faith, and by drawing on the theological tradition, as well as on philosophers such as Nietzsche. We shall examine here, in their relation to Nietzsche, three of the most prominent of these existential theologians: Martin Buber, Barth and Tillich. The fact that each of them is often considered among the most important theologians of the twentieth century attests to the profundity of Nietzsche's impact on theological thought.

Buber: "Nietzionism"

Martin Buber (1878–1965) was a Polish-Jewish theological scholar. He was an important contributor to the early Zionist movement, and his major work *I and Thou* ([1923] 1970) contains themes that have often led to him being labelled an existentialist. Zionism is a movement that contains great diversity, but which centres on the aim of creating a Jewish nation in Israel. It began in the 1890s, largely as a secular, political movement. Buber contributed a strong cultural and spiritual dimension to the movement. Like some other early Zionists, Buber was influenced by Nietzsche at an early age. He discovered Nietzsche at fourteen, and at seventeen he began (but never completed) a translation of *Zarathustra* into Polish. Buber's first published essay was on Nietzsche: "A Word about Nietzsche and Life Values" (1900). In later life, Buber denounced Nietzsche's influence, describing it as an "invasion" that robbed him of his freedom, and which he took a long time to overcome. However, scholars such as Jacob Golomb have argued that despite this explicit renunciation, Nietzschean themes persist even in Buber's later thought (Golomb 2004).

While Nietzsche sometimes criticizes Judaism for the same reasons that he criticizes Christianity, he also suggests that there was a life-affirmative Hebraic religion that was later corrupted, and he praises Jews for their strength as a culture, and gives them a special role in some of his prophetic musings about the future of Europe. These are some of the reasons why the perhaps unlikely pairing of Nietzsche and Zionism became possible. Some early Zionists were also attracted by Nietzsche's negative theme of "the death of God" in so far as they felt the need to throw off traditional religious Judaism – belief in "God the father" – in order to create a new form of Jewish identity. However, Golomb (2004) argues that it is the positive existential theme of self-creation, and the focus on creativity as constitutive of a strong culture, that most significantly account for the interest of Buber and other early Zionists in Nietzsche.

Buber argued that prior to the creation of a Jewish state, it was necessary for Jews to establish their own self-identity both as individuals and as a culture, and Nietzsche's works helped to inspire this view. He argued for a "Jewish Renaissance" that would produce a "new kind of Jew". Buber advocated the creation of a new Jewish identity through creative productivity, which he understood in a Nietzschean sense as a process of tapping into and unleashing vital life forces. In unmistakably Nietzschean terms, Buber defined Zionist politics as "a transvaluation (*Umwertung*) of all aspects of … the life of people to its depths and very foundations. It must touch the soul … We must unlock the vital powers of the nation and let loose its fettered instincts" (quoted in *ibid.*: 168). Golomb suggests that Buber's Zionist writings are so infused with Nietzschean language and ideas that the neologism "Nietzionism" is an apt characterization (*ibid.*: 166). Moreover, against the purely political aims of founding Zionists such as Theodor Hertzl, Buber advocated cultural and spiritual education. As Golomb notes, one of the key tensions in Buber's Zionism is the question of how to reconcile Nietzsche's individualist ethic of self-creation with the ideal of a cultural self-creation with a specifically Jewish content.

Golomb argues that while Buber's Zionist writings in the early years of the twentieth century represent his most Nietzschean period, his most original and influential book, *I and Thou*, also bears the mark of Nietzsche's influence. In this philosophical and theological work, Buber argues for a basic distinction between two types of relation, the "I–It" and the "I–Thou".

KEY POINT *Buber's I and Thou*
- *The "I–It" relation*: One relates to something as an object, to be understood through abstract universal categories, appropriated and manipulated for one's own ends.
- *The "I–Thou" relation*: One relates to another subject in a dynamic process of mutual respect and enrichment.

Buber argues that the "I–It" relation is necessary for many of our practical engagements in the world, and is an essential part of the scientific endeavour. However, he criticizes the contemporary tendency towards an excess of "I–It" relationality, which, he believes, is encroaching on the territory of the properly "I–Thou". These latter kinds of relations are ones that allow genuine respect and reciprocal self-actualization through dialogue. "I–Thou" relations can be between persons, but also with nature, with works of art, and with spirit or God (which Buber calls the "eternal Thou"). Buber's emphasis on relations with others was a tremendous influence on the phenomenological philosopher Emmanuel Levinas (1906–95), and it impacts on existentialist themes in so far as these concern relations with others, the uniqueness of human existence and relations with God.

Golomb argues that there is a striking similarity between Nietzsche's categories in *On the Genealogy of Morality* and Buber's in *I and Thou*: the "I–It" relation is a form of slave morality, while the "I–Thou" relation is a master morality. The slave moralist relates to other persons as objects or

"It"s, attempting to reduce them to objects of manipulation over which they have power, as a way of asserting dominance from their own weak position out of a feeling of desperation. The master moralist, to the contrary, is secure in their power and is able to relate to the other as another subject because they do not feel threatened by the other. Moreover, Golomb notes that there are evident vindications of Nietzsche's atheism in *I and Thou* from Buber's own theological position. Most significantly, he suggests that it is the *type of relation* that determines that it is God to whom one relates, rather than "what" one believes one relates to. Thus, he writes: "Whoever abhors the name and fancies that he is godless – when he addresses with his whole devoted being the You of his life that cannot be restricted by any other, he addresses God" (quoted in Golomb 2004: 178). As Golomb interprets this, it means that when Nietzsche was addressing the ideal of the *Übermensch*, he was addressing God (*ibid.*). Despite Nietzsche's apparent atheism, then, Buber implies that what is essential to religious belief is evident in the relations to ideals present in Nietzsche's texts.

Barth: theology beyond religion

Giles Fraser (2002: 8) notes that Nietzsche's proclamation of God's death influenced many early-twentieth-century theologians to explore the idea that a certain conception of religion and theology was dead, and to try to reinvent theology for the contemporary context. Karl Barth (1886–1968) was one of the first, and probably the most prominent, of the theologians to undertake this task. Barth was a Swiss Protestant, and one of the most influential theologians of the twentieth century. Barth had frequently been associated with existentialism, primarily because of his early works *The Epistle to the Romans* ([rewritten 2nd edn 1922] 1968) and *Church Dogmatics* ([1927] 2010). In these works he was influenced by figures such as Kierkegaard, Nietzsche and Nietzsche's friend Franz Overbeck in the task of criticizing religion. By "religion", Barth means the modern idea that God can be known by human means, such as through rational argument, or through interpreting history. He thus agrees with Nietzsche that "God is dead" in so far as the idea of a knowable God who is present in the human world and gives meaning to history is dead. In relation to such an idea of God and the kind of religion that bases itself on such a notion, Barth agrees that we should be atheists. However, Barth insists on the living reality of God in an ontological sense, and believes that the proclamation "God is dead" expresses only a cultural event. Barth understands this event as the end of the *modern* understanding of God, and as opening the possibility of a new kind of faith.

> **KEY POINT**
> Barth asserts that God is "Wholly Other" to human beings, and describes this radical otherness with a phrase derived from the Danish existentialist Kierkegaard: "infinite qualitative difference". Because of this radical otherness, we cannot know anything of God in human terms.

Barth asserts that God is knowable, but only through his revelation of himself to us, which is, in effect, a miracle. The precondition for such knowledge is an abandonment of rational, human theological knowledge and frames of reference. Barth is thus existentialist in insisting on the groundlessness of our existence in the face of reality, and the fact that we cannot rely on any rational certainties to form the basis of our faith and our basic attitudes towards life. In other words, for a genuine faith to be possible, one must first face up to what Nietzsche calls "nihilism". André J. Groenwald notes that in Barth's early work, Nietzsche was Barth's ally in his aim to "free God from the views of the modern period" (2007: 1441–2); that is, to overcome the "religious God" of rational proofs, and to establish God as the "Wholly Other".

In his later *Church Dogmatics*, Barth takes a more critical approach to Nietzsche, accusing him of an excessive *individualism* incompatible with any adequate ethics. Barth criticizes Nietzsche (and not just Nietzsche, but many other modern thinkers) for endorsing what he calls "humanity without the fellow-man". He sees radical individualism asserted in Nietzsche's concept of the noble or master in *On the Genealogy of Morality*, where such a strong type affirms themselves in complete independence of others. Relations with others seem to have a primarily negative meaning for Nietzsche, since the slave type define themselves through a negative relation to the other (*ressentiment* and the desire for revenge), while the master type have no real need for others at all, but are self-sufficient. This would appear to be a very different reading of Nietzsche from that which Golomb suggests in relation to Buber's thought (see above), and Barth in fact draws on Buber's notion of the "I–Thou" relation in what he understands as a necessary *corrective* to Nietzsche.

Tillich: God beyond God

Paul Tillich (1886–1965) was, along with Barth, one of the most influential Christian theologians of the twentieth century. Tillich also took an interest in Nietzsche, and was also associated with existentialism. Tillich was both a philosopher and a theologian, and in his works he often seeks to establish a dialogue between the two disciplines. Tillich argues against the conception of God as an "object" of thought, and seeks to reconceive God as above and beyond any predicates (i.e. statements of fact, or descriptions of qualities) we might ascribe to him. Tillich calls this non-objective conception of God "the God beyond God". Similarly, he sometimes defines God in a rather open fashion as simply "ultimate concern", that is, what concerns us most about our lives, the world, and the meaning and significance we ascribe to things. His conception of religious belief is similarly expanded to cover anything that involves such ultimate concern.

Tillich encountered Nietzsche in a variety of texts, and a variety of ways. In his most popular book, *The Courage to Be* ([1952] 2000), he includes a discussion of Nietzsche in his attempt to establish an onto-logical sense of courage. Perhaps most significantly for his theology, however, Tillich argues elsewhere that Nietzsche shows that God nec-essarily survives even "the death of God". This argument is made in a short sermon, "The Escape from God" ([1945] 2001). Here Tillich compares Psalms 139 and the section "The Ugliest Man" in Nietzsche's *Zarathustra*. Tillich asserts that "Friedrich Nietzsche, the famous atheist and ardent enemy of religion and Christianity, knew more about the power of the idea of God than many faithful Christians" (2001: 174). He notes that both texts concern the theme of God's omnipresence and omniscience, that is, the fact that he is everywhere and knows every-thing. Both texts express a horror, and even a hatred, towards God, in response to the thought that nothing can be hidden from this "absolute witness". The Ugliest Man, whom Tillich understands as symbolizing the ugliness within us all, states that this is why God needed to be killed: because the individual cannot tolerate such an omniscient witness.

Tillich sees great value in the recognition of this horror in the face of God. He suggests that if one has never known the desire to escape God, then one has never really known God (only an idolized image of God, who represents nothing but what is good and easy in life). This, then, is one reason he attributes such insight to Nietzsche: he has the courage to face the aspects of God that frighten us, as many Christians never do. However, Tillich takes his analysis an important step further by asserting that Nietzsche also demonstrates the "utter impossibility" of killing God. While the Ugliest Man asserts that God is dead (indeed, he has killed him), Tillich argues that Zarathustra then becomes the focus of his "ultimate concern". As such, Tillich sees the Ugliest Man as "resurrecting" his belief in God in a secular form. The moral is that for the atheist, God (as a figure of "ultimate concern") will always be revived in *something*. Thus, while Tillich agrees that a certain kind of God – God considered as an "object" of theoretical speculations – does not exist, he asserts that there is a higher form of God – the "God beyond God", or "ultimate concern" – that cannot die, and which survives all proclamations of his death. Thus, Tillich argues that beyond the death of God, there is a God that survives. As Craig Wiley (2009: 511) notes, however, Tillich's reformulation of the notion of God as "ultimate concern" has led some to the conclusion that Tillich is not really a theist at all, since he concedes a great deal to the atheist position. That is, the conception of God he endorses is so open that it is difficult to see it as a necessarily "theological" belief.

Radical theology: "God is dead"

As signalled at the beginning of this chapter, Nietzschean theology gained a certain notoriety in the 1960s, particularly in America. There, a number of theologians who had been pursuing their confrontations with Nietzsche individually began to speak to one another, and the movement variously known as "radical theology", "death of God theology" and sometimes even "theothanatology" began to crystallize. Key figures in this movement included Thomas J. J. Altizer, Gabriel Vahanian, William Hamilton and Paul van Buren. We shall take the views of Altizer as our key example of this movement here, but before turning to him specifically, we may note in a general sense the defining features of radical theology.

In a preface to their *Radical Theology and the Death of God*, Hamilton and Altizer note that radical theology "is, in effect, an attempt to set an atheist point of view within the spectrum of Christian possibilities" (Hamilton & Altizer 1966: ix). That is, radical theology is a kind a Christian atheism; a religious point of view that affirms Christianity while denying the existence of God. It is concerned to take the widespread secularism of our contemporary world seriously, and to try to reconcile it with a Christian position. As such, it is a response to a perceived crisis brought about by the end of Christendom (that is, the political and social dominance of Christianity) and the widespread contemporary loss of faith. Second, the authors suggest that the phrase "the death of God" is central to this position, and that determining exactly what is meant by it is the best way to begin to interpret radical theology (*ibid.*). From a list of possible meanings of this phrase, they isolate the following as the sense in which radical theology affirms the death of God. It means:

> [t]hat there once was a God to whom adoration, praise and trust were appropriate, possible, and even necessary, but that now there is no such God. This is the position of the death of God or radical theology. It is an atheist position, but with a difference. If there was a God, and if there now isn't, it should be possible to indicate why this change took place, and who was responsible for it. (*Ibid.*: x)

As this indicates, radical theology asserts that the death of God is a kind of *event*. Unlike theologians such as Barth, who concede only that this is a cultural event, the radical theologians assert it as a real ontological event. We shall turn to the details of this event with Altizer's understanding of it below, but as a final general point, it is important to note that while Hamilton and Altizer warn that the phrase "death of God" should not be linked to Nietzsche alone (*ibid.*: ix), he is undoubtedly the central reference and inspiration for the "radicality" of radical theology.

Altizer began exploring the central themes of radical theology from his first publications on the religious scholar Mircea Eliade and oriental mysticism, but his views achieved their most well-known form in the mid-1960s, with books such as the above-mentioned *Radical Theology and the Death of God* (with Hamilton), and *The Gospel of Christian Atheism* (1966). In addition to Nietzsche, Altizer takes William Blake and Hegel as key sources, and, as we shall see, a kind of dialectical thought inspired by Hegel is central to his vision of radical theology.

Altizer explains the death of God in the following way. It is an event, something that has occurred, but it is not an occurrence that can be identified with a single moment in historical time. Its central meaning is that God – as a transcendent, supernatural being – died when he incarnated in the form of Jesus Christ. For Altizer, the original and central meaning of Christianity is this "self-annihilation" of the transcendent God in the choice to take on the human form of Christ. For him, this event was irrevocable, irreversible: God cannot "resurrect himself" and once again become transcendent. However, the realization of this event in human history has unfolded progressively, and it is only with the advent of widespread secular atheism in the nineteenth century that the event of God's death gains its true meaning. For Altizer, then, this event is a real cosmological and ontological event, which has an "objective" reality; it is not simply a widespread loss of human *belief* in God, as is sometimes supposed. This is significant, because many theologians respond to the contemporary perceived crisis of faith by attempting to renew belief in the transcendent God. For Altizer, this is undesirable, because he believes that God really has died. Rather than being simply a lamentable crisis, then, according to Altizer contemporary secular atheism unfolds the true meaning of Christianity and constitutes an unprecedented opportunity for a new and authentic form of Christian faith.

KEY POINT

For Altizer and the radical theologians, the "death of God" is a real ontological event: God died as a transcendent being when he incarnated in Jesus Christ. But the true meaning of this event becomes evident only in the contemporary world of secular atheism, in which a new form of Christianity becomes possible.

Altizer praises:

> the gospel, or the "good news," of the death of God: for the death of God does not propel man into an empty darkness, it liberates him from every alien and opposing other, and makes possible his transition into what Blake hailed as "The Great Humanity Divine," or the final coming together of God and man.
>   (1966: 107)

Altizer underscores the fact that Christianity is distinguished from all other religions by the way that the Incarnation signals a transformation of the sacred into the profane. He writes: "it is Christianity alone which witnesses to a concrete and actual descent of the sacred into the profane, a movement wherein the sacred progressively abandons or negates its particular or given expressions, thereby emptying them of their original power" (*ibid.*: 104). Altizer thus understands Christianity as having a kind of secular vocation; it is the religion that contains the essence of secularization within itself as its own destiny. Nietzsche becomes an important marker of this process of "profanation" because he signals the "becoming conscious" of the death of God.

Despite his emphasis on secular atheism, however, Altizer affirms a real "spiritual" meaning to Christianity, and this possibility becomes evident through his recourse to Hegelian dialectical thought.

Altizer understands the death of God as a dialectical process of "self-
negation of Spirit". There is thus an important sense in which the negation of divinity will transform into an affirmation of divinity: from the
opposites of atheism and religious belief, a synthesis will be possible.
The dialectic is, then, the key that allows Altizer to affirm the seemingly paradoxical position of the Christian atheist, and to argue that
the contemporary secular age will make possible a *new form* of divinity.

Altizer takes his bearings from Kierkegaard, because he asserts
that Kierkegaard inaugurates dialectical thinking in the context of
Christianity. However, he argues that with Kierkegaard, dialectical
thought remains incomplete: he stays with negation, and does not follow
through with affirmation. This is played out in the way that Kierkegaard
stresses the radical otherness of God, and asserts that we cannot rationally know his existence, nor can we know what he wants us to do.
Famously for Kierkegaard, one must take a "leap of faith" (although
he never actually uses this term), and the meaning of religious belief is
to be found in *passionate commitment* to an entirely subjective notion
of truth, which finds no guarantee in objectivity. Moreover, after he
personally experienced a "second conversion", Kierkegaard abandoned
engagement in philosophical debate in order to focus on criticizing the
established Church: an entirely negative undertaking.

In contrast, Altizer sees Nietzsche as a dialectical thinker (*contra*
Deleuze, for example; see Chapter 2) who completes the dialectical process with an affirmation. On Altizer's reading, the negative moment of
Nietzsche's thought involves his many criticisms of religious, transcendent thought (summarized with the slogan "God is dead"). However,
Nietzsche follows through with a positive moment, which is his attempt
to affirm the secular world after God's death. Altizer focuses here on
Nietzsche's doctrine of the eternal return, and he draws a (perhaps surprising) parallel between Nietzsche's eternal return and the "kingdom of
heaven" announced by Jesus Christ. Both visions of the world, he asserts,
are affirmations of the meaning and value of the *immanent* world, after
the categories of meaning provided by the *transcendent* God have lost
their currency. Dialectically, Altizer argues, Nietzsche is able to affirm

a new kind of divinity precisely on the basis of the absolute negation of the old (transcendent) kind of divinity. Thus, he sees Nietzsche as the key moment in the revelation of the full meaning of the original event of the death of God in his incarnation in Christ.

In what can be taken as a good summary of his position, Altizer writes:

> So far from regarding the vacuous and rootless existence of modern man as the product of an abandonment of faith, the radical Christian recognizes the spiritual emptiness of our time as the historical actualization of the self-annihilation of God, and despite the horror and anguish embedded in such a condition of humanity, the radical Christian can greet even this darkness as a yet more comprehensive embodiment and fulfillment of the original passion of Christ.   (1966: 110)

Weak theology

A relatively recent development in theology may be described as "weak theology". The term itself was coined by John D. Caputo, and developed in his book *The Weakness of God* (2006), but is also associated with other thinkers, such as Vattimo (as discussed below). In short, weak theology combines the insights of "death-of-God" theology with developments in contemporary continental philosophy in the post-Heideggerian tradition, such as deconstruction and weak thought. These philosophical developments propose a radical ontology of "weakness", and resonate with death-of-God theology in so far as they reject the "strong" metaphysical concepts that previously defined God in the Western theological and philosophical traditions. Jefferey W. Robbins (2004) usefully situates weak theology in relation to the theological movements and thinkers we have already discussed by characterizing it as the latest development in a genealogy of changes in theology underway since the beginning of the twentieth century. This genealogy represents the progressive expansion and deepening of theology's own immanent critique and self-dissolution. The three genealogical moments he identifies are as follows.

- *Neo-orthodoxy:* Theologians such as Barth critiqued "modern liberal theology" and the historical critical method of biblical scholarship. These trends attempted to make theology coincide with rational enquiry, and the critique of this approach coincided with the end of Enlightenment optimism after the First World War.

- *The end of Christendom:* After the Second World War, theologians such as Tillich and Rudolph Bultmann (1884–1976) engaged with secular society, taking seriously the end of Christendom.
- *Weak theology:* As Robbins explains this moment in his genealogy of theological dissolution, "death of God theology is wedded with deconstructive philosophy, thereby completing this dissolution by stripping theology of its very content by calling into question such supposed fundamentals as God, religion, revelation, and faith" (2004: 1).

Weak theology is thus characterized by Robbins as a radical development in the process by which theology has been questioning itself, and, as we have already seen, Nietzsche has, for many theologians, been a touchstone in this process of self-questioning. Robbins further explains that weak theology is marked by both a lack of constraint by ecclesiastical authority, and the return of religion in a contemporary global culture that is somehow at once both secular, and multi-faith (*ibid.*: 2–3). In this context, weak theology attempts to explain the possibility of the coincidence of secularism and religious belief by drawing on the notions of "weak ontology" in contemporary philosophy. While Caputo draws most significantly on Derrida and deconstruction, we shall focus here on Vattimo. Vattimo presents an interesting case, because he has long been an influential Nietzsche scholar, and he has recently recounted his own return to religion, and his attempt to reconcile it with his Nietzscheanism, in terms that are both personal and philosophical.

Vattimo: to believe that one believes

Gianni Vattimo (b. 1936) is a prominent Italian philosopher, politician and public intellectual, who has, since the 1990s, developed a unique form of Nietzschean theology. Vattimo has long been one of the most significant interpreters of Nietzsche in Italy, having been invited to the famous Royaumont colloquium in 1964, and having published numerous books and articles on Nietzsche. Vattimo is also a Heidegger scholar, and he reads both philosophers in a way that has allowed him to formulate his own philosophy: a kind of postmodern hermeneutics that became known as "weak thought" (*il pensiero debole*) in the 1980s. As a public intellectual, a Nietzschean and an openly gay man, Vattimo has often vocally criticized the Catholic

Church, and for much of his career his thought appeared to embrace a decidedly secular bent. (It is notable that one of the first books on his philosophy, Dario Antiseri's *The Weak Thought and its Strength* (1996), spends much time chastising him for ignoring the possible place of God in his ontology). More recently, however, Vattimo has taken a "theological turn", without, however, backtracking on the lessons he has learned from Nietzsche. His own brand of weak theology thus provides an interesting example of how Nietzschean philosophy might be reconciled with theology.

Much of the thrust of Vattimo's work has concerned the formulation of a *positive* conception of nihilism, in which Nietzsche's "death of God" has been understood in the metaphysical sense Heidegger gave it. While Heidegger considered nihilism as the oblivion of Being, and hoped for some sort of overcoming of nihilism through a "turn" in Being, Vattimo develops a progressive reading of Nietzsche and Heidegger that argues that this oblivion of Being is itself the only hope we have for over-coming the problems of metaphysics. Vattimo thus advocates a kind of heroic, anti-nostalgic embrace of the very contemporary conditions Nietzsche and Heidegger believed were evacuating meaning from the world. Vattimo's view is that nihilism is our only hope for a kind of emancipation in the contemporary world. His surprising understanding of nihilism can be understood in the following way.

Vattimo's "postmodern" philosophy of weak thought opposes itself to the classical and modern conceptions of ontology (the nature of real-ity) and epistemology (the grounds of knowledge) glossed by the term "metaphysics". Metaphysics understands Being as a permanent, stable structure or enduring presence. Epistemology is understood as a search for truth, understood as universal, necessary and objective. Following Nietzsche and Heidegger, Vattimo takes a critical attitude towards meta-physics. However, drawing also on other thinkers, such as Adorno and Levinas, he frequently emphasizes the *ethical* dimension of metaphysics, arguing that it licenses violence in the name of a superior knowledge of reality. Citing our postmodern, multicultural society, marked by con-flicting worldviews that exist in overlapping textures in the single space of media communication networks, Vattimo argues that metaphysics threatens a violent silencing of dissenting voices (a violence made pos-sible by the claim to an objective reality, and an exclusive truth that represents it). (See e.g. Vattimo 1997: ch. 3, "Ethics").

Vattimo advocates his "positive" conception of nihilism as a solution to the problems of metaphysics. He understands this nihilism through, first, an "ontology of decline". This ontology proposes that today, there is very little of Being left, in so far as it is understood in the traditional sense as a stable and objective structure of reality. Instead, he argues, Being must be understood – in the Heideggerian sense as that which "gives" or reveals beings (the particular things that exist) as what they are – not as a stable structure, but as a historically changing horizon of interpretation. For Vattimo, things are what they are because of the way we interpret them, and these interpretations are made possible by the linguistic structures of the culture we inhabit. From this perspective, the ontology of decline means that not only should we understand Being as historically shifting rather than stable, but also our current horizon of meaning is far from stable and binding. In other words, instead of living in a culture where meanings are fixed by traditions and authoritative institutions, we live in a multicultural world where horizons are open and in flux. This openness of interpretive horizons is perhaps the most important, and most progressive, of the meanings of Vattimo's ontological nihilism.

Second, Vattimo's nihilism is epistemological, and embraces a radical interpretation of Nietzsche's well-known dictum, "there are no facts, only interpretations" (WP 481). In line with his ontology of decline, Vattimo denies that there is any interpretation-independent, objective reality *of* which it would be possible for us to have true knowledge. Therefore, he embraces a kind of epistemological relativism, and emphasizes the fluidity and plurality of interpretations. However, Vattimo gives this relativism an important qualification by orienting it towards history, nihilism and the value of the reduction of violence. For Vattimo not all interpretations are equal, and the ones he privileges are the ones that take their bearings from the historical situation in which we find ourselves (and which, according to him, is precisely a nihilistic situation). Moreover, according to Vattimo's (certainly arguable) interpretation, the central value governing our nihilistic situation (that is, the decline of metaphysics) is the value of violence reduction. Therefore, according to his epistemology, while there are no facts, only interpretations, we can give direction to our thought through the principle that nihilistic, violence-reducing interpretations are to be favoured over others.

KEY POINT *Vattimo's "positive" nihilism*
For Vattimo, nihilism is a solution to the violence of metaphysical thinking. Nihilism is ontological (there is little of Being left in the strong sense of a permanent structure of reality) and epistemological (there are no facts, only interpretations).

A useful segue from Vattimo's general philosophy to his religious thought is provided by his characterization of the postmodern era as one marked by "the secularization of secularization". While modernity was marked by secularization – the replacement of mythic and religious explanations of the world with scientific ones – Vattimo argues that the postmodern era has seen a breakdown in faith in the ability of science to provide such alternative structures. As Nietzsche pointed out, science retained many remnants of metaphysics, and Vattimo insists that these elements – belief in objective reality and truth – have increasingly been undermined by developments in science studies, and in science itself (see e.g. Vattimo 1997: ch. 2, "Science"). Moreover, as Heidegger and many others have argued, science can tell us nothing of many of the issues of deepest human interest and significance. Thus, Vattimo speaks of a "secularization of secularization" in the current age, by which he means that we have lost faith in secular metaphysical explanations. Importantly, for him this means that the postmodern age is once again open to a return of religious belief, although by no means in its pre-modern (or even modern) metaphysical form.

Vattimo's mature "reconversion" to a kind of religious belief was announced by a book translated under the title *Belief* (1999), but a closer translation of its original Italian title – "To believe that one believes" – gives a much clearer statement of Vattimo's position. The book is a somewhat personal memoir of the author's return to faith. Raised in the Catholic faith as a child, and taking an active role in Catholic organizations as a young adult, Vattimo tells us that he turned away from the Church, owing in part to his studies (of, significantly, Nietzsche), and in part to his developing sexuality. The book tells the story of his return to a kind of religious belief, but in an ironic, weakened form. The title comes from a turning point in Vattimo's spiritual life: during a telephone conversation with a colleague, and in response to the pressing question of whether at bottom he still believed in God, Vattimo replied that he believed that he believed (1999: 70). This spontaneous eruption was then followed by intellectual reflection, and Vattimo hit on a way of reconciling his re-found faith with his Nietzscheanism.

The key concept in Vattimo's Nietzschean theology is *kenosis*, a theological term that refers to the incarnation of God in the form of Jesus Christ. The term implies a weakening, emptying out or decreasing of God's power through human incarnation. It is a kind of "self-debasing" of God in Christ. This term has allowed Vattimo to associate Christianity with his ontology of decline, his positive conception of nihilism and the Nietzschean "death of God". Vattimo argues for a powerful association between Christianity and secularization: in so far as it is the religion of God made flesh, it implies the weakening of metaphysical structures (of God as the permanent foundation of reality). In a way similar to that which we have already seen with the radical theologians, the incarnation of God in Christ is then understood by Vattimo as the original event of the "death of God", the original event inaugurating nihilism in the West.

Since Christianity presents us with a weakened God, Vattimo argues, it also licenses a weakened faith. His statement of religious faith, "I believe that I believe", is an ironic one that works precisely to bracket belief in a metaphysical God: a really and objectively existing, supernatural, highest being. Instead, by "belief" Vattimo signals an acknowledgement of the continuing validity of the Christian tradition as a vital aspect of Western culture. While belief in a transcendent, metaphysical God may no longer be plausible, the Christian tradition continues to condition the horizons of our world. Vattimo singles out *caritas* (charity) as the central value of this culture: a value that strongly supports his emphasis on the reduction of violence and openness to all voices, no matter how dissenting and multifarious. (In addition to the book *Belief*, see Vattimo 1997: ch. 4, "Religion", for a brief outline of many of these themes.) Through this series of remarkable moves, Vattimo may appear to give us a Nietzschean theology that is equally removed from Nietzsche and from traditional theology. Since *Belief*, however, Vattimo has gone on to refine and develop his views, in conversation with other philosophers and theologians (such as Caputo, René Girard and Richard Rorty), and by finding precursors to some of his views in the theological tradition, such as Joachim of Fiore (see Vattimo & Caputo 2007; Vattimo & Girard 2010; Vattimo & Rorty 2005; Vattimo 2002).

Recent developments

New Nietzschean theologies

Two recent books, both published under the title *Nietzsche and Theology*, signal the currency of this trend, and the fact that original work continues to be done in this area. Nietzsche's impact on theology is far from over, and continues to be appreciated in new ways. While earlier Nietzschean theologians focus on the ontological dimensions of Nietzsche's "God is dead" and often ignore his critique of Christian values, David Deane's *Nietzsche and Theology: Nietzschean Thought in Christological Anthropology* (2006) focuses on this critique and reclaims it for Christian purposes. According to Deane's interpretation, Nietzsche helps us to understand the nature of sin, fallenness (our distance from God) and reconciliation (our union with God). Thus, as his subtitle indicates, his intent is to situate Nietzschean thought within a "Christological anthropology", that is, a theory of human being that takes the creation of humanity by God and redemption through Christ as central. Deane argues that there is a notion of sin associated with the *biological drives* (rather than simply conscious intent), and deploys Nietzsche's genealogical analyses of such drives within the framework of a theology inspired by Barth.

Craig Hovey's *Nietzsche and Theology* (2008) aims to show that Christians ought not reject Nietzsche outright as "wicked", and that, quite to the contrary, theology can benefit from him. Hovey argues that theology is not a self-sufficient discourse; its purpose is to serve the active and present Christian community and aid the worship of God. Therefore, theology is not simply an academic discipline in the normal sense. Hovey argues that Nietzsche can aid theology in resisting ossification into an academic disciple by helping it to engage in "an uncompromising and fearless self-criticism" (2008: 11). Hovey argues that Christians ought to welcome Nietzsche's very foreignness as allowing pause for reflection, allowing a critical distance that theologians risk losing if they listen only to each other. The book is written for those within the field of theology, as an introduction to Nietzsche and as a meditation on the meaning of reading his works for those who hold a Christian faith.

Continental philosophy's "theological turn"

Finally, before we close this chapter, it is worth briefly considering how there has been what some term a "theological turn" in recent continental philosophy, which signals a move away from Nietzsche, in so far as it positively revalues the legacy of St Paul (which, as we have seen, is a primary target in Nietzsche's attack on Christianity). Paul has been the subject of renewed positive attention by three of the most prominent European philosophers of the first decade of the twenty-first century: Giorgio Agamben, Alain Badiou, and Slavoj Žižek. While each of these philosophers is an avowed atheist, they find in Paul an ethical and political significance that they believe is valuable for the contemporary age.

For Badiou, for example, the significance of Paul lies in his universalism (see Badiou 2003). Paul was the apostle who decisively steered

Christianity away from being simply a Jewish movement, and insisted on its relevance for everyone. For Badiou, and for Žižek following him, this universalism stands as a necessary corrective to the widespread relativism of postmodern times: it asserts the legitimacy of a truth for all, not just for the individual. Moreover, for these philosophers Paul represents the possibility of a radical *event*, a genuine break with the past and the promise that the entire world might be transformed. As such, Pauline Christianity offers a renewal of the revolutionary impulse, which declined with the postmodern eclipse of Marxism, and Žižek has attempted to reconcile Marxism with Christianity in what he sometimes calls a "Christian materialism" (see Žižek 2009). While Agamben has argued against Badiou's reading of Paul's message as one of universalism, he nevertheless understands his significance in a similarly political, and secularized, sense. Agamben draws on Walter Benjamin's understanding of "the messianic" as an understanding of time that he sees as challenging the contemporary sociopolitical order, and argues that Paul's letters are deeply significant in this sense because they are the original messianic texts of the West (see Agamben 2005). While there is a remarkable coincidence of prominent continental philosophers turning to Paul and, in this sense, away from Nietzsche, a Nietzschean strand of the theological turn is represented by the work of Vattimo, examined above.

Summary of key points

Nietzsche's anti-Christianity

Nietzsche criticizes Christianity in the strongest possible terms, but his opposition centres on Paul and what he made of Christianity, rather than Jesus and his message. For Nietzsche Jesus abolished the metaphysical "two-world" view and taught a way of life in which the here and now could be affirmed as a "kingdom of heaven". His death on the cross exemplified a rejection of all *ressentiment*. However, Paul turned Christianity into a nihilistic religion by restoring the metaphysical world and the notion of sin, emphasizing belief rather than a way of life, and centring it on a slave morality.

Existential theology

In general, existential theologians assert the radical difference of God from humanity, and his unknowability by us in human, rational terms.

To this extent, they agree with Nietzsche's announcement that "God is dead", and believe that we need to confront nihilism in the contemporary age. Yet they continue to believe in the existence of a transcendent deity.

- *Martin Buber* was influenced by Nietzsche in his Zionist project for a creative, vital renewal of Jewish cultural identity, and in his distinction of "I–Thou" and "I–It" relations.
- *Karl Barth* used Nietzsche as an ally in his attempt to overcome the modern conception of God as knowable in human terms, and to establish God as "Wholly Other".
- *Paul Tillich* believed that Nietzsche showed that atheism is impossible, and that by facing up to "the death of God" we are able to recognize a "God beyond God".

Radical ("death-of-God") theology

Radical theology is "Christian atheism". It asserts that the death of God is a real event that occurred when the transcendent God died by becoming flesh in Christ, the full meaning of which is only now being revealed in contemporary secular, atheistic culture. For Altizer, Nietzsche is a dialectical thinker who shows how the death of God can reveal a new, immanent form of the sacred: Nietzsche's eternal return is equivalent to Jesus's kingdom of God on earth.

Weak theology

Weak theology attempts to interpret the theological tradition in terms of the contemporary weakening of metaphysical claims in recent philosophy (after Nietzsche and Heidegger in particular). Vattimo develops a positive interpretation of nihilism as the weakening of both metaphysics and violence, and argues that Nietzsche's "death of God" is equivalent to the Christian *kenosis*, the "emptying out" of the transcendent God's metaphysical power. Vattimo argues that we can no longer believe in theological themes in a metaphysical sense, but must affirm Christianity as a living tradition in Western culture. He expresses this through the ironic formula "I believe that I believe".

Recent developments

- New Nietzschean theologies: Deane has appropriated Nietzsche's work on morality to establish a new understanding of sin and fallenness within a Christological anthropology. Hovey has argued for the value of reading Nietzsche for Christians, in so far as it opens up a vital avenue of self-criticism that protects theology against dogmatic complacency.

- There has been a "theological turn" in recent continental philosophy that has taken a variety of forms. Philosophers such as Agamben, Badiou and Žižek have challenged Nietzsche's reading of the legacy of Paul. Philosophers such as Vattimo retain a certain fidelity to Nietzsche within this turn.

six

Nietzscheanism and posthumanism

I write for a species of man that does not yet exist.

(WP 958)

Posthumanism is a recent intellectual and popular trend in which Nietzsche has been both an influence and a focus for debate. Most basically, posthumanism means "beyond humanism". Like most –isms, however, the term posthumanism is used in a number of differing ways. Here we shall use the term in two ways that are antagonistically related. First, it is used more or less synonymously with "transhumanism" (to be defined below). Second, it refers to antihumanist currents of thought in the recent and contemporary humanities. After a first approach to Nietzsche's relation to transhumanism, we shall see how posthumanism in the second (antihumanistic) sense can also be found in Nietzsche's thought, and how this can in fact be used to critique transhumanism.

Transhumanism

Transhumanism is a relatively new movement, the origin of which can be traced to the early 1990s. It crystallized with Ed Regis's humorous survey of some of the "wacky" ideas being pursued by some scientists, *Great Mambo Chicken and the Transhuman Condition* (1990). Transhumanism admits of a number of currents, including Max More's extropianism ("extropy" is a term coined to express the opposite of entropy, that is, unlimited development), singularitarianism (which endorses the idea of a sudden coming of the posthuman condition through a rapid technological acceleration, dubbed "the singularity"), David Pearce's "Hedonistic Imperative" (a hedonistic utilitarian form of transhumanism), democratic transhumanism (which foregrounds social and political issues) and survivalist transhumanism (which focuses of the achievement of longevity) (see Bostrom 2001). However, there are certain key themes and values all forms of transhumanism hold in common. Simply put, transhumanism is a movement that seeks to overcome the current limitations of the human condition with the help of science and technology. It posits the imminent arrival of a new species beyond the human, the members of which are referred to as "posthumans". Posthumanity is conceived as the next evolutionary step after humanity, and transhumanists believe that this evolutionary step will have the special characteristic of involving technological, not simply biological and organic, developments. Transhumanists think of themselves as "transitional humans" who accept transhumanism and prepare the way for the coming of posthumans.

The posthuman condition is conceived as an expanded sphere of human potential that will make possible new modes of being, composed of a range of thoughts, feelings, experiences and activities that our current biological nature prevents us from accessing (Bostrom 2005: 2). These expanded possibilities are thought of by transhumanists as at least potentially valuable, and worth pursuing for that reason. As Nick Bostrom puts it:

> It is not farfetched to suppose that there are parts of this larger space [i.e. of posthuman modes of being] that represent extremely valuable ways of living, relating, feeling, and thinking ... there is at least a serious possibility of there being something very precious outside the human sphere. This constitutes a reason to pursue the means that will let us go there and find out. (Bostrom 2005: 2-3)

What will posthumans be like? Transhumanists typically resist a definite answer, suggesting that we cannot yet imagine all the possibilities the posthuman condition will make available, many of which will be bound up with technologies yet to be invented. However, they give frequent indications of how the human condition might be transcended in ways we can conceive of, with the help of sciences and technologies now being developed. Transhumanists often cite life extension, the improvement of health and the extension of cognitive and communicational capacities through computing, information and media technologies. Artificial intelligence, robotics, nanotechnologies, genetic engineering, prosthetic enhancements, virtual realities and space colonization are all common transhumanist themes. Transhumanists hope for enhancements in all dimensions of the human being, including the physiological, emotional and intellectual (Sorgner 2009: 36–7). They seek to eliminate pain and suffering, and expand our capacities for pleasure, enjoyment and happiness. The dreams of transhumanists range from the relatively humble, such as life extension through improved nutrition, exercise and medical science, through the unusual but conceivable, such as giving humans the power of flight with prosthetic wings, to the distant, ultimate dream of transforming humanity into God-like beings able to transcend the current limits of time and space and survive the eventual "heat death" of the universe (for more on this, see the section on Ansell-Pearson below).

Nietzsche as transhumanist

The question of Nietzsche's relation to transhumanism has recently been raised and debated in the *Journal of Evolution & Technology*. The article that raised the issue, Stefan Sorgner's "Nietzsche, the Overhuman, and Transhumanism" (2009) claims Nietzsche as a predecessor and ally of transhumanism. Twelve years earlier, Ansell-Pearson had radically problematized simplistic conceptions of the transhuman with reference to Nietzsche in his book *Viroid Life* (Ansell-Pearson 1997). (Sorgner acknowledges Ansell-Pearson's work, but does not engage with it.) Despite this chronological ordering, for thematic reasons I shall in this section first present Sorgner's case for Nietzsche's closeness to transhumanism, before presenting Ansell-Pearson's Nietzschean critique of transhumanism. This will then allow us to examine Nietzsche's posthumanism in the antihumanist sense as bearing on the debate over Nietzsche and transhumanism. Thus we shall again see that, as in so many areas, Nietzsche's work provides a pivot around which contrary sides on a particular issue can be taken, each side taking his work to support their own position.

Sorgner argues two main points. First, against previous disclaimers by another transhumanist (Bostrom), he argues that there are significant similarities between Nietzsche's thought and transhumanism. Second, he argues that Nietzsche's work can usefully be used to supplement transhumanism because it gives us stronger *reasons* to be transhumanists than anything current in transhumanist discourse, because of Nietzsche's reflections on meaning and value in the scientific age. Sorgner advances his first argument by identifying correspondences between some of the key transhumanist principles (identified by Bostrom), and principles in Nietzsche's thought. Briefly, these correspondences are as follows. Both Nietzsche and transhumanists hold *a dynamic view of nature and values*. That is, both view the world and human nature as undergoing constant processes of change (here, Sorgner refers to Nietzsche's "cosmological" conception of the will to power – the world as a constant flux of forces). Next, both Nietzsche and transhumanists have an outlook on the world that diverges from Christianity, and both posit a "revaluation of values" in which *a scientific form of thinking replaces the religious*. Furthermore, both Nietzsche and transhumanists value the *enhancement* of human beings. While the means of enhancement differ, both hold enhancement of the scope of human powers and capacities as a value. Moreover, both Nietzsche and transhumanism value *self-overcoming* as a key aspect of such enhancement.

KEY POINT *Nietzsche and transhumanism: some basic terms*
- *Posthuman*: A member of the new species that represents a further stage of evolution, whose capacities greatly exceed those of human beings.
- *Transhuman*: A "transitional human", in the process of becoming, or preparing the way for, posthumans.
- *Overhuman*: Nietzsche's *Übermensch*, understood by some as the same thing as the posthuman.
- *Higher type*: A superior human who is a precursor of the *Übermensch*.

Sorgner further argues that Nietzsche's concept of the *Übermensch* (or "overhuman") has much in common with transhumanism. Sorgner's argument is that Nietzsche's terms "higher type" and "overhuman" can be seen as represented in transhumanist discourse with the terms "transhuman" and "posthuman": according to Sorgner, these terms, in fact, refer to the same thing. For Nietzsche, no overhuman has yet lived, but there have been higher types (such as Napoleon, Cesare Borgia, Goethe, etc.) who have indicated the way to surpassing humanity. Higher humans still belong to the human species, but have some capacities the overhuman will possess (Sorgner 2009: 38). Similarly, transhumanists believe that there are now, or soon will be, transhumans who prepare the way for posthumans through their usage of technology, their cultural values, and their lifestyles (Bostrom 2005: 12). For both Nietzsche and the transhumanists, the beings that will transcend humanity cannot be adequately conceived by us; we cannot really know what they will be like. But we can prepare for their coming by extending current human capacities as far as we are able.

Sorgner rightly points out that Nietzsche's conceptions of self-overcoming and his ideal of the overhuman are focused on education, the development of intellectual capacities and the ability to interpret. Nietzsche does not suggest technological means of improvement (Sorgner 2009: 38). However, Sorgner contends that nor does Nietzsche rule out such means, and his view that the coming millennium will be governed by the scientific spirit gives credence to the association of Nietzsche with transhumanism (*ibid.*). Summing up this contention, Sorgner writes: "The overhuman comes about via an evolutionary step which originates from the group of higher humans. Nietzsche does not exclude the possibility that technological means bring about the evolutionary step" (*ibid.*). In a follow-up note to Sorgner's article, More (2010) adds that the advent of transhumanism, at least in some of its influential forms, not only bears unconscious similarities to Nietzsche's thought, but was in fact directly influenced by Nietzsche. More claims that it was he who introduced the term transhumanism (for a key early writing see More [1990]), and in doing so he was directly influenced by Nietzsche (who he also occasionally quotes in his seminal writings on the topic).

As a second part to his argument, Sorgner suggests that Nietzsche is not merely a forerunner to transhumanism, but has something of significant positive value to add to the movement. He writes, "Transhumanists, at least in the articles which I have consulted, have not explained why they hold the values they have, and why they want to bring about post-humans" (2009: 39). In Sorgner's view, Nietzsche fills this gap by explaining the values underlying his positing of the overman. For Nietzsche, philosophers are creators of values. Moreover, Nietzsche's worldview is supposed to appeal to the scientific spirit; his philosophy is, then, aimed at creating values appropriate to the scientific age. In Christianity, the personal afterlife is what gives a sense of meaning to life (the transcendent world gives value to the immanent one). Nietzsche's challenge, then, is to create a basis for meaning and value in a world that has replaced the transcendent, religious worldview with an immanent, scientific one. According to Sorgner, the overhuman and the eternal recurrence are Nietzsche's "scientific" answer to the Christian afterlife: they constitute an idea of "this-worldly" salvation. For Nietzsche, the overhuman "represents the meaning of the earth" (*ibid*). Thus, the overhuman is the "meaning-giving" concept in Nietzsche's philosophy. This meaning lies in self-overcoming, the ultimate form of which is the overcoming of the human species (it is "in the interests" of higher humans to permanently overcome themselves). In this way, the overhuman gives meaning to human beings: the meaning of our lives is, through self-overcoming, to be a bridge to the overhuman. Sorgner states that this "is not a transcendent meaning but an earthly immanent one which is appropriate for scientifically minded people who have abandoned their belief in an after world" (*ibid.*). Sorgner rightly notes that the transhumanist concept of the posthuman cannot be fully appreciated without taking into account meaning-giving and quasi-religious aspects of the phenomena (*ibid.*: 39–40). Summing up his argument, Sorgner explains that transhumanism can act as a value structure that gives meaning to human life in a secular, scientific age: "I suspect that the value of the bringing about of the posthuman cannot be ultimately justified, except to an individual who believes that the concept makes his life meaningful: 'I wish to be the ancestor of a posthuman'" (*ibid.*: 40).

Ansell-Pearson on Nietzsche and the transhuman condition

The transhuman condition has become transformed into a classic expression of an ancient ideal – the *ascetic ideal.*

(Ansell-Pearson 1997: 33)

In Ansell-Pearson's 1997 collection of essays *Viroid Life*, he sets out to "question, problematise, overturn, revalue, announce, renounce, advocate, interrogate, affirm, deny, celebrate, critique, the 'transhuman condition', exploring the human as a site of contamination and abduction by alien forces and rendering, in the process, the phenomenon polyvalent and polysemous" (1997: 1). As this and the book's subtitle indicate, Ansell-Pearson presents a number of *perspectives* on the transhuman condition, using Nietzsche as a frequent reference point. In short, Ansell-Pearson aims to critique and problematize a popular, simplistic and "determined" understanding of the transhuman, and to open up the possibility of thinking the transhuman condition more adequately, that is (according to him), in an open, "undetermined" manner. In other words, he critiques what he sees as false and inadequate answers to problems so that the problems themselves can be thought anew. Ansell-Pearson's many criticisms of "simplistic" transhumanism are summarized in the box opposite.

First, Ansell-Pearson sees transhumanism as a new "metanarrative". This is a term drawn from Lyotard, who famously defined the postmodern condition as characterized by "incredulity toward metanarratives"

(Lyotard 1984: xxiv). Metanarratives are stories that give meaning to human life by explaining it as part of a historical process with a final goal. Examples of metanarratives include the Christian story of personal salvation through redemption from sin, the Hegelian story of the progressive development of *Geist* (mind or spirit) towards the Absolute, the Marxist story about the meaning of history as class struggle, aimed towards the classless society, and the Enlightenment story about the emancipation of human life through the progressive development of reason. According to Lyotard, metanarratives used to function as frameworks that justified research and development, but he saw them as breaking down in the late twentieth century for a number of reasons: perhaps the most readily appreciated is that certain events of the twentieth century, such as the Holocaust, have destroyed our belief in progress (see Lyotard 1992). However, Ansell-Pearson believes Lyotard spoke too soon – transhumanism has since appeared as a new metanarrative (or, as Lyotard also calls it, a "grand narrative"):

> The grand narrative today is likely to take the form of a facile quasi-Hegelianism in which the rise of the machine is construed in linear and perfectionist terms: the ever-growing inhuman character of "technology" resides in the "simple" fact that it is machines that are proving to be more successful in creating an adequate response to the tasks laid down by evolution than the creatures whose existence first gave rise to it.
> (Ansell-Pearson 1997: 4)

Lyotard is critical of metanarratives because they present a narrow view of the meaning of human history that excludes or marginalizes minorities (for example, metanarratives of civilization and progress were used as a justification for the exploitation of the resources of supposedly less civilized peoples in colonization). More generally, he is "incredulous" towards metanarratives because – as Ansell-Pearson points out – the view that human history is a coherent story proceeding towards a meaningful ending, rather than an accidental and meaningless series of events, is simply a bizarre idea. In other words, like Nietzsche's argument about the existence of a "true world", we simply have no good reason to believe in metanarratives. In fact, metanarratives have a similar structure and psychological function to belief in an afterlife; they simply posit redemption at a future time in this world rather than in another world, and for humanity as a whole rather than for the individual.

More polemically, Ansell-Pearson draws further on Lyotard (despite some criticisms) in order to show how transhumanism is complicit with, and can function as an ideological support for, capitalism and imperialism. In several essays (see e.g. Lyotard 1991), Lyotard tells an ironic fable that sounds very much like the dreams of at least some transhumanists. In 4.5 billion years, the sun will explode. The earth and its inhabitants will be eradicated. But perhaps something of humanity will survive in posthuman form. Lyotard notes that the nature of what might survive the solar catastrophe is not something we can now imagine, but he suggests that the problem of how to survive is the most urgent one facing us today. He presents a historical narrative in which the subject is not humanity as such, but the evolutionary process, understood as a negentropic process of increasing complexification. Present-day humanity is just a step in this evolutionary process, in which better, more complex forms are destined to be selected while inefficient forms are selected out. Lyotard's postmodern fable is ironic because he himself is very opposed to this way of thinking (his assertion of the importance and urgency of this problem – we only have 4.5 billion years! – is particularly rich with irony). The problem, he suggests, is that on this view, the entire third world becomes superfluous (to take just one example). More generally, the point is that this evolutionary theory seems to have no place for justice; it acts to justify what may be morally wrong with appeal to supposedly natural (and implicitly therefore both right and inevitable) processes. Moreover, such evolutionary narratives can act as an ideological support for capitalism, by arguing (as has happened in particular since the collapse of communism in Eastern Europe in 1989) that the socioeconomic combination of democracy and capitalism has proved to be the superior system of human organization because it has survived while others have, it is claimed, been "selected out" by natural processes.

Ansell-Pearson also argues that much of the discourse on transhumanism employs overly simple dichotomies that Nietzsche's work helps to properly problematize. Such dichotomies include the following. Transhumanists tend to present a categorical divide between the *human* and the *posthuman*, unreasonably valuing the latter and unreasonably devaluing the former. Ansell-Pearson comments that "A recent popular account of 'postbiological man', for example, treats the human condition as an affliction which shouldn't happen to a dog" (1997: 32). Likewise, the posthuman condition is often eulogized as an immensely worthwhile aspiration at the same time as the assertion is made that it may be so far beyond the human condition that we are not now able to even imagine it. What this dichotomy forgets, Ansell-Pearson argues, is the "human" *in* "posthuman". For Nietzsche, the *Übermensch* is an outgrowth from, ideal of and self-overcoming of the human, and cannot be thought independently of human history. Ansell-Pearson asserts:

> From a "Nietzschean" perspective, in the sense in which the term possesses "meaning", recent reports on the transhuman condition ironically amount to an annulment of that condition, to an erasure of the "memory" of man out of which the promise of the overman can be thought. (*Ibid.*)

One of the primary themes of transhumanism (which all concede is not to be found in Nietzsche) is the idea that technology is the new vehicle for evolution: the posthuman may be an entirely technological, non-organic being, and one of the key ambitions of the transhumanist movement is the technological enhancement of the organic human body. According to many transhumanists, we are now on the cusp of a major evolutionary event: the transition from the *organic* to the *technological*. Ansell-Pearson points out that many recent and contemporary theorists in the continental tradition (for example, Deleuze and Guattari) reject any absolute distinction between these terms (*ibid.*: 123). Moreover, from their origins, human beings have been evolving in ways that necessarily incorporate the technical (the use of tools, for example, has helped to govern the evolution of human beings).

Both the above dichotomies (human/posthuman, organic/technological) are organized in transhumanist discourse in terms of a historical dichotomy between the *past* and the *future*. That is, the past is construed as human and organic, while the future is projected as posthuman and technological. Ansell-Pearson argues that in this way the transhumanists employ a progressive notion of history that is little more than a fantasy, and in fact erases any real historical memory. His point is that these dichotomies cannot be supported on the basis of real history. Ansell-Pearson's most striking example is perhaps this: in response to the common proclamation that we are now entering an entirely new "silicon age" because of the advent of computers and robot intelligence, he points out that bacteria used magnetite for internal compasses about three thousand million years ago (*ibid.*: 124). Thus, the supposedly recent nature of the technological, as well as its supposed human origin, are not supported by the facts.

The most central and most repeated claim throughout the essays collected in *Viroid Life* is that transhumanism is unknowingly and problematically anthropocentric. This is announced in Ansell-Pearson's introduction: " what I take issue with in this study is the anthropomorphic claim that the process of complexification is 'inhuman' and the expression of 'life'" (*ibid.*: 5). Simply put, transhumanism is guilty of anthropocentrism because, as we have already seen, it takes the form of a metanarrative. Transhumanism projects human values onto what it erroneously takes to be natural, evolutionary processes. It does this by positing a progressive image of evolution, where progress is understood as increasing complexity. Increased complexity is thought to expand the possibilities of existence, and this is taken as a good. However, Ansell-Pearson draws on Nietzsche's arguments concerning the relativity of human value-positing to show that transhumanism involves anthropomorphic projections onto nature. He writes:

> Considered psychologically – that is, from the perspective of a psychological *a priori* – human values are the result of utilitarian perspectives that have been designed to enhance human control and mastery over nature and the external world but which in the process have been falsely projected into the essence of things … [WP 12(B)]. The positing of themselves as the meaning and measure of evolution is the anthropocentric conceit of humans that is exposed with the advent of nihilism. (*Ibid.*: 161)

Anthropomorphism, then, involves the misguided interpretation of nature according to perspectives that are grounded only in the fact that they are useful for human survival.

The problem, in short, is that transhumanism unknowingly and problematically takes "human, all too human" values and naturalizes them, understanding them not simply as human "errors" (which they are), but as fundamental facts of life. Moreover, Ansell-Pearson notes, some transhumanists anthropomorphize evolution more blatantly by ascribing to it a conscious will and intelligence:

> Evolution, we are told, has been "searching" the planet to find ways of "speeding itself up", not because it is anthropomorphic but because "the speeding up of adaptation is the runaway circuit it rides on" (Kelly 1994: 361). The excess of contingent evolution in the domain of technology is treated as if it revealed a necessary and conscious "desire" on the part of evolution (it "wants" to become metal). Kelly speaks of "what evolution really wants" as if evolution wanted anything.   (1997: 31–2)

This anthropomorphism is dangerous because it provides an apparent naturalistic grounding for contingent and erroneous perspectives that, as we have seen, can work to support a political and economic *status quo* that perpetuates injustice. Transhumanism thus appears – at least in one popular form – as an ideological support for the current global system of technological and economic development.

Finally, Ansell-Pearson argues, the anthropomorphic values fancifully ascribed to evolutionary processes by the transhumanists are not just any values, but the values of the ascetic ideal. That is, transhumanism is a contemporary form of religious nihilism, which condemns human life here and now and projects a redemptive future. It is not God who will redeem us however, but the natural selection of more complex processes. What ties transhumanism most strongly to the ascetic ideal is the desire to completely overcome suffering, and the inability to affirm suffering as a part of life. As Ansell-Pearson notes, for the transhumanists "All that which Nietzsche regarded as providing fertile soil for an immanent process of continual self-overcoming is here treated as a condition that is to be escaped from" (*ibid.*: 32–3). According to Ansell-Pearson, transhumanism in its most popular form is the new "Platonism for the people" (as Nietzsche characterized Christianity), and "never has such an unintelligent hybrid – that of 'bio-technological' vitalism – been more suspect and in need of 'critique'" (*ibid.*: 2). Nevertheless, Ansell-Pearson is no "bio-conservative" (as the transhumanists sometimes label those who reject transhumanism *tout court*), and he uses his readings of Nietzsche to advocate a more adequate thinking of the transhuman.

Since we have already intimated some of these more positive points above, we may deal with them more briefly. First, Ansell-Pearson wants

> **KEY POINT** *Towards a more adequate thinking of the transhuman condition*
> 1. We need to think the transhuman condition as an "open" problem.
> 2. Thinking the transhuman condition should involve "anthropological deregulation".
> 3. Evolution needs to be artificialized and politicized.
> 4. Nietzsche can help us to think the transhuman more adequately.
> 5. New sciences, such as complexity theory, can help us to think the transhuman more adequately.

to displace the transhuman from a relatively fixed set of ideas and values (those established by the current popular writers on transhumanism), and open it up to a wider field of questioning. We need to think the transhuman as an "open" problem, not a "closed" one. In response to the central problem of anthropomorphism plaguing transhumanism, Ansell-Pearson argues that attempting to think the transhuman should involve a radical and widespread "anthropological deregulation". According to him, from a Nietzschean perspective, "The transhuman condition is not about the transcendence of the human being, but concerns its non-teleological becoming in an immanent process of 'anthropological deregulation'" (*ibid.*: 163). This means, first, that thinking the transhuman condition more adequately means remembering the human condition and our anthropocentric prejudices. But it also means trying to shift those perspectives, trying (for example) to undermine the prejudices of humanistic thinking by opening thought to the insights of the natural sciences, while resisting the temptation to anthropomorphize those sciences in turn.

In response to the way that transhumanism can act as a metanarrative supporting a political *status quo*, Ansell-Pearson advocates the artificialization and politicization of evolutionary theory (*ibid.*: 172). Even as we attempt to "anthropologically deregulate" our perspectives, we need to recognize that we cannot easily transcend our human condition, and that evolutionary theory remains a human theory marked by anthropological limitations and political resonances. This conscious artificialization and politicization undermines the ideological effects of naturalization.

A point that needs little further elaboration – since it has been illustrated throughout this discussion – is that, for Ansell-Pearson, Nietzsche can help us to think the transhuman beyond the dangerous simplifications of the contemporary transhumanists. One point worth emphasizing, however (and we shall come back to this at the end of the chapter), is that while transhumanists tend to think the posthuman primarily in terms of the technological expansion of physical limitations, Nietzsche's thinking takes place primarily on the level of *values*. The main force of Ansell-Pearson's critique lies in the fact that while transhumanists advocate technological change, their values remain conservative, and conserve most of what Nietzsche understands as nihilistic. One of Nietzsche's great insights was that humanistic atheism remained religious in essence because it conserved Christian values: Ansell-Pearson shows us how Nietzsche can reveal the same thing about transhumanism.

Finally, in *Viroid Life*, Ansell-Pearson also ranges far beyond Nietzsche to show how recent sciences can shed light on a more adequate way to think the transhuman. As has already been noted, he points out that many of the conceptions of the transhumanists do not hold up under the pressure of comparison with recent findings of the natural sciences. In fact, he argues that transhumanism employs an outdated, pre-Darwinian conception of evolution to support its thesis. As we have seen, transhumanism is *teleological* – that is, it understands evolution as a process directed towards a goal (complexity). Moreover, at least some transhumanists understand the ultimate goal of the evolutionary process – the ultimate goal of life – as the survival of the heat-death of the universe. The prospect that at a very distant future point the universe will suffer a "heat-death" is speculated as a consequence of entropy. Simply put, entropy is the principle of the dissipation of energy in a system. Difference in energetic potential is what gives a system its dynamism and allows it to function. To take a very simple example, when you open a door between a room with relatively hot air and a room with relatively cold air, a dynamic system is created as hot air (which has greater kinetic energy) flows into the cooler room. What soon happens, however, is that both rooms achieve an even temperature, and the air stops moving: the system has achieved equilibrium and stasis. The theory of entropy allows this simple model to be applied to all physical systems, and thus to the universe as a whole: the universe is subject to the gradual entropic dissipation of energy, and eventually a "heat-death", in which all life, as well as all organized matter, will dissolve into an amorphous, inert "soup".

Transhumanists often construe evolution as a *neg*entropic process (that is, a process that counters entropy), and complexity is thought to embody negentropy (the more complex the system, the further away from, and more resistant it is thought to be to, an entropic lack of differentiation, or "heat-death"). For example, "extropy", a key term in one form of transhumanism, is a neologistic equivalent to negentropy. The evolutionary development of life to the point where it will be able to survive the heat-death of the universe (perhaps by reinjecting new energy into the old universe, or perhaps even by creating a new one for it to inhabit) appears as a new theory of salvation in transhumanist thought; no longer is it a religious doctrine about the salvation of the individual soul from physical death, but about the salvation of life itself from the death of the physical universe.

Ansell-Pearson argues that this view of life and evolution is predicated on false and outdated science. First, Darwinian evolutionary theory is (precisely) not teleological. In fact, it has played a large role in undermining the idea that there is any teleology (directedness towards aims or goals) in nature. Before Darwin, it was often thought that living beings needed to be explained in teleological terms (for example, the stomach would be explained by its purpose of digesting food). This teleological view was often thought to provide support for the existence of an intelligent designer (i.e. God as creator), since life appeared to be designed in a complex way with definite purposes in mind. However, Darwinian evolution made teleological explanation obsolete by demonstrating how complex living systems could have come about purely by chance and natural selection given a long enough time frame (thus, the stomach is not designed for the purpose of digesting food, but because this function is conducive to survival, it has been selected by blind evolutionary processes).

Second, however, there is no scientific support for the view that evolution *selects* complexity over simplicity. In fact, the opposite often seems to be the case: simple systems seem to be better adapted for survival, and evolutionary theory finds it challenging to explain the prevalence of complex forms of life. So while evolution can explain the existence of complex living systems without need of teleological or theological theories, it does not give any kind of privilege to complexity itself. Neither can evolution be accurately seen as progressive in so far as it supposedly produces organisms with a "better" adaptation to conditions: both conditions and organisms are constantly changing in complex ways, and adapting in relation to each other, showing no evidence of "progress". Seeing complexity or better adaptation as the goal of evolution, as something it "wants" and "seeks out", is thus an anthropomorphic conceit.

Third, Ansell-Pearson attacks the apparent transhumanist assumption that evolution is a process subject to relative equilibrium and continual negentropic progress. Against this, he cites recent theories such as chaos theory (non-linear dynamics) and "punctuated equilibrium", which see complexity theory as a way to reconcile entropy and evolution, or dissipation and creative adaptation (1997: 185). Ansell-Pearson cites the work of Ilya Prigogine, who, with Isabelle Stengers in their book *Order Out of Chaos* (1985), popularized the idea that dissipative structures can in fact give rise to complex adaptive systems. On this view, there is no need to posit entropic and negentropic processes as opposing each other, and the transhumanist valorization of the "heroic" negentropic processes of evolution striving to outwit the seemingly inexorable entropic laws of the universe loses credibility. Finally, Ansell-Pearson notes that new developments in geology undermine the gradualist idea of evolution implicit in Darwin and suggest that evolutionary processes are subject to a great degree of chance and contingency. One of the most dramatic expressions of this tendency is the geochemist Ross Taylor's assertion that if the asteroid thought to be responsible for wiping out the dinosaurs by colliding with the earth had missed, it is unlikely that human beings in anything like their current form would have evolved (cited by Ansell-Pearson 1997: 185). Thus, instead of being anything like a gradual process of development aimed towards a specific goal, evolution appears to be a highly contingent and random process, in which not only the fittest, but also the *luckiest*, survive.

What these new sciences reveal is the degree to which popular conceptions of the transhuman condition remain anthropomorphic. These new sciences can thus free us from such conceptions, and present challenges to human thinking and our self-conception that can prompt our self-overcoming. Thinking the transhuman condition thus means rethinking the place of human life in the universe given the changing conception of the universe revealed by the natural sciences. This is a challenge precisely because the sciences undermine our old metanarratives, our religious as well as humanistic conceptions of meaning. Nietzsche's recognition and exploration of this problem is one of the main reasons for his continued importance (a point I underline in the conclusion to this book). I suggested above that while transhumanism focuses on technological change, Nietzsche reminds us of the importance of *value* in human life. If popular transhumanism remains humanistic at the level of values, another current form of posthumanism draws on Nietzsche's work to challenge the very idea of the human and the values it has grounded.

Antihumanism

The term "humanism" admits of quite a few varieties and meanings, and in approaching the issue of "*anti*humanism", we must bear this cautiously in mind. Broadly speaking, antihumanism is the rejection of the particular type of humanism that asserts that the human being is the origin of meaning and the centre of significance in the world. Again quite broadly, we can position this issue in relation to the intellectual movements considered in earlier chapters of this book by saying that existentialism is in general humanistic, and poststructuralism in general antihumanistic. In this section we shall focus on the famous antihumanism of the poststructuralist Nietzschean Foucault (for other aspects of Foucault's Nietzscheanism, see Chapter 2), followed by a brief consideration of Nietzsche's own motives for critiquing humanism. As we shall see, the antihumanistic pole of posthumanism is in some important respects opposed to the transhuman posthumanism we have just examined.

Foucault: the end of man

Foucault is famous for his thesis of "the end of man", announced in the oft-quoted final passage of his book *The Order of Things*:

> [Man] was the effect of a change in the fundamental arrangements of knowledge. As the archaeology of our thought easily shows, man is an invention of recent date. And one perhaps nearing its end.
>
> If those arrangements were to disappear as they appeared, if some event if which we can at the moment do no more than sense the possibility – without knowing either what its form will be or what it promises – were to cause them to crumble, as the ground of classical thought did, at the end of the eighteenth century, then one can certainly wager that man would be erased, like a face drawn in sand at the edge of the sea.
>
> (Foucault 1994: 387)

What is far less well appreciated, however, is the specific sense in which Foucault understands "man", and the deep influence of Nietzsche on his thesis of the end of man. In approaching Foucault's thesis, it is first worth noting the following remarkable passage from *Human, All Too Human*. While to my knowledge this passage was not one to which Foucault made any special reference, I would suggest that it is one that outlines much of his project, including his "anti-humanism":

> *Family failing of philosophers.* – All philosophers have the common failing of starting out from man as he is now and

thinking they can reach their goal through an analysis of him. They involuntarily think of "man" as an *aeterna veritas*, as something that remains constant in the midst of all flux, as a sure measure of things. Everything the philosopher has declared about man is, however, at bottom no more than a testimony as to the man of a *very limited* period of time. Lack of historical sense is the family failing of all philosophers; many, without being aware of it, even take the most recent manifestation of man, such as has arisen under the impress of certain religions, even certain political events, as the fixed form from which one has to start out. They will not learn that man has become, that the faculty of cognition has become; while some of them would have it that the whole world is spun out of this faculty of cognition. Now, everything *essential* in the development of mankind took place in primeval times, long before the four thousand years we more or less know about; during these years mankind may well not have altered very much. But the philosopher here sees "instincts" in man as he now is and assume that these belong to the unalterable facts of mankind and to that extent could provide a key to the understanding of the world in general: the whole of teleology is constructed by speaking of the man of the last four millennia as of an *eternal* man towards whom all things in the world have had a natural relationship from the time he began. But everything has become: there are *no eternal facts*, just as there are no absolute truths. Consequently what is needed from now on is *historical philosophizing*, and with it the virtue of modesty.   (HAH 2)

Foucault's project may be broadly described as just such a "historical philosophizing". As discussed in Chapter 2, Foucault rejects the notions of timeless essences, eternal facts and absolute truths, and instead seeks to show how our ideas have changed over time. His questioning of the supposed eternal verity of the concept "man" is one of his most well-known provocations.

Foucault's announcement of the end of man takes place in the context of his archaeological project, and in order to understand it we need to appreciate a few basic points about this project. When we first encountered Foucault in Chapter 2, we briefly noted the following points about his "archaeology", the methodological approach that governs his early works (including *The Order of Things*): (i) the focus of interrogation is *knowledge*; (ii) archaeology seeks to identify the *conditions* for the *possibility* of systems of knowledge; (iii) archaeology focuses on studying how knowledge is formed and expressed through *uses of language* and *systems of communication*. We can now add the following.

In his archaeological phase, Foucault is primarily interested in the way that what has been taken to be true knowledge has changed through time. In his first major book, *The History of Madness* (1961), for example, he examines the way in which the concept of "madness" came into historical currency. Foucault's attempts to find conditions for knowledge were sometimes understood as aligning him with the structuralist project of uncovering deep, hidden structures, and this led him to be identified as a structuralist in the archaeological phase of his work. However, Foucault sought to distance himself from structuralism, and his work differs from most structuralists in that he does not see these conditions as unified structures, or as deeply hidden, or as in any way *permanent, fixed* or *necessary*. Rather, he emphasizes the *arbitrary* nature of such structures, the fact that they existed and exist by historical chance, and the fact that they could have been otherwise. Against various dominant theories (e.g. Marxist, Hegelian, etc.), which see history as continuous, progressive or deterministic, Foucault asserts the importance of the discontinuities, the shifts and the arbitrary nature of historical facts.

Archaeology is an enquiry that attempts to uncover the "*historical a priori*" of knowledge. It is not so much interested in what specific knowledge claims are made, but in the implicit rules that underlie the claims themselves: the frameworks of thinking that allow certain claims to knowledge and disallow others. Foucault uses the term *episteme* to describe the general framework of thought – the general *a priori* conditions for the production of discourses of knowledge – which might be said to characterize certain historical eras. (Foucault's idea of the *episteme* is often compared with philosopher of science Thomas Kuhn's idea of the *paradigm*, which describes different, incommensurable theoretical frameworks in the history of science.)

The Order of Things is "an archaeology of the human sciences" (which is the subtitle of the book). Foucault examines the historical *a priori* frameworks of knowledge that have made possible the disciplines grouped as the "human sciences" in France, focusing on philology (the study of ancient texts), biology and economics. He identifies four broad epistemes: the "Renaissance", the "Classical", the "Modern" and a new, unnamed episteme emerging from the collapse of the Modern episteme.

Foucault proposes that "man" emerged in the Modern era, and the collapse of the Modern episteme correlates with the famous proclamation of the "end of man". It is essential to appreciate that the concept of "man", as it functions in *The Order of Things*, is not simply the idea of the human being, which of course predates the Modern episteme and will probably outlive it, but is a specifically *epistemological* construct (see Gutting 2008). In simple terms, in the Modern episteme, "man" becomes the central category thought to ground knowledge.

Foucault locates the explicit formulation of this Modern grounding of knowledge in the concept of "man" in the philosophical anthropology of the great modern philosopher Immanuel Kant. In his *Logic*, Kant identifies four central questions around which he believes the production of knowledge should revolve, indicating that the first three are reducible to the fourth. These questions are: (i) what can I know; (ii) what must I do; (iii) what am I permitted to hope; and (iv) what is man? Kant writes: "The first question is answered by *Metaphysics*, the second by *Morals*, the third by *Religion*, and the fourth by *Anthropology*. In reality, however, all these might be reckoned under anthropology, since the first three questions refer to the last" (Kant's *Logic*, quoted in Schrift 1990: 80).

Foucault thus proposes that "man" acts as a grounding and centralizing principle for all knowledge in the Modern episteme. In effect, this means that all things are referred back to a particular idea of the human and human capacities: the question of knowledge becomes a question of what knowledge man is capable of, questions of language become questions of how it can be used by man and so on. Foucault argues that this anthropological grounding of knowledge acts as a kind of dogmatism that restricts thought in a way that is illegitimate, and ultimately sterile, and argues that we are overcoming the Modern episteme in the contemporary era. Foucault's famous proclamation of "the end of man" really means only this, that "man" is ceasing to be a grounding and centralizing concept in the "human sciences".

More technically, Foucault calls the Modern concept of man the "empirico-transcendental doublet" (1994: 318). In short, this means that man is considered to be both the (empirical) object of knowledge, or what is studied, and also the (transcendental) subject of knowledge, or what does the studying. According to Foucault, man, as an empirico-transcendental doublet, contains an epistemological problem at its heart. On the one hand, man is an empirical being, that is, part of the world and subject to all the contingencies and limitations of history. On the other hand, man is thought as a transcendental subject, who constitutes the possibilities of knowledge through his mental faculties, and who grounds the possibility of knowledge because these faculties are universal, beyond historical contingencies. (Otherwise, our knowledge itself would just be the product of historical trends, and we could not consider it "true" knowledge). The problem, in short, is that man has to be both *in* empirical history and *transcendent* to it.

KEY POINT

For Foucault, "man" is a specifically epistemological concept, the "empirico-transcendental doublet". This image of man acts as a grounding for all knowledge. The "end of man" in the transition from the Modern episteme to the contemporary one means that man is no longer considered the ground of knowledge, as epistemology turns its focus to language.

Foucault proposes that the Modern episteme is coming to an end because no adequate solution to the epistemological problem of the empirico-transcendental doublet has been found, despite many attempts. Moreover, Foucault sees this end as emerging with a new grounding for knowledge not in man, but in language. Simply put, Foucault proposes that man is disappearing because a return of language in contemporary thought is making this grounding figure obsolescent. It is no longer the transcendental faculties of man that are thought to provide the conditions of knowledge, but the extra-subjective structures of language (which had retreated from such a role in the Modern episteme). While *The Order of Things* gives far more detailed analyses to a range of other thinkers, and it is evident that the rise of structuralism is at least in part what Foucault implicitly references with the "return of language", it nevertheless situates Nietzsche as a central pivot in the collapse of the Modern episteme and the transition to a new mode of thought. Nietzsche's importance here, according to Foucault (*ibid.*: 305), is that he was the first to connect the philosophical task with a radical reflection on language. Furthermore, Foucault links "the end of man" with Nietzsche's announcement of the coming of the *Übermensch*. This concept is first introduced in tandem with another, "the last man", in the prologue of *Thus Spoke Zarathustra*. The figure of "the last man" represents the one who has killed God, but set up man in God's place: as a foundation for all thought. In Nietzsche's account of the processual development of nihilism, the last man – and all of "humanism" with him – is one of the "shadows of the dead God" that must be vanquished after God himself is declared dead (GS 108). In Foucault's archaeology of the human sciences, the last man corresponds roughly with the Modern episteme. The coming of the *Übermensch* thus corresponds, for Foucault, with the end of the figure of "man" as the foundational principle for thought, and the opening of a new era of thought based on new reflections on the constitutive function of language.

In *The Order of Things*, Foucault presented an enormously influential "antihumanist" thesis, directly inspired by Nietzsche. This thesis linked Nietzsche's thought with, among other things, the antihumanist trends of structuralism and poststructuralism (see Chapter 2), and Foucault's work continues to be important for contemporary antihumanist versions of posthumanism in the humanities today (see e.g. Badmington 2000). However, Foucault's reading of Nietzsche's antihumanism is annexed to his own archaeological project and epistemic interests. In concluding this chapter, we can note a more specifically "Nietzschean" sense in which Nietzsche was an antihumanist, and this will allow us to more clearly contrast the *anti*humanist side of Nietzschean posthumanism with the *trans*humanist side.

The "more Nietzschean" approach I am suggesting here is that Nietzsche's antihumanism be considered in terms of his own privileged terms of analysis, that is, in terms of *values*. Nietzsche's own critiques of humanism, embodied in the figure of "the last man" but also present elsewhere in his works, revolve around the complaint that humanism (often unknowingly) perpetuates the same values as the Christian-moral interpretation of the world (and thus remain nihilistic in the same sense). For example, in *Twilight of the Idols* Nietzsche criticizes George Eliot's supposed atheism for perpetuating the same *morality* for which the theological worldview provided a support (TI "Expeditions" 5). For Nietzsche, the death of God and of the last man, and the advent of the *Übermensch*, has significance above all in relation to his project of a "revaluation of all values".

Significantly, transhumanists frequently align themselves with the values of Enlightenment humanism, and even of religious worldviews. While transhumanism appears radical with respect to the *forms* transhumanists endorse for intelligent life – technology rather than organic material – the underlying values and aims of transhumanism often appear relatively conservative from the perspective of Nietzsche's project. Following Enlightenment humanism, transhumanism endorses the idea of the emancipation of humanity through the development of reason (with the modification that a truly emancipated state will involve a transition to "posthumanity"). Moreover, as we have seen, transhumanism also often appears as a quasi-religious doctrine of salvation: a manifestation of the ascetic ideal. Nietzsche's antihumanism questions the values that underlie these projects at a deep level. (We have seen some of these values questioned already in our discussion of

Ansell-Pearson's critique of transhumanism, and further relevant points are discussed in the next chapter in relation to Nietzsche's project of "naturalizing" both humanity and the world.) From the perspective of values, then, we can see a significant contrast between two notable forms of contemporary Nietzschean posthumanism: transhumanism on the one hand, and antihumanism on the other.

Summary of key points

Transhumanism

Transhumanism is a movement based on the desire to transcend the human condition through the development and application of technology. Transhumans are "transitional humans" who, through their ideas and lifestyles, aim to produce posthumans, members of a new and higher species, beyond the human.

Sorgner on Nietzsche as precursor to transhumanism

Nietzsche and transhumanism have the following points in common:

- a dynamic view of nature and values;
- a "revaluation of values" in which a scientific form of thinking replaces the religious;
- a valuing of the enhancement of human beings; and
- a valuing of self-overcoming.

In addition, Nietzsche's work can be used to supplement transhumanism because it gives us stronger *reasons* for being transhumanists: principally, the ideal of the overhuman/posthuman provides a sense of meaning and value in the scientific age.

Ansell-Pearson on Nietzsche and the transhuman condition

Ansell-Pearson critiques popular conceptions of transhumanism primarily because they are unknowingly and problematically anthropomorphic. That is, they project human values onto natural processes in a way that sustains the ascetic ideal, construing evolution in terms of a teleological history of progressive, negentropic complexification, aimed towards the ultimate salvation of intelligent life processes from the heat-death of the universe. Moreover, transhumanists posit a transition from organic to technological life that problematically assumes a simple distinction between these categories. Ansell-Pearson critiques these problematic aspects of transhumanism with reference both to Nietzsche and to contemporary science, and advocates a more "open" approach to the transhuman condition that would involve a constant "anthropological deregulation".

Antihumanism

Antihumanism rejects the philosophical ideas that human beings are the origin of meaning and significance, and that the category "man" (or "the human") should be the unifying basis of our knowledge. Structuralism and poststructuralism have antihumanistic tendencies, perhaps the most famous expression of which is Foucault's proclamation of "the end of man", a thesis explicitly influenced by Nietzsche. For Nietzsche himself, the problem with humanism is that it enshrines particular, nihilistic values as essential; he looks forward to the "overhuman", a more powerful creator of new, life-affirmative values.

seven

Nietzscheanism, naturalism and science

The aim of this final chapter is to survey some of the main trends in recent Nietzsche scholarship and influence, that is, roughly over the past twenty years. While there have been many such Nietzschean trends in this period, we shall focus on two major themes: naturalism and science. Nietzsche's relation to science, and the interpretation of Nietzsche as primarily a naturalist philosopher, have been variously cited as the main trends in recent Nietzsche scholarship (see, respectively, Diethe 2006: xl; Ansell-Pearson 2011, respectively). These two themes are related. Naturalism, in the one of its several forms we shall focus on here, is the idea that thought needs to connect with and be grounded in the natural sciences. While the importance of the natural sciences for Nietzsche has long been recognized, it is only recently that this relatively underexplored topic has begun to receive the attention it deserves.

Naturalism

> When will all these shadows of god no longer darken us?
> When will we have completely de-deified nature? When may
> we begin to *naturalise* humanity with a pure, newly discovered,
> newly redeemed nature?   (GS 109)

Reading Nietzsche as a naturalist is one of the dominant trends in recent Nietzsche scholarship. In a general sense, naturalism is perhaps most usefully approached by contrasting it with *supernaturalism*, that is, the belief in the kinds of supernatural ideas Nietzsche frequently attacks, such as God, a divine will, a true world and so on. Christianity and metaphysics are replete with such supernatural ideas. More specifically, naturalism appeals to the natural sciences as better principles of explanation than the supernaturalism of religion and metaphysics. Christoph Cox (1999: 5) notes that the use of the term "naturalism" in contemporary philosophy stems primarily from the work of the American philosopher W. V. Quine (1908–2000), who characterizes it as the rejection of first philosophy, the priority of natural science and the redescription of philosophy as continuous with science. Cox goes on to say that while Nietzsche never used the term "naturalism", he called for a "de-deification of nature" and a "naturalization of humanity" (see above), and much of his work can be understood as expressing the themes Quine identifies with naturalism.

However, exactly what naturalism means, and the sense in which Nietzsche might be said to be a naturalist, is not agreed on. Ansell-Pearson (2011: 292) points to at least three types of naturalistic reading of Nietzsche: methodological naturalism (Leiter), existential naturalism (Hatab) and artful naturalism (Christa Davis Acampora). Here, after some initial orienting comments on what naturalism might mean, we shall content ourselves with an examination of two contrasting approaches: Leiter's methodological naturalism and Cox's "interpretive" naturalism. These two approaches bring out clearly what issues are at stake in understanding Nietzsche as a naturalist. For Leiter and interpreters in a similar vein (broadly construed this includes Richard Schacht, Maudemarie Clark, Ken Gemes and others), the naturalistic reading of Nietzsche should be understood in opposition to the "postmodern" reading, a reading closely related to the material covered in the chapter "Nietzscheanism and Poststructuralism", and variously named "the poststructuralist Nietzsche", "the deconstructionist Nietzsche", "the new Nietzsche" and "the French Nietzsche". While these terms embody a range of different views of Nietzsche, the frequent commonality the description "postmodernist Nietzsche" picks out is a scepticism about truth and reality. Simply put, the postmodernist reading has it that Nietzsche holds that there is no true knowledge, and no reality to have true knowledge of. Leiter's naturalist interpretation opposes the postmodernist one by defending the view that Nietzsche did endorse the possibility of true knowledge, which is precisely the knowledge of "facts" concerning reality. Moreover, it defends Nietzsche's alleged view that the natural sciences give us privileged access to such facts. In contrast to this approach, Cox presents a reading that, in effect, attempts to reconcile the naturalistic and postmodernist readings, by showing that Nietzsche's commitment to naturalism is not inconsistent with his rejection of facts and assertion of the ubiquity of interpretation.

Leiter's methodological naturalism

Leiter gives an overview and defence of his naturalist reading of Nietzsche in the first chapter of his *Routledge Philosophy Guidebook to Nietzsche on Morality* (2002). In order to situate Nietzsche as a naturalist, Leiter first gives an analysis of naturalism, discerning various types as follows.

KEY POINT *Types of naturalism*
1. *Methodological* (M-naturalism): philosophical enquiry should be *continuous* with empirical enquiry in the sciences.
   Two meanings of "continuity":
   • results continuity: philosophical theories must be supported or justified by the results of the sciences;
   • methods continuity: philosophical theories should emulate the methods of enquiry of successful sciences.
2. *Substantive* (S-naturalism): either the (ontological) view that the only things that exist are *natural* (or perhaps simply physical) things; or the (semantic) view that a suitable philosophical analysis of any concept must show it to be amenable to empirical enquiry (Leiter 2002: 3–6).

On the basis of this typology of naturalism, Leiter situates Nietzsche as fundamentally a *methodological* naturalist, concerned primarily with methods continuity; he is primarily a naturalist in so far as he is concerned with making philosophy continuous with the methods of the natural sciences. This does not mean that Nietzsche thinks philosophers should do empirical experiments with laboratory equipment and so on, but that they should emulate the rigorous truthfulness and objectivity of the natural sciences, as well as employ models of explanation adopted from the natural sciences, such as explaining effects by identifying their causes. However, Leiter also says there is a type of results continuity in Nietzsche's naturalism, in so far as he wishes to build his philosophical views on certain results of science, such as evolutionary theory. Moreover, Leiter identifies an *ontological* type of *substantive* naturalism in Nietzsche in so far as he wants to eliminate anything supernatural from his view of reality. However, Leiter insists that there is nothing to suggest that Nietzsche would have been sympathetic to *semantic* substantive naturalism, which suggests that everything can be reduced to and explained in terms of the natural sciences (including such things as beauty and love).

Leiter explains Nietzsche's naturalistic project here primarily in terms of his critique of morals (the subject of the book). According to Leiter, Nietzsche's naturalism can be understood as a methodology in service to the philosophically independent project of the "revaluation of all values". As Leiter glosses it, Nietzsche criticizes existing values and morality because they are a threat to human excellence and greatness (2002: 26). Naturalization is a method for conducting such a critique. Leiter outlines a "typical Nietzschean argument" as follows: "a person's theoretical beliefs are best explained in terms of his moral beliefs; and his moral beliefs are best explained in terms of natural facts about the type of person he is" (*ibid.*: 9). According to Leiter, then, Nietzsche's naturalism appeals to what he calls "type-facts". On this view, each person has a fixed psycho-physical constitution, which defines him or her as a particular *type* of person. Explanations of a person's theoretical or moral beliefs are thus given in terms of facts about what type of person they are, typically of a psychological or physiological nature. The will to power, for example, is a type-fact with perhaps the widest scope of application in explaining human motivation and behaviour (including beliefs). This form of argument is naturalistic because it deflates supernatural accounts of human beliefs and morals by construing them as effects for which there are natural causes. Leiter defends this naturalistic reading of Nietzsche from five theses that he presents as common among postmodernist Nietzscheans, and which would seem to be objections to this reading, as follows.

Truth and knowledge

As noted above, Nietzsche has often been held to reject the notions of truth and knowledge. Leiter asserts that this interpretation is largely based on Nietzsche's early, unpublished text "On Truth and Lying in a Non-moral Sense" (TL), and that Nietzsche's views changed significantly over time (a point that, he suggests, the postmodernists often forget). Following an argument by Maudemarie Clark, Leiter asserts that Nietzsche's last six books (beginning with the *On the Genealogy of Morality*) exhibit no significant scepticism with regard to truth and knowledge, and thus express a mature position in Nietzsche's thought that is consistent with the naturalist interpretation. Moreover, Leiter notes that Nietzsche frequently employs "epistemic value terms", such as true/false, real/unreal, justified/unjustified and so on. Significantly (and this is a point Cox's reading will dispute), Leiter insists that "a class of claims can only be *epistemically* privileged if it is possible for there to be *objective* truths about them and for us to have *objective* knowledge of those truths" (2002: 14). Moreover, Leiter interprets Nietzsche's famous "perspectivism" as being consistent with objective truth and reality: while any knowledge claim will be limited to a certain perspective on an object, this does not deny the existence of a really existing, perspective-transcendent object, nor that some perspectives on it are clear (true) and others distorted (false). Leiter thus argues that Nietzsche's philosophy implies that he *knows* certain *truths* that others – Christians, most philosophers, moralists – fail to comprehend (*ibid.*: 14).

Scepticism about science

Nietzsche is often held to be sceptical about the epistemic value of science, understanding it as one interpretation among others with no special relation to truth or reality. Against this, and following from the argument above, Leiter suggests that the mature Nietzsche was not sceptical about the epistemic value of science. In his late works, he is concerned to point out that science cannot create values – the necessary purview of philosophy – but this does not imply a scepticism towards the epistemic value of science as such.

Scepticism about causation

As we saw above, Leiter's naturalistic interpretation of Nietzsche involves a kind of causation: Nietzsche seeks to identify natural causes (generally physiological and psychological facts) for human beliefs. However, Nietzsche is often thought to reject the very idea of causation. Again, Leiter claims that this rejection does not appear in Nietzsche's mature works. Moreover, he interprets an apparent critique of causation in *Beyond Good and Evil* (BGE 21) as arguing only that causality does not apply to "things-in-themselves", but only to appearances. On Leiter's reading, the idea of a realm of things-in-themselves is rejected in Nietzsche's late works, and we are left with *this* world – the only world – discoverable by empirical science, to which causation legitimately applies.

Hostility towards materialism

Leiter acknowledges that Nietzsche makes explicit disavowals of the materialist position, a position that it might be thought necessary for a naturalist to endorse. However, he points out that Nietzsche's rejection of materialism has a specific character: it is a rejection of the reduction of any and all facts to a mechanistic materialist view of the universe (for Nietzsche's views on mechanism, see the section on science below). This means that Nietzsche's attacks on materialism amount to a rejection only of a restricted type of naturalism: substantive naturalism of the semantic variety. Nietzsche's views thus remain perfectly consistent, Leiter asserts, with a thoroughgoing methodological naturalism, as well as ontological substantive naturalism (the rejection of supernaturalism).

Scepticism about human nature and essence

Nietzsche has often been thought to be sceptical about human nature, a scepticism in line with his rejection of metaphysics and the ascription of essential properties to anything. However, Leiter notes that Nietzsche *does* make claims about essences. Those who believe Nietzsche is sceptical about all essences, Leiter suggests, conflate the rejection of *non-naturalistic claims* (that is, the identification of supernatural or metaphysical essences) with a rejection of any and all claims about essence (2002: 26). With reference to Quine, he notes that there is a way of ascribing "natural" essences to things that is perfectly consistent with both naturalism, and with Nietzsche's rejection of supernatural essences. (For more on Nietzsche and human nature, see Chapter 6).

In sum, then, Leiter believes that the common "postmodernist" theses about Nietzsche that would present objections to the naturalistic interpretation he espouses are all incorrect, or at least not sufficiently correct to count as objections. A principal point of Leiter's arguments is the claim that Nietzsche's mature works are free of his earlier published views, which would conflict with naturalism.

Cox's interpretive naturalism

Cox's *Nietzsche: Naturalism and Interpretation* (1999) presents a reading of Nietzsche that we might call "interpretive naturalism". Cox follows the broad definition of naturalism, outlined in the introduction to this section, as the attempt to make philosophy continuous with science. To this extent his naturalistic thesis is compatible with Leiter's reading.

However, Cox differs with respect to Nietzsche's views of truth and reality, and follows the "postmodernists" in underscoring Nietzsche's rejection of "facts" in favour of perspectives and interpretations. For Cox, although he does not use precisely these terms, the naturalist and postmodernist interpretations are compatible because it is precisely Nietzsche's naturalism that leads him to "postmodern" epistemological and ontological views. That is, Nietzsche's reconsideration of philosophy on a scientific basis leads him to reject the "God's-eye view" in epistemology, and the "pre-given world" in ontology. We shall here outline Cox's interpretation of Nietzsche's naturalized epistemology and ontology, and show how – according to Cox – Nietzsche's naturalistic project proceeds along two main lines: the "naturalization of humanity" and the "de-deificatation of nature".

Epistemology naturalized

According to Cox, Nietzsche rejects the most popular views in philosophical epistemology on naturalist grounds. In order to understand Nietzsche's naturalized epistemology, we first need to have a basic grasp of what these popular views are. Traditionally, the two dominant approaches to the acquisition and justification of knowledge in the Western philosophical tradition have been *rationalism* and *empiricism*. Rationalism is the view that human reason gives us access to truth through "innate ideas" that naturally inhere in the mind, and which, once accessed, give us a true understanding of reality. (Plato is the "grandfather" of the rationalist thesis, while Descartes is its modern "father".) Empiricism, on the other hand, is the view that all our knowledge is derived from, and justified by, sensory experience. (Aristotle is empiricism's grandfather, and John Locke its father.) In the late eighteenth century, Kant attempted to reconcile rationalism and empiricism with his extremely influential theory of *transcendental idealism*. According to Kant, knowledge is produced by a synthesis of sensory experience and necessary, *a priori* categories supplied by the mind. The mind thus organizes our experience and makes it intelligible, but knowledge claims are justified only if they can point to objects of sensible experience.

According to Cox, Nietzsche rejects all three of these views in most of their forms, and opts for a qualified empiricism. Nietzsche argues that the ideas or categories that shape our interpretations of the world are not simply reflections of an objective reality, but have, rather, evolved over time under evolutionary pressures and constraints. Thus, Nietzsche suggests that the ideas that human beings are inclined towards persist because they have proved to be advantageous to the species, not because of some supposed connection they have to "reality". This goes not just for substantive beliefs (such as the existence of God, the soul or the afterlife), but for the applications of reason that have often been thought to express the most basic structures of rationality: language, logic, mathematics and the "categories". These are thoroughly bound up with one another and serve the same basic evolutionary role: functions of consciousness that serve to simplify and schematize the sensuous manifold into a calculable and communicable system (Cox 1999: 83). Logic and mathematics are both concerned with making things equal and constructing identities. The categories are concepts or intellectual forms, such as quality, quantity, substance, place, time and so on, which are thought to be basic to organizing our experience and understanding the world. For Nietzsche, the evolutionary value of thinking in the categories is that it simplifies and organizes our reception of sensuous experience so that we can more quickly and easily cope with the challenges of our environment. Finally, language enables us to communicate with others on the basis of this simplified world (*ibid.*).

Nietzsche's naturalized epistemology rejects rationalism and the Kantian supposition of the universal and necessary, unchanging nature of the categories. For Nietzsche, there is nothing necessary nor fixed about the way we categorize our experience: even rational functions as basic as the law of identity, the ability to recognize one thing as identical to another, Nietzsche understands as contingent products of evolutionary pressures, open to alteration. Rejecting *a priori* ideas, Nietzsche's naturalized epistemology is a form of empiricism in so far as it accepts that all knowledge derives from the senses. However, according to Cox, Nietzsche rejects what he calls *reductionist empiricism*, "which holds that all knowledge and experience is reducible to immediate observations that deliver a unique and full meaning" (*ibid.*: 93). Nietzsche is strongly hostile to the idea that sensory experience gives immediate certainties about the nature of things, and praises the capacity to think beyond what is most apparent to sensory experience. Nietzsche rejects a distinction between the immediate givenness of sensory data and the interpretive activity of the mind on it, and asserts that all sensory perception takes place within a web of what are already interpretive perspectives. This perspectivist account of knowledge is a direct consequence of Nietzsche's naturalization of epistemology, and these views resonate with his rejection of a "pre-given world", which we shall consider below.

It is necessary to note first, however, how Cox's account of Nietzsche's epistemology stands in relation to the problem of relativism. Relativism, and how to avoid it (at least in its most pernicious forms) is one of the perennial problems for any philosophical theory of knowledge. Relativism, in its simplest form, is the idea that all knowledge claims are of equal value, so it is impossible to privilege one over the other. This is equivalent to epistemological nihilism: the view that we can have no knowledge of anything, since any knowledge claim might be as equally true or false as any other claim. On the one hand, Cox's interpretation of Nietzsche's epistemology would seem to invite relativism because he insists that, for Nietzsche, the claims of empirical science and of natural-ized philosophy are themselves interpretations and perspectives, open to the same scepticism regarding perspective transcendence as any other knowledge claims. However, Cox argues that Nietzsche's epistemology is saved from relativism because it includes a criterion for privileging some knowledge claims over others.

As noted earlier, Leiter insists that "a class of claims can only be *epis-temically* privileged if it is possible for there to be *objective* truths about them and for us to have *objective* knowledge of those truths" (2002: 14). However, Cox's interpretation of Nietzsche differs on this point, because he suggests another way in which claims can be epistemically privileged, a way that does not depend on objective truth. On Cox's interpretation, for Nietzsche not all knowledge claims are of equal value because epis-temic privilege is given to *naturalized* interpretations and perspectives. Cox writes: "Nietzsche holds that perspectives and interpretations are, in large part, developed to help us cope with our sensuous imbrication in the natural world. A basic standard for interpretations, then, is how well they do this" (Cox 1999: 99).

Cox's interpretation seems to imply, then, that despite the evolution-ary advantages that have accrued to religious and metaphysical beliefs in the past, naturalized interpretations are ultimately superior with respect to their value in helping us cope with "our sensuous imbrication in the natural world". On Cox's interpretation, then, it is not objective truth – itself a human idea open to critique – that acts as the criterion for epistemic privilege, but the naturalistic criterion of coping with our environment. In short, then, on Cox's interpretation Nietzsche holds both that (i) there are no facts, only interpretations, and (ii) some inter-pretations (naturalistic ones) are better than others.

Ontology naturalized

Cox analyses Nietzsche's naturalization of ontology as proceeding along the two lines of a naturalization of humanity, and a de-deification of nature. That is, Nietzsche presents a naturalized ontology of human beings, and of the cosmos. Nietzsche's project of "naturalizing humanity" means translating human beings entirely into a natural worldview, rejecting any appeal to supernatural entities or principles of explanation. This project involves rejecting the disjunctions that philosophers have traditionally used to mark out human beings as somehow exceptional: reason/nature, mind/body, consciousness/instinct and so on (Cox 1999: 99). Instead, Nietzsche sees these terms on a continuum, where the specifically human term is a modification and outgrowth of the "animal" term, and one that should not be understood as higher or superior, but simply different.

As a corollary to Nietzsche's epistemology, the world is de-deified in an ontological sense. Nietzsche rejects not just a "God's-eye view", but also the idea of an absolute object that could be seen from this point of view. Nietzsche understands this idea of the world as it really is in-itself, the perspective-transcendent "fact" of the world, as a manifestation of religious nihilism. Cox explains: "The notion of the world 'as it really is' or 'as it is in itself' is simply fabricated through a *negation of*, a *desire to transcend*, the world we know (the world as it is constructed by the many interpretations/perspectives)" (*ibid.*: 96).

As a religious idea, the notion of the objective, factual nature of reality is undermined through naturalization. As we have seen, for Cox's Nietzsche not only conceptual categories but also sensory experiences are always-already interpretive, so any apprehension of the world, including empirical science and naturalized philosophy, will have the character of an interpretive perspective.

According to Cox's interpretation, Nietzsche's project of de-deifying nature involves revealing the perspectival and interpretive character of the world and our relation to it. The project involves the removing of all categories through which the world has been understood as divine: "purpose, order, aim, form, beauty, wisdom, eternal novelty, law, hierarchy, and so forth" (1999: 103). What is uniquely distinctive about Nietzsche's naturalism here is that he believes scientific perspectives themselves to bear strong traces of the religious and metaphysical perspectives they are replacing. Nietzsche's naturalist project, then, does not take the scientific description of nature at face value, but criticizes this description in the name of a more radical naturalism. This is evident in the following note: "My task: the dehumanisation of nature and then the naturalisation of the human after it has gained the pure concept of 'nature'" (KSA 9, 11 [211], quoted in Moore 2004: 6).

What, then, is this "pure concept of nature" Nietzsche seeks to attain? It is the image of the world once the theistic and metaphysical categories – purpose, order, aim and so on – are removed from it. Cox elaborates on this by outlining how it is also an image of the world without the four "causes" identified by Aristotle, which have been an influential framework for formulating metaphysical conceptions of nature. These four Aristotelian causes, and their theistic modifications, are as follows.

KEY POINT *The four causes*
- The *efficient cause* of something is the force that has brought about a change to produce that thing. (God as prime mover – the force that originally brought about motion in the cosmos.)
- The *formal cause* is that in virtue of which something is what it is; in Aristotelian metaphysics, its form. (The world understood as organism, as cycle, as machine and as law-abiding.)
- The *final cause* is the purpose, aim or goal for the sake of which a change is brought about. (The purpose of the universe as equilibrium, progress or happiness.)
- The *material cause* is the "stuff" out of which something is made. (materialistic atomism, pantheism, etc.) (see Mautner 1999: 90; Cox 1999: 104).

What is left of the world once these theological notions have been removed? Nietzsche sometimes describes his de-deified image of nature as "chaos" or as "the innocence of becoming", but the most famous de-deified image of the world to appear in his thought is the world as "will to power". In this interpretation, the world is understood in terms of a single explanatory principle, that of dynamic quanta of force in ever-changing relations. Nietzsche reveals this image in the famous final note collected in *The Will to Power*:

> This world: … a play of forces and waves of forces, at the same time one and many, increasing here and at the same time decreasing there; a sea of forces flowing and rushing together, eternally changing, eternally flooding back, with tremendous years of recurrence, with an ebb and a flood of its forms …
> (WP 1067)

Significantly for Nietzsche's doctrine of perspectivism, these quanta of force are what interpret, and every interpretation is a manifestation of the will to power. Every interpretation – including Nietzsche's interpretation of the world as will to power – is invested with its own interests and desire for expansion. Nietzsche's de-deified nature, understood as chaos, becoming and will to power, is thus not presented as a perspective-transcendent fact, but as one interpretation among others. As Cox explains, "it is not a question of distinguishing the real from the apparent world but of distinguishing different ways of constructing apparent worlds" (1999: 103).

While this is not the place to debate the respective merits of Leiter's and Cox's brands of naturalism, the following considerations may briefly be noted. Leiter's interpretation has the advantage of aligning Nietzsche with a widely accepted and commonsensical view of truth and science, and, on this basis, of making sense of projects such as the *Genealogy*, which have often puzzled readers. However, this advantage comes at the expense of restricting our perspective on Nietzsche to the last six published works. Cox's interpretation, on the other hand, has the advantage of making sense of a much wider range of Nietzsche's texts (including the late unpublished notes and the earlier published works), and of attributing to Nietzsche a more original, but also more challenging, view of truth and reality and their relation to science.

Science

From the earliest interpretations of Nietzsche's works in the late nineteenth century, the relationship between Nietzsche's thought and science was often noted, particularly in relation to specific ideas that seem to bear a "quasi-scientific" character, such as the will to power and the eternal return (we shall note some of these early studies in the discussions of these ideas below). A notable work that discussed several of these themes was the French Nietzsche scholar Charles Andler's massive study *Nietzsche, sa vie et sa pensée* (Nietzsche, his life and his thought), published in six volumes between 1920 and 1931. However, Nietzsche's relation to the natural sciences has become more widely recognized as a fecund ground for new explorations over roughly the past thirty years. Gregory Moore (2004: 10) notes the likely significance of the publication of the Colli–Montinari critical edition of Nietzsche's collected works as a spur to tracking down and examining the works of natural science Nietzsche read and referred to in his notes. Diethe (2006: xl) attributes responsibility for "spearheading" the trend of scholarship on Nietzsche and science, at least among British scholars, to Ansell-

Pearson. (Ansell-Pearson's work in this area is examined in Chapter 6.)

Notable works within this recent period which have examined particular aspects of Nietzsche's relation to science include: George J. Stack's *Lange and Nietzsche* (1983); Laurence Lampert's *Nietzsche and Modern Times* (1993); Babette E. Babich's *Nietzsche's Philosophy of Science* (1994); Babich and Robert S. Cohen's edited volumes *Nietzsche and the Sciences I: Nietzsche, Theories of Knowledge, and Critical Theory* (1999a) and *Nietzsche and the Sciences II: Nietzsche, Epistemology, and Philosophy of Science* (1999b); Robin Small's *Nietzsche in Context* (2001), Moore's *Nietzsche, Biology and Metaphor* (2002); and John Richardson's *Nietzsche's New Darwinism* (2004). However, as Moore notes, the first, and so far only, attempt at a systematic and comprehensive study has been Alwin Mittasch's book *Nietzsche als Naturphilosoph* (1952; cited in Moore 2004: 10). Moore notes, however, that this book is significantly flawed. Moreover, not only does Nietzsche's relation to science lack a comprehensive study, but various areas of likely significance have received little or no attention. For example, Thomas H. Brobjer (2004: 41) notes that the important influence on Nietzsche's thought of two positivist (or, as they were called at the time, "criticoempiricist") philosophers of science, Richard Avenarius and Ernst Mach, has been curiously overlooked. This influence is significant because it shows that Nietzsche was familiar with, and to some degree influenced by, the ideas that helped shape the Vienna Circle positivists and the analytic tradition of philosophy in the twentieth century (*ibid.*). Thus, Nietzsche's relation to science remains a rich area of research and exploration in the twentieth-first century.

At the outset, it is worth noting some general points regarding Nietzsche's relation to science. Like so many other things in Nietzsche's *oeuvre*, the status of science manifests a great deal of ambiguity. Nietzsche's changing attitude to science is, in fact, one of the key markers differentiating the three periods into which his work is usually divided. Science was a deeply significant topic in European intellectual culture generally in the nineteenth century, and Moore suggests that "One might even argue that the various positions vis-à-vis science which Nietzsche adopts throughout his life recapitulate in a single career the different stages in the development of the relationship between science and philosophy in the nineteenth century" (2004: 8). Nietzsche wrote in the context of a great ferment regarding the cultural significance of science, and in particular of two scientific theories that seemed directly to undermine religious faith: the Darwinian theory of evolution, which decentred and desacralized the nature of human beings; and the second law of thermodynamics (entropy), which suggested an eventual "heat-death" of the universe and affronted the notion that creation is a divine and eternal phenomenon. (Entropy is discussed in Chapter 6.) As Moore further notes, however, Nietzsche's original contribution to the science debates was in seeing that the undermining of explicitly religious beliefs also has the consequence of undermining the moral and normative values on which much of our social structure rests (Moore 2004: 6).

Nietzsche's first reactions to science – in the period of *The Birth of Tragedy* and the *Untimely Meditations* – is primarily negative. He understands science as an outgrowth of the Socratic elevation of knowledge over art, and as having a primarily negative value for life. In its uncompromising search for truth, science strips away both the Apollonian veil of illusion and the Dionysian intoxication that enable us to affirm suffering, and which act as stimuli to life. In his "middle period", however – from *Human, All Too Human* to *The Gay Science* – a radical change seems to take place: now Nietzsche highly esteems science precisely for its uncompromising honesty, and pursues the task of unmasking moral conceits and prejudices by "naturalizing" morality (that is, explaining our moral sentiments according to the knowledge afforded by the natural sciences). The following passage from *The Gay Science* exemplifies this approach:

> *Long live physics!* .... We, however, want to *become who we are* – human beings who are new, unique, incomparable, who give themselves laws, who create themselves! To that end we must become the best students and discoverers of everything lawful and necessary in the world: we must become *physicists* in order to be creators in this sense – while hitherto all valuations and ideals have been built on *ignorance* of physics or in *contradiction* to it. So, long live physics! And even more long live what *compels* us to it – our honesty!   (GS 335)

Nietzsche's third period – from *Zarathustra* on – sees a final change of attitude, which is in a way a nuanced combination of the previous two positions. Nietzsche continues to value the *scientific method* for its critical potential and intellectual discipline, but once again becomes critical of science as such and many dominant scientific theories, seeing them as based in the same values as religious nihilism. In addition to this broad outline of Nietzsche's changing explicit views on science, the influence of the natural sciences is frequently manifested in the concepts, metaphors and terminology he employs throughout his works:

the "chemistry of concepts and sensations", the "physiology of art", the struggle for existence, the conservation of energy, concepts from the psychological theory of his day and so on (Moore 2004: 9).

Below, we shall examine in more detail two principal areas that have recently attracted the attention of scholars of the Nietzsche/science interface: (i) Nietzsche's "philosophy of science", that is, his views regarding the status of science both in terms of its claims to knowledge and its cultural and existential value; and (ii) his knowledge of the natural sciences, and the way such knowledge impacted on and influenced his philosophical work.

Nietzsche's philosophy of science

One scholar who must be considered among those who have done the most to explore Nietzsche's relation to science is Babich. She has published a monograph on Nietzsche's philosophy of science (Babich 1994), and co-edited two volumes of essays on "Nietzsche and the Sciences" (Babich & Cohen 1999a,b). Babich's monograph is titled *Nietzsche's Philosophy of Science: Reflecting Science on the Ground of Art and Life*, and its subtitle neatly encapsulates her argument. While acknowledging that Nietzsche in no sense had a fully developed philosophy of science of the kind that goes under that name today, she nevertheless argues that Nietzsche's philosophy – and, in particular, his reflections on epistemology and scientific method – has important implications for the philosophy of science. Babich's study is predicated on the critical claim that contemporary philosophy of science, especially as it is practised in the Anglo-American "analytic" tradition of philosophy, lacks a critically reflexive orientation to science (which, she further argues, is a necessary condition for philosophy as such). The problem, as she sees it, is that philosophy of science lacks a ground other than science itself from which it can reflect on science. As the subtitle of her book suggests, Babich finds the possibility of such a ground (or grounds) in Nietzsche's work, where they take on the forms of art and life. Here, she recalls the statement Nietzsche makes in the later, self-critical preface attached to *The Birth of Tragedy* in its 1886 edition, regarding the task he first attempted in that book: "*to look at science through the prism of the artist, but also to look at art through the prism of life*" (BT "Preface" 2). Babich thus proposes an *aesthetic* critique of science: a critical take on science from the perspective of art, and a connection of this critical perspective with Nietzsche's views on the values and demands of life.

Babich develops a critical perspective on science by drawing out Nietzsche's critique of truth, knowledge and scientific method. Simplifying greatly, Nietzsche's critical perspectives on science can be boiled down to the following two points. First, Nietzsche criticizes what he sees as a scientific pretension to a single, absolute truth, and contrasts this with his own perspectivalist account of truth and knowledge. Babich characterizes Nietzsche's account of knowledge according to what she calls an "ecophysiological" approach: knowledge is produced by the body and by the world, and through their interrelation. Given the limitations placed on the nature of human bodies in general (as well as on the specific bodies of enquirers), and the limited scope of their interactions with the world, knowledge will have an inevitably perspectival character. In particular, Nietzsche argues that human knowledge is produced in accord with the realities and needs of our species's adaptation to the environment. From this perspective, science is a type of illusion not in so far is it is untrue as such, but in so far as it is a partial perspective that takes itself to be an absolute vantage point able to access absolute truths. Nietzsche presents both art and science as illusions, but art at least has the virtue of recognizing itself as such. In Nietzsche's view, science needs an aesthetic culture: art can act as a corrective to science by revealing its kinship as a form of illusion.

Second, Nietzsche questions the value of truth, knowledge and science by enquiring into the existential and psychological dimensions of what it is in us that wants truth, scientific regularity and (by extension) technological mastery (Babich 1994: 298). Nietzsche presents what he calls the "will to knowledge" as a species of the will to power, and sees an intimate connection between the desire to know the world and the desire to master it. Thus, while Nietzsche views the reality of the world as a flux of becoming (the metaphysical dimension of the will to power; a view that Babich calls Nietzsche's "hyperrealism"), science cuts its objects from this flux and stabilizes them in order to apprehend and control them. Again, while this affords a degree or perspective of knowledge about the world, it remains illusory in so far as it covers over and denies the more primary flux of becoming, which allows things to manifest in multiple ways.

Furthermore, and most decisively, Nietzsche sees the will underlying science as a manifestation of the ascetic ideal, and, as such, a continuation of religious nihilism under a radically different guise. Babich draws out the ascetic nature of science most strongly through the motivation of the modern scientific project to preserve life. As she presents it, the ascetic ideal is "the means whereby a reactive or weak Will to Power can become superordinately creative, representing its own standard as universally binding" (*ibid.*: 8). For Nietzsche, religion, and the Judaeo-Christian tradition in particular, manifests the ascetic ideal as a mechanism that preserves life by creating a system of values appropriate for those with a low level of will to power (hope placed in salvation in a world beyond as compensation for an inability to bear the suffering of this life), and universalizing those values to create social conditions also conducive to such life preservation. According to Nietzsche, the project of modern science continues the religious nihilism of the ascetic ideal by other means by aiming principally at the preservation of any and all (human) life, even the most impoverished, by mastering and taming the natural world. As Babich emphasizes, this impetus to life preservation is actually nihilistic – it actually negates life – because according to Nietzsche the full and affirmative expression of life requires an *expenditure* of life. In other words, affirming life by living to the maximum requires risk, the expenditure of energy and the embrace of forces inherent to life, which from a limited perspective appear to be counter to it: change, decay and death. Thus, the development of Nietzsche's "philosophy of science" in Babich's work underlines Nietzsche's critique of science from the perspective of life, from which perspective it appears as a manifestation of the will to knowledge and the ascetic ideal. These aesthetic and vitalist critiques would not seem to call for an abandonment of science, but a revaluation that demotes it from an exclusive claim to truth, to its positioning within culture that places due weight on the demands stemming from art and life.

The significance of science for Nietzsche

In addition to Nietzsche's broad attitudes towards the epistemic, cultural and existential value of science as such, scholars have been interested in determining exactly what science Nietzsche was familiar with, and how it impacted on his philosophy. They have also been concerned to determine how his philosophical ideas cohere with nineteenth-century science, and how they sometimes seem to presage more recent developments in the sciences (Moore 2004: 11). Archival material, such as Nietzsche's notebooks, and the often-annotated books in his private library, has allowed scholars to undertake detailed research into these questions. A good example of such research is that conducted by Brobjer (2004).

Nietzsche, trained as a philologist, lacked any significant formal training in the natural sciences. However, he undertook periodic serious attempts to make up for this lack in his education by ordering and reading numerous books on the sciences, and even planned at one stage to study science at the University of Vienna for ten years to rectify this lack (a plan never carried out).

After detailing the numerous books by scientists, science writers and philosophers of science that Nietzsche studied and wrote notes on, Brobjer concludes that "Nietzsche was better informed and more engaged in questions relating to natural science than has generally been assumed" (*ibid.*: 46). In general, the sciences that most interested Nietzsche were biology, physiology and physics (and, if we include the "social sciences", psychology and sociology; Moore 2004: 11). While there are a large number of scientists and scientific theories that influenced Nietzsche, we shall restrict ourselves here to discussion of the three areas that have received the most attention: Lange and materialism, Darwinism and the question of its relation to the *Übermensch*, and the relation of physics to the ideas of the will to power and the eternal return.

Lange and materialism

It has long been well known that one of Nietzsche's earliest, and most significant, continuing influences as far as science is concerned, was Friedrich Albert Lange's *History of Materialism* ([1886] 1950), a book he read on its first publication, and periodically re-read and minutely studied up to and including his later period, re-reading it in 1883, 1884 and 1885, and buying and reading the third edition in 1887 (Brobjer 2004: 27). Stack, in his detailed study *Lange and Nietzsche* (1983), argues that:

> It would not be too much to say that many of the essential issues that Nietzsche grapples with throughout his creative life can only be clarified when placed against the background of Lange's remarkable study ... Many of the insights, flashes of thought and intuitive interpretations found in Nietzsche's writings owe their inspiration to what can only be characterised as Nietzsche's microscopic study of Lange's exposition, commentary and interpretation of the history of materialism from pre-Socratic thought up to the latter part of the nineteenth century. (Stack 1983: 1)

So what was Lange's work about, and what was its significance for Nietzsche?

Friedrich Albert Lange (1828–75) was a professor of philosophy at Zürich and Marburg universities, and one of the founders of the influential movement in German philosophy of the late nineteenth and early twentieth centuries known as "neo-Kantianism". (As the name suggests, philosophers such as Lange sought to return to the philosophy of Kant, but in ways that updated his work, and which varied between different schools and philosophers, collectively known as neo-Kantian.)

Lange's *History of Materialism* is an impressively erudite work, which not only outlines the history of materialist thought from the Presocratic philosophers (such as Democritus) to the present, but contains overviews and criticisms of many of the key figures in the history of philosophy, as well as a comprehensive summary of the branches of natural science and their results up to the time of its publication (1866). It was very influential at the time, and continued to be used as a standard textbook into the twentieth century. Lange's work had significance for Nietzsche in a wide variety of areas and at many subtle levels of influence (Nietzsche called Lange's work a "treasure-house"; Stack 1983: 12), but this significance can be summarized around the following points.

KEY POINT *Lange's significance for Nietzsche*
1. Providing a grounding knowledge of philosophy and science.
2. Enabling a more critical relation to Schopenhauer, and other philosophers.
3. Stimulating an interest in materialism.
4. Guiding an approach to the relation between science and meaning.

First, then, Nietzsche gained much of his initial knowledge of philosophy and the sciences from Lange's book. As far as science is concerned, Stack comments that "Lange's erudition is such that it is no exaggeration to say that one could acquire a basic understanding of the methods and results of the sciences up to the 1870s by a careful reading of his work" (*ibid.*: 8).

Second, it is notable that Nietzsche's discovery of Lange followed shortly after his discovery of Schopenhauer (a philosopher who used many examples from science to support his metaphysics) – Schopenhauer in 1865, and Lange in the latter half of 1867 – and, along with Wagner as well, was one of the most significant influences on Nietzsche's early thought. In his first extant mention of Lange – in a letter to Carl von Gersdorff dated August 1866 – Nietzsche interprets the work in a way that coheres with his admiration for Schopenhauer.

In the letter, Nietzsche summarizes Lange's conclusions in the following three propositions:

- the world of the senses is the product of our organization;
- our visible (physical) organs are, like all other parts of the phenomenal world, only images of an unknown object;
- our real organization is therefore as much unknown to us as real external things are. We continually have before us nothing but the product of both (Nietzsche 1996a: 18–19).

Nietzsche concludes from this in turn that Lange gives philosophers a free hand so long as they edify us (since they can neither judge nor be judged concerning the "thing-in-itself"). Art also falls into this category. Nietzsche then construes philosophy as an art with the function of edifying, and concludes that Schopenhauer stands firm, and is the most edifying of philosopher-artists.

However, elsewhere Nietzsche draws out some of Lange's conclusions in a way that is more critical of Schopenhauer. The main thrust of this criticism is an extension of the criticism regarding the possibility of any pronouncements whatever on the thing-in-itself, including construing it as a "negative" of appearances, and of identifying it with the will (Schopenhauer's position). (See e.g. the early unpublished essay "On Schopenhauer", in Ansell-Pearson & Large 2006: 26). Thus, while Lange was a self-professed neo-Kantian, he criticized some of Kant's ideas such as the thing-in-itself, which in turn acted as the basis for Nietzsche's criticisms of Schopenhauer, as well as other philosophers. In fact, Stack remarks, many of Nietzsche's criticisms of other philosophers – such as Plato – seem to be taken in their entirety from Lange (Stack 1983: 2).

Third, Nietzsche's study of Lange stimulated his interest in materialist philosophy in general. It is frequently necessary to explain to beginning students of philosophy the difference between materialism as a philosophical doctrine and the meaning the term has in popular parlance (where it refers to the valuing, typically excessive, of material objects and "the things money can buy"). The philosophical doctrine of materialism is a metaphysical thesis about the nature of reality that asserts that only material things exist. It is traditionally contrasted with idealism: the view that only minds and their products exist. As Brobjer has charted it, Nietzsche's interest in materialism is first manifested in his early (April 1862) unpublished essay "Fate and History", where he writes that "World history is, then, the history of matter" (quoted in Brobjer 2004: 25). During 1861–62, Nietzsche's interest in materialism was primarily influenced by the philosopher Ludwig Feuerbach, and by a journal called *Anregungen für Kunst, Leben und Wissenschaft* (Suggestions for art, life and science), which, as well as discussing artistic and cultural issues such as the music of Wagner, was a forum for materialist philosophy. Lange was a more decisive influence in this regard, however, and Brobjer reports that Nietzsche's notebooks in the years immediately following his discovery of Lange (1867–68) are littered with references to materialist thinkers such as Laplace, Gassendi, La Mettrie, Büchner and Moleschott (Brobjer 2004: 26). Lange also provided a likely impetus for Nietzsche's study of the Presocratic materialist philosopher Democritus in this period, a study that fed into his lecture course *The Pre-Platonic Philosophers* (Nietzsche 2000) and the book that he based on it, *Philosophy in the Tragic Age of the Greeks* (Nietzsche 1996b) (Brobjer 2004: 27).

Finally, it remains to ask the obvious question: was Nietzsche a materialist? As Stack notes, in Nietzsche's work we find both an admiration for, and an insistence on, the importance of scientific materialism, and clear tendencies towards idealism. As with many points, it is tempting to accuse Nietzsche here of contradiction or inconsistency, or of simply changing his mind. But Stack suggests that a reading of Nietzsche in the light of Lange clarifies this issue and provides it with a greater coherence than it may appear to have on a surface reading (Stack 1983: 8). While Lange's work is to a large extent an endorsement of materialism, there is an important further dimension, in which he attempts to reconcile materialism and idealism. Lange acknowledges that while scientific materialism frees us from superstition and works to improve humankind in many respects, a scientific materialist worldview creates a spiritual vacuum by evacuating meaning from the world and human life. In response, he advocates what he calls "the standpoint of the ideal": "a poetic representation of an ideal that is not represented as a metaphysical certainty, but as a goal for the future" (*ibid.*: 5). That is – as Nietzsche's early summary of Lange indicates – Lange preserves a space beyond materialism for art, mythology and philosophy: for "ideals" that have no metaphysical status, but which are necessary to give human life meaning. Lange discusses the necessity of creating a new collective mythology and religion to take the place of religious beliefs founded on erroneous metaphysical ideas, and it is easy to see how these ideas fed into Nietzsche's thought, especially in its early stages, when he saw a rebirth of tragedy in Wagner's music-dramas. Thus Nietzsche, like Lange, often broadly advocates a materialistic viewpoint, but he is also deeply concerned with the problems of value that such a view inculcates, and he tends towards idealism in some of his attempts to address this problem. Summarizing the extent of Lange's influence on Nietzsche, Stack writes that, "The grenade-like explosions of thought we encounter when reading Nietzsche are often detonations of the explosive material that Lange had already provided" (*ibid.*: 8).

Darwinism and the Übermensch

As Moore (2004: 10) notes, Nietzsche's idea that has attracted the most attention within the field of his relation to science has been the *Übermensch* ("superman", "overman" or "overhuman"), in its relation to Darwinism and evolution. Darwin's *On the Origin of Species* appeared in 1859, and his *Descent of Man* in 1871. While evolution was not a new idea, Darwin's work was decisive in refining the theory according to the mechanism of natural selection, and in achieving its widespread acceptance in the scientific community. Darwin's works were also vastly influential with respect to culture and the general public, and Nietzsche's writings were set against the background of widespread interest in, and controversy concerning, Darwinism. Nietzsche appears never to have read Darwin's principal works on evolution, nor those of his principal vocal supporters such as T. H. Huxley or Ernst Haeckel (Brobjer 2004: 23). Nevertheless, he read many secondary texts on Darwinism and evolution, and his thought bears the deep imprint of this influence.

Many commentators have interpreted the *Übermensch* in a Darwinian sense as a further step in the evolutionary path; a new biological species beyond *Homo sapiens*. This view attracted attention as early as 1886, with an interpretation of the *Übermensch* in evolutionary and biological terms appearing in Helene Druskowitz's *Moderne Versuche eines Religionsersatzes: Ein philosophischer Essay* (Moore 2004: 10). Nietzsche's idea of the *Übermensch* was also appropriated by social Darwinists and eugenicists such as Alexander Tille and Maximilian Mügge. However, many commentators have also noted that in so far as Nietzsche's thought concerns evolutionary theory, the ideas of pre-Darwinian evolutionists such as Jean-Baptiste Lamarck (1744–1829) seem to be a more decisive influence. Claire Richter argued this in *Nietzsche et les theories biologiques contemporaines* (1911). A major work on Nietzsche that also contributed to this line of argument was Andler's (1920–31) study, which pointed to the importance for Nietzsche of non-Darwinian evolutionists such as Ludwig Rütimeyer (a colleague of Nietzsche's at Basel), William Rolph, and Wilhelm Roux (Brobjer 2004: 10–11). More recently, one of the most significant contributions to the question of

Niezsche's relation to Darwinism has been Wolfgang Müller-Lauter's "The Organism as Inner Struggle" (1999). Moore's *Nietzsche, Biology and Metaphor* (2002), as Moore himself summarizes the book, extends Müller-Lauter's attempt to trace and contextualize Nietzsche's borrowings from the natural sciences, attempts to provide a definitive account of Nietzsche's understanding of organic change in general and considers the importance of his evolutionary perspective for the development of his moral and aesthetic philosophy (Moore 2004: 11). Ansell-Pearson's *Viroid Life* has also made significant contributions to this issue (some of which have been discussed in the previous chapter). Finally, one of the most important recent engagements with this topic has been Richardson's *Nietzsche's New Darwinism* (2004). Richardson argues that, despite Nietzsche's often hostile overt remarks about Darwin, a deep Darwinian influence can be discerned in his philosophy, an influence manifest through his naturalistic interpretation of values.

Brobjer (2004: 23) simplifies our task of coming to terms with this large body of literature (only the most notable examples of which have been mentioned here) by summarizing it in terms of two major schools of thought on Nietzsche and Darwinism:

- Nietzsche was a Darwinist.
- Nietzsche was an anti-Darwinist.

As Brobjer notes, in a way both these views are correct, and each finds significant supports in Nietzsche's works. The view that Nietzsche was a Darwinist is supported by the apparently evolutionary terms in which the concept of the *Übermensch* is introduced in *Thus Spoke Zarathustra*:

> *I teach you the overman.* Human being is something that must be overcome. What have you done to overcome him?
> All creatures so far created something beyond themselves; and you want to be the ebb of this great flood and would even rather go back to animals than overcome humans?
> What is the ape to a human? A laughing stock or a painful embarrassment.
> You have made your way from worm to human, and much in you is still worm. Once you were apes, and even now a human is still more ape than any ape. (Z "Prologue" 3)

Moreover, Nietzsche emphasizes the importance of physiology and breeding, of struggle and competition, and he seemingly adopts the

Darwinian rejection of the idea that nature is teleological (that is, has a purpose or goal) (Brobjer 2004: 23).

On the other hand, the interpretation of Nietzsche as an anti-Darwinist is supported by explicit criticisms of Darwin and Darwinism (see e.g. TI "Expeditions" 14, "Anti-Darwin"). Nietzsche rejects the idea that self-preservation is the most fundamental drive (a rejection akin to his rejection of Schopenhauer's interpretation of the will as a "will to life"), and rejects the Darwinian thesis of the passive adaptation of an organism to its external environment. In opposition to both these points, he proposes the will to power as an internal creative force. Furthermore, he rejects the idea of *progress* implicit in Darwin's theory (life as producing ever more perfect forms). Most decisive for the anti-Darwinist camp, perhaps, is Nietzsche's apparent disavowal of the Darwinist interpretation of the *Übermensch* in *Ecce Homo* (EH "Books" 1), where he quips about the "learned cattle" who suspect him of Darwinism (Brobjer 2004: 23).

Once again, Nietzsche appears ambiguous. However, in this case both views can be seen as consistent if we consider that Darwinism can be taken (as it often is) as synonymous with evolutionism. In short, Nietzsche was undoubtedly an evolutionist in that he believed that human beings evolved from other forms of animal life. However, he disputed aspects of the specifically Darwinian theory of evolution. Given the amount of attention the topic has received, it is worth noting Nietzsche's relation to Lamarck and the character of his own views on evolution.

Lamarck holds a place of distinction in the history of biology as the thinker who first proposed a full-blown theory of evolution. The idea that organic life had changed over time, rather than having been created in its current form, was extant since the eighteenth century, and evidence for such a view – principally the collection of numerous fossils and the recognition of "vestigal organs" (such as the obsolescent vestiges of legs on sea creatures who never walked on land) – had been steadily mounting for some time, but Lamarck was the first to formulate a coherent theory of evolution as such. It has often been commented that Nietzsche was more Lamarckian than Darwinian because of the way Lamarck understood evolutionary change in terms of the inheritance of *acquired traits*. Before the discovery of genes, it was not known how traits were transmitted from parents to offspring. Lamarck's theory was that traits could be acquired by animals and passed on to their offspring. For example, if a giraffe often stretched its neck to eat high leaves from trees, its neck would grow, and this trait would be passed on to its offspring. After several generations, the inherited trait would achieve significant development. This view seems to accord with Nietzsche's emphasis on the importance of the individual's will to self-enhancement. While we now know that traits acquired by an individual in their lifetime will not be inherited organically by their offspring (since inheritance is transmitted through fixed genetic material), the idea has seemed to many to be resonant with Nietzsche's theory of the *Übermensch* in so far as he urges human beings wilfully to overcome themselves, thus making themselves a "bridge" to a higher type.

Despite the oft-repeated suggestion that Nietzsche was more Lamarckian than Darwinian, however, there is an important sense in which his views about evolution are closer to Darwin than to Lamarck. Lamarck endorsed a teleological and progressive view of evolution in which the process is driven forwards by an "arrow of complexity": organic life forms become increasingly more complex through evolutionary change. While the notion of progress is arguably still implicitly present in Darwin, he explicitly rejected the idea that evolution proceeds towards any goal, or that it necessarily brings about more complex forms of life. While Lamarck did not recognize extinction, Darwin recognized that many lines of evolution are "dead ends", and that the whole process is a blind, mechanical one, without meaning or purpose. This rejection of teleology is strongly endorsed by Nietzsche, so in this sense he is more Darwinian than Lamarckian. (For more on this, see Chapter 6.)

Nietzsche was ultimately far more concerned with the cultural and existential implications of evolution than the details of its biological mechanisms. In the essay "On the Uses and Disadvantages of History for Life", he writes of evolutionary theory that "should these ideas be more widely disseminated, the fabric of society will disintegrate as moral and legal codes lose their binding force" (HL 9; as glossed in Brobjer 2004: 24). So the science of evolution, for Nietzsche, is one of the key discoveries contributing to the general breakdown of the worldview organized around the "highest values posited so far", and designated by the shorthand expression "the death of God". Evolution radically undermines the traditional Christian worldview by providing an explanation for life that makes a creator God obsolescent, and by suggesting that human beings are not special creatures of divine significance, but simply a curious kind of animal. So far as the *Übermensch* is concerned, Nietzsche was far more interested in the production of a "higher type" understood in terms of their will to power and ability to *interpret* the world and *create values* than he was in any notion of the production of a biologically different species. Nevertheless, as we have seen he does employ evolutionary and biological terms to describe the *Übermensch* on occasion, and to what extent these are merely metaphors or something more remains an open question for future research.

The physics of the will to power and the eternal return

In addition to the *Übermensch*, Nietzsche's other two most well-known original ideas, the will to power and the eternal return, have an important relation to science. As we saw in the Introduction, in addition to being a kind of psychological trait or principle of explanation, the will to power is proposed by Nietzsche as a metaphysical and physical theory of reality. In Nietzsche's words:

> My idea is that every specific body strives to become master over all space and to extend its force (– its will to power:) and to thrust back all that resists its extension. But it continually encounters similar efforts on the part of other bodies and ends by coming to an arrangement ("union") with those of them that are sufficiently related to it: thus they then conspire together for power. (WP 636)

At the most fundamental level, these "specific bodies" are quanta of force, and the "inner will" that drives them to extend themselves is the will to power.

Nietzsche's quasi-scientific descriptions of the will to power are based in a critique of mechanistic atomic theory, and influenced by the atomic theory of Roger Boscovich (1711–87). Nietzsche criticizes the mechanistic view of the universe as composed of atoms understood as the tiniest things, existing in a system governed by necessary laws of cause and effect. (This view was the dominant scientific one of the time, and is still influential in some respects today.) In Nietzsche's view, mechanism perpetuates belief in a "true world", and is underpinned by the same anthropic projections and prejudices as traditional metaphysics. He argues that the understanding of atoms as "things" imputes to them a unity not found in any scientific data, which is simply a projection of our own (illusory) sense of ourselves as unified subjects. Furthermore, he argues that motion and the ideas of cause and effect are projections of our perceptions and of our psychological habits of associating impressions, which again have no real justification in the data of science. He then arrives at his "scientific" theory of the will to power by removing these anthropic projections:

If we eliminate these additions, no things remain but only dynamic quanta, in a relation of tension to all other dynamic quanta, in their "effect" upon the same. The will to power not a being, not a becoming, but a *pathos* – the most elemental fact from which a becoming and effecting first emerge –.

(WP 635)

Scholars have noted the influence on this theory of Boscovich, one of modern atomic theory's founding fathers. The first to identify and discuss this influence was Andler, while scholars who have followed up this theme include Anni Anders and Karl Schlechta, George J. Stack, Alistair Moles and Greg Whitlock (Moore 2004: 11). For Boscovich, atoms are not substantial "things", but points of force with mass, but without extension (termed *puncta*). As in Nietzsche's theory of the will to power, it is the relations between the atoms that generate structures and "things". On this view, atoms are not themselves small units of matter, but extensionless (that is to say, they do not "take up space") points of force that interact to produce matter. Nietzsche's view of the will to power is indebted to Boscovich because of the way his extensionless view of atoms eliminates the metaphysical assumptions of mechanism, and accords with Nietzsche's idea of the "will", the inner compulsion that drives these points of force.

KEY POINT *The will to power and atomic theory*
Nietzsche's metaphysical conception of the will to power is indebted to Roger Boscovich's atomic theory. The will to power is composed of multiple "points of force" that seek to expand their power in relation to each other.

The influence of science on Nietzsche's conception of the eternal return is perhaps even more evident. While the idea has a number of different formulations, and can be interpreted simply as a "thought experiment" with existential value (if you live *as if* the eternal return were true, this will positively impact your life), Nietzsche clearly thought it was also a physically accurate description of the universe that could, in principle, be scientifically proved. In fact, Nietzsche calls the eternal return "the most *scientific* of all possible hypotheses" (WP 55). He thought of studying science formally in order to be in a position to formulate such proofs. While he never carried these plans to fruition, unpublished notes collected in *The Will to Power* outline his scientific ideas regarding the eternal return in skeletal form.

As with the will to power, the physical conception of the eternal return proceeds on the basis of a critical rejection of the idea of a mechanistic universe. Nietzsche understands mechanism as implying a final state in which an equilibrium of forces is achieved, whether this equilibrium is understood as a static, unchanging universe, or as a nothingness produced by the degeneration and destruction of everything. He takes this view that mechanism must lead to a final state from the scientist William Thomson (WP 1066), and argues against it as follows. If such a state is possible, given the hypothesis of an infinite time stretching back into the past (which Nietzsche endorses), such a state must already have been achieved. Since it has not been achieved, Nietzsche reasons, it will not and cannot be achieved. Nietzsche takes this as a refutation of the mechanistic conception of the universe in favour of a dynamic one, in which change is constant, and no final state will ever be achieved. The eternal recurrence of all things is then deduced from the further rejection of the idea that the universe may be capable of infinite novelty (and thus never repeat the same states). Nietzsche sees this thesis of infinite novelty as essentially a form of the old, religious way of thinking, in so far as it imputes to the universe the intention and the ability "to control every one of its movements at every moment so as to escape goals, final states, repetitions". For Nietzsche, this implies an "infinite, boundlessly creative God" (WP 1062). Thus, if the universe is capable of only a finite number of states, then given an infinite time, Nietzsche reasons that it must repeat those states an infinite number of times.

Critical attention was given to the scientific status of these reflections early in the twentieth century. In 1907, Georg Simmel's *Schopenhauer and Nietzsche* ([1907] 1991) contained what Walter Kaufmann calls a "very elegant" refutation of Nietzsche's supposedly scientific hypothesis (1968: 327). Kaufmann summarizes Simmel's refutation as follows.

> Even if there were exceedingly few things in a finite space in an infinite time, they would not have to repeat the same configurations. Suppose there were three wheels of equal size, rotating on the same axis, one point marked on the circumference of each wheel, and these three points lined up in one straight line. If the second wheel rotated twice as fast as the first, and if the speed of the third wheel was $1/\pi$ of the speed of the first, the initial line-up would never recur. *(Ibid.)*

The scientific status of Nietzsche's hypothesis was also criticized by Walter Löb (1908). In a brief note Nietzsche invokes the first law of thermodynamics, that of the conservation of energy, as support for eternal return (WP 1063). Löb's study investigates this possibility, and concludes that Nietzsche was mistaken in thinking that thermodynamics provides a basis for eternal return. While Nietzsche may have been wrong, more recently Small has shown that his ideas had a basis in contemporary scientific ideas, such as those of Robert Mayer, Johann Gustav Vogt and Johann Friedrich Zöllner (Small 2001; cited in Moore 2004: 11). Note, also, that these refutations of Nietzsche's scientific musings do not themselves refute the hypothesis of the eternal return as such, but simply the "scientific" *reasons* Nietzsche had for supposing it to be true. It might still be the case that the theory of the eternal return is true, even if Nietzsche's reasons for thinking it true are wrong.

In contemporary cosmology, there are three dominant and competing hypotheses concerning the ultimate fate of the universe: the "big freeze", the "big rip" and the "big crunch". In the "big freeze" scenario, all the heat in the universe will dissipate through the law of entropy, leading to a static and undifferentiated, soup-like state (again, for more on entropy, see Chapter 6). In the "big rip" scenario, the forces driving the expansion of the universe from the point of the Big Bang (which are currently accelerating) exceed the gravitational forces of attraction holding things together, and will eventually tear everything in the universe apart. The "big crunch" is the opposite hypothesis: it posits that gravitational forces will halt the expansion of the universe at some point and everything will begin to contract, ultimately compacting into an infinitely dense point. Some scientists have suggested that this point will then expand outwards once again in another big bang, creating a new universe, and this cycle of expansion and contraction will repeat infinitely. In general, Nietzsche's positing of a universe without beginning or end appears to be out of step with contemporary cosmology, which endorses the idea of a beginning in the Big Bang, and a final state in one of the three forms described. However, the last hypothesis does suggest the possibility of something like the eternal return.

Summary of key points

Naturalism

In general, naturalism seeks to replace all supernatural (that is, mythical or religious) explanations of phenomena with natural explanations. It seeks to make philosophy continuous with the natural sciences (physics, chemistry and so on).

Leiter's methodological naturalism

Leiter identifies various types of naturalism, and identifies Nietzsche as a *methodological* naturalist primarily concerned with *methods continuity*. That is, he is concerned with making philosophy continuous with the methods of the natural sciences.

Leiter opposes the naturalistic reading of Nietzsche to the "postmodern" reading, and defends it from the latter on the following points:

- truth and knowledge;
- scepticism about science;
- scepticism about causation;
- hostility towards materialism; and
- scepticism about human nature and essence.

Cox's interpretive naturalism

In contrast to Leiter, Cox proposes a reading of Nietzsche that combines the naturalistic and postmodern approaches. According to him, Nietzsche's naturalism leads to his emphasis on the ubiquity of interpretation (there are no facts, only interpretations).

- *Epistemology naturalized:* Nietzsche rejects the main traditional theories of knowledge – rationalism, empiricism and transcendental idealism – and adopts a qualified form of empiricism. For him, all our knowledge comes from the senses, but does not access "facts" about the world. Rather, our knowledge claims are only *perspectives*, conditioned by our perceptions and concepts, which have been fashioned under the pressures of evolution. Our knowledge is good for our survival, but that doesn't make it "true".
- *Ontology naturalized:*
  - A naturalization of humanity: Nietzsche seeks to undermine any notion that human beings are divine or exceptional, and positions them as continuous with animals.
  - A de-deification of nature. Nietzsche seeks to remove all traces of a supernatural worldview, including those that he believes remain in scientific theories. His de-deified theory of the world

is given by the will to power and the eternal return: a world without design, purpose or meaning.

Science

Nietzsche's philosophy of science
According to Babich, while Nietzsche did not have a developed "philosophy of science", his views on science can act as a corrective to contemporary philosophy of science. Philosophy of science fails to achieve a significant critical perspective because it has no independent ground from which to reflect on science. Nietzsche provides this independent ground by reflecting on science from the perspectives of art and life.

The significance of science for Nietzsche
- Lange and materialism: Lange provided Nietzsche with much of his knowledge of science, stimulated his interest in materialism, gave him a ground from which to criticize philsosophers and stimulated his thinking on the relation between science and meaning.
- Darwinism and the *Übermensch*: Nietzsche was a Darwinian in so far as he embraced the idea that humans are animals. However, the *Übermensch* is a higher type of human with respect to his or her ability to interpret life and create values, not a new biological species in a Darwinian sense.
- The physics of the will to power and the eternal return:
  - The will to power: influenced by Boscovich's atomic theory, in which atoms are dimensionless "centres of force".
  - The eternal return: extrapolated by Nietzsche from the law of the conservation of energy. Given finite matter and infinite time, all arrangements of matter must repeat infinitely.

Conclusion

If you have read through the preceding chapters of this book, or even just a few of them, you will hopefully have begun to appreciate in how many areas, and in how many varied ways, Nietzsche's influence has been felt. You will perhaps have begun to feel a little at home in the Nietzschean "archipelago", and perhaps you will feel inspired to explore it further. Rather than attempt anything like a summary of the variegated field of Nietzscheanism we have explored here, I would simply like to conclude with an observation concerning Nietzsche's continued relevance, and why I believe the field of Nietzscheanism is likely to continue to expand for a long while to come.

Nietzsche can be seen as a Janus-like figure, presenting us with two faces: one turned towards the ancients, the gods, the rhythms of nature, the sweetening balms of the arts and the encircling lifeworld, which keeps our horizons securely grounded in tradition; one turned to the future, the heavens, the infinite, the inhuman, the excoriating power of reason, technology, science and that which is hardest in human hearts and most uncompromising in human heads. In different phases of his career (most clearly exemplified by the "early" and "middle" periods), one of these faces showed itself almost to the exclusion of the other. Yet perhaps what is most distinctive about Nietzsche is that he possessed, and he presents us with, both faces. Moreover, from the first, Nietzsche tries to reconcile, balance or somehow come to terms with both of these sides within himself, from the meaning of tragedy as an ideal combination of the Apollonian and Dionysian aesthetics in *The Birth of Tragedy*, to the "bicammeral system of culture" (both art and science) in *Human, All Too Human*, to the nuanced and synthetic approach of the late writings.

These two sides within Nietzsche reflect the two sides of the great cultural conflict with which he tried to come to terms, and which constitutes the problem of nihilism: the eclipse of the traditional, mythic, religious and artistic worldview by the scientific, rationalist, demythologizing one. This is one meaning of Nietzsche's claim that he is "the first perfect nihilist of Europe, who, however, has even now lived through the whole of nihilism, to the end, leaving it behind, outside himself" (WP "Preface" 3). For in a very real sense, our contemporary nihilist predicament is precisely this: how to embrace the "positivist", scientific side of our culture, which seems inexorably to be advancing, without entirely losing sight of what makes our lives not only bearable, but meaningful, which was previously the province of mythic and religious culture: to know how to find meaning within the new horizons opened up, out on Nietzsche's "new seas" (see Gillespie & Strong 1988).

Despite all the faults, limitations and dangers in Nietzsche's work, one main reason he continues to be read, and will very probably continue to be read for a long time to come, is because he has bestowed to us the testimony of a powerful mind who tried to think through this confrontation of the "religious" and the "scientific" worldviews, a confrontation with which we continue to grapple in many ways today. (And as Nietzsche instructs us, aspects of the religious worldview are often still operative in our ways of thinking, even when we think we have explicitly rejected it.) Certainly Nietzsche did not think all of the problems that remain to be thought; certainly his works contain many dead ends and infertile ciphers. And yet, Nietzsche thought more deeply about many of these issues than anyone before or since, and his works – despite more than a century of interpretation – remain a labyrinth to be explored and mined. Many of Nietzsche's prophetic notions seem to be playing out in our own age, and others, which he did not specifically envisage, are undermining our fundamental concepts and values in ways to which his work seems to speak: the generalized reduction of all value to economic value in a globalized economic system; the evacuation of religion from the state and the religious fundamentalist backlash; the changing fabric of social life brought about by the increasingly mediatized nature of our personal interactions; the alteration of the relations between knowledge and culture brought about by the information and computing revolution; and the calling into question of fundamental, received notions about what it means to be human through the development of biotechnologies such as cloning. As the horizons of our world continue to shift, Nietzsche continues to stand as a key intellectual figure: he is one of the most significant thinkers since the Enlightenment, who remains an indispensable companion as we navigate our continuously unfolding, contemporary situation.

Chronologies

Nietzsche's life and work

15 October 1844	Friedrich Wilhelm Nietzsche born in Röcken, Saxony. Father Karl Ludwig Nietzsche; mother Franziska Nietzsche.
1846	Sister Elisabeth born.
1848	Brother Joseph born. Nietzsche's father dies. Joseph dies. Family moves to Naumburg
1858	Attends the prestigious grammar school Pforta.
1864	Graduates from Pforta; begins studies in theology at the University of Bonn.
1865	Transfers to Leipzig and studies philology under Ritschl. Discovers Schopenhauer. Reads Lange's *History of Materialism*.
1867–68	Military service in Naumburg, until discharged due to a riding accident.
1868	Meets Wagner.
1869	At the recommendation of Ritschl, Nietzsche is appointed Extraordinary Professor of Classical Philology at Basel University (aged 24). Awarded a doctorate without examination. Frequently visits the Wagners at Tribschen.
1870	Two weeks' service as medical orderly in the Franco-Prussian war; discharged after contracting dysentery and diphtheria. Beginning of friendship with theologian Overbeck. *The Birth of Tragedy* *Untimely Meditations*

1875	Meets Gast, who becomes his disciple and secretary.
1876	Attends Bayreuth Festival but leaves early. Beginning of break with Wagner.
	Beginning of friendship with Rée.
1878	Break with Wagner definitive.
1878–80	*Human, All-Too-Human*
1879	Resigns position at Basel owing to declining health. Starts to live in boarding houses in Switzerland and Italy.
1881	*Daybreak*
6 August	"Revelation" of the eternal return near the Surlej boulder on the shores of Lake Silvaplana at Sils-Maria, in the Upper Engadine mountains of Switzerland.
	The Gay Science
	Meets Salomé; proposes marriage to her and is declined.
1883	Richard Wagner dies.
	Thus Spoke Zarathustra
1886	*Beyond Good and Evil*
	Prefaces for second editions of *The Birth of Tragedy, Human, All-Too-Human*.
	On the Genealogy of Morality
	Prefaces for second editions of *Daybreak, The Gay Science, Thus Spoke Zarathustra*.
	In Turin. Writes *The Case of Wagner, Dionysian Dithyrambs, The Twilight of the Idols, The Anti-Christ, Ecce Homo*, and *Nietzsche contra Wagner* (each published separately between 1889 and 1908).
	Mental breakdown. Admitted to a psychiatric clinic at the University of Jena.
	Cared for by his mother in Naumburg.
	The Will to Power
1897	Nietzsche's mother dies. He is taken to Weimar by his sister.
25 August 1900	Nietzsche dies in Weimar.

Nietzsche reception

1888	Brandes gives the first lectures on Nietzsche's work, in Copenhagen.
1892	Beginning of publication of the first collected edition of Nietzsche's works, the *Grossoktavausgabe*.
1893	Nordau, *Degeneration*.
1894	Elisabeth Nietzsche founds the Nietzsche Archive in Naumburg.
	Salomé, *Nietzsche*

1896　Elisabeth moves the Nietzsche Archive to Weimar.

1907　Simmel, *Schopenhauer and Nietzsche*

1918　Bertram, *Nietzsche: Attempt at a Mythology*

1920–31　Andler, *Nietzsche: His Life and His Thought*

1926　Klages, *The Psychological Achievements of Friedrich Nietzsche*

1931　Baeumler, *Nietzsche: Philosopher and Politician*

1934　Spengler, *The Decline of the West*

1935　Löwith, *Nietzsche's Philosophy of the Eternal Recurrence of the Same*

1936　Jaspers, *Nietzsche: An Introduction to the Understanding of his Philosophical Activity*

1936–41　Heidegger's lectures on Nietzsche at the University of Freiburg.

1944　Bataille, *On Nietzsche*

1950　Kaufmann, *Nietzsche: Philosopher, Psychologist, Antichrist*

1954　Schlechta, *Nietzsche's Great Noontide*

1954–56　Schlechta's edition of Nietzsche's complete works, *Werke in drei Bänden* (*Works in Three Volumes*)

1956　Lukács, *The Destruction of Reason*
　　　Wolff, *Friedrich Nietzsche: The Way to Nothingness*

1960　Fink, *Nietzsche's Philosophy*

1961　Heidegger, *Nietzsche* (lectures from 1930s, in 4 vols)

1962　Deleuze, *Nietzsche and Philosophy*

1964　Royaumont Colloquium on Nietzsche.

1965　Danto, *Nietzsche as Philosopher*

1966　Granier, *The Problem of Truth in the Philosophy of Nietzsche*

1967　Beginning of publication of the Colli-Montinari edition of Nietzsche's complete works.

1969　Klossowski, *Nietzsche and the Vicious Circle*

1971　Müller-Lauter, *Nietzsche: His Philosophy of Contradictions and the Contradictions of His Philosophy*

1972　*Nietzsche aujourd'hui* conference at Cerisy-la-Salle.
　　　The journal *Nietzsche Studien* founded.
　　　Kofman, *Nietzsche and Metaphor*

1978　Derrida, *Spurs: Nietzsche's Styles*

1980　North American Nietzsche Society founded.
　　　Irigaray, *Marine Lover: Of Friedrich Nietzsche*

1985　Nehamas, *Nietzsche: Life as Literature*

Questions for discussion and revision

one Nietzscheanism and existentialism

1. What are the main points that characterize existentialism?
2. How is existentialism connected with life-philosophy and value-theory?
3. Explain what Jaspers thinks is the "use" of Nietzsche's philosophical activity.
4. How does Nietzsche believe we can create ourselves?
5. What do Sartre's existentialism and Nietzsche's philosophy have in common?
6. What is absurdity, and what does Camus' response to it owe to Nietzsche?
7. Why does Camus criticize Nietzsche in *The Rebel*?
8. On what points does Kaufmann think Nietzsche can be characterized as an existentialist?
9. Summarize the basic points of Heidegger's philosophical project.
10. Why does Heidegger characterize Nietzsche as "the last metaphysician"?
11. Taking the entire chapter into account, on what points can Nietzsche be characterized as an existentialist?

two Nietzscheanism and poststructuralism

1. What is "poststructuralism"?
2. Why was Nietzsche such a pivotal reference for the poststructuralists?
3. Summarize the important points on which Bataille's and Klossowski's readings of Nietzsche influenced the poststructuralists.
4. How does Deleuze understand the will to power? How does he understand the eternal return?
5. What is Deleuze's "logic of difference", and how does it differ from a logic of opposition?
6. What was Foucault's project? How was it influenced by Nietzsche?

7. For Foucault, what is the difference between semiology and hermeneutics? Which approach to interpretation does Foucault see in Nietzsche?
8. What is "différance"? How is this idea influenced by Nietzsche?
9. How can Derrida's reading of Nietzsche be seen as an alternative to Heidegger's reading (see Chapter 1)?
10. Summarize the reasons why some recent French philosophers have turned away from and criticized Nietzscheanism.

three Nietzscheanism and politics

1. What political events of Nietzsche's time can be seen as influencing his political views?
2. Outline some of the interpretations of Nietzsche that made his work ripe for co-optation by National Socialism.
3. What are the key points that make Nietzsche's views incompatible with National Socialism?
4. What is at stake in the question of whether or not Nietzsche was a political thinker?
5. Explain why Nietzsche endorses aristocratism, and criticizes socialism.
6. How can Nietzsche's thought be made compatible with liberalism?
7. Can Nietzsche's work be used to support democracy? Explain both sides of the debate.
8. How did Klossowski's reading of Nietzsche help the poststructuralists to develop a new understanding of "the political"?
9. Why do Lukács and Habermas criticize Nietzsche?
10. According to Adorno and Horkheimer, what aspects of Nietzsche's work make him useful for critical theory?

four Nietzscheanism and feminism

1. In what ways has Nietzsche been thought of as expressing misogynistic views?
2. Why did Nietzsche oppose women's liberation?
3. What were some of the main points of difference between varieties of early Nietzschean feminism?
4. Contrast the figures of Circe and Baubô in Kofman's reading of Nietzsche. What do each mean in relation to truth and perspectivism?
5. According to Kofman, what positive image of woman can be found in Nietzsche's texts?
6. According to Irigaray, how have women been excluded from the Western tradition of thought?
7. On what points does Irigaray accuse Nietzsche of masculine bias?
8. How does Irigaray see Nietzsche as contributing to the feminist cause?
9. What are the two ways of understanding textuality (reading and writing) that Oliver discerns?

10. In what ways does Oliver believe Nietzsche continues to exclude the feminine from a position in philosophy?

five Nietzscheanism and theology

1. Why is Nietzsche so vehemently opposed to Christianity?
2. How is it that some theologians have managed to find value in Nietzsche's thought?
3. In what way can theology be "existential"?
4. Explain the key features of Buber's "Nietzionism".
5. Why does the early Barth see Nietzsche as an ally?
6. Explain how it is that Tillich believes God survives even "the death of God".
7. What distinguishes the radical theologians' understanding of "the death of God" from that of the existential theologians?
8. According to Altizer, what is the importance of Nietzsche?
9. How does Vattimo manage to reconcile his Nietzscheanism with his Christianity?
10. How does the recent "theological turn" in continental philosophy challenge Nietzsche's interpretation of the Christian legacy?

six Nietzscheanism and posthumanism

1. What are the main types of posthumanism?
2. Explain "transhumanism".
3. Why does Sorgner see Nietzsche as a forerunner to transhumanism?
4. Summarize Ansell-Pearson's main criticisms of "popular" transhumanism.
5. How does Ansell-Pearson think the transhuman condition *should* be understood?
6. Explain "antihumanism".
7. What does Foucault mean by "the end of man"?
8. Why does Nietzsche criticize humanism?

seven Nietzscheanism, naturalism and science

1. Explain "naturalism".
2. According to Leiter, what are the main types of naturalism? What kind of naturalist is Nietzsche?
3. Explain the contrast, on Leiter's view, between the naturalistic and postmodern interpretations of Nietzsche.
4. How does Cox reconcile Nietzsche's naturalism with his emphasis on interpretation?
5. According to Cox, how does Nietzsche naturalize ontology?

6. How does Babich believe Nietzsche's views on science can contribute to contemporary philosophy of science?
7. Explain Lange's significance for Nietzsche.
8. In what sense was Nietzsche a Darwinist? In what sense was he an "anti-Darwinist"?
9. Explain the role of physics in Nietzsche's idea of the will to power.
10. Explain the role of physics in Nietzsche's idea of the eternal return.

Further reading

Full bibliographical details appear in the Bibliography.

Nietzsche

Reading Nietzsche's own writings is, of course, absolutely indispensable in coming to terms with his thought. The standard edition of the complete works in Nietzsche's original German is the *Kritische Gesamtausgabe: Werke* (Colli & Montinari 1967–). In the case of most of Nietzsche's books, there are several English translations to choose from. The first, and to date only full English translation of his complete works (Levy 1909–13), is now considered unreliable and is generally avoided. A translation of the complete works based on a shorter version of the Colli and Montinari edition is currently underway, but so far only three volumes of the projected twenty have appeared (Magnus *et al.* 1995–). Cambridge University Press has recently published good critical editions of all Nietzsche's major works (it is these editions that I have generally referenced throughout this book; bibliographic details can be found in the Abbreviations). Penguin also publishes inexpensive editions of most of Nietzsche's major works, many in classic translations by Kaufmann and R. J. Hollingdale.

There are also several popular collections of selected works by Nietzsche. Kaufmann's *The Portable Nietzsche* (1977) contains several full-length books and a selection of letters, while his *Basic Writings of Nietzsche* (1968) contains several further complete books. Hollingdale's *A Nietzsche Reader* (1977) contains thematically organized selections for works Nietzsche published (nothing from the *Nachlass* is included). Ansell-Pearson and Duncan Large's *The Nietzsche Reader* (2006) contains a wide selection, including many early unpublished writings, as well as an excellent commentary.

Many short introductions to Nietzsche's thought are also available, of which I shall mention two as particularly recommended. Ansell-Pearson's *How to Read Nietzsche*

(2006a) brings to bear the author's vast scholarly knowledge on the topic, but is short, engaging and accessible to the reader new to Nietzsche. Vattimo's *Nietzsche: An Introduction* (2001) is a good introductory overview of Nietzsche's thought that contains a useful overview of the history of Nietzsche reception. Several biographies of Nietzsche are also available, which also serve as introductions to his thought. The classic in English is Hollingdale's *Nietzsche: The Man and His Philosophy* (1999). More recent biographies are Ronald Hayman's *Nietzsche: A Critical Life* (1980), Safranski's *Nietzsche: A Philosophical Biography* (2003), and Julian Young's similarly-titled *Friedrich Nietzsche: A Philosophical Biography* (2010). Safranski's book is a particularly good introduction to Nietzsche's thought, focusing more on his philosophical development than the events of his life, and drawing on recent research.

History of Nietzsche's reception and influence

For a relatively condensed overview of the international history of Nietzsche reception, see the appendix to Vattimo's *Nietzsche: An Introduction* (2001). Ernst Behler provides a brief overview of the reception of "Nietzsche in the Twentieth Century" (1996). Another condensed overview of Nietzsche's reception, but one that restricts itself to treatments of the eternal return, is Löwith's "On the History of the Interpretation of Nietzsche (1894–1954)", in *Nietzsche's Philosophy of the Eternal Recurrence of the Same* (1997). For a more comprehensive study, with separate sections devoted to different international regions, see Diethe's *Historical Dictionary of Nietzscheanism* (2006). There have been several monographs charting the history of Nietzsche's reception in specific countries. On Nietzsche in Germany, see Steven E. Aschheim's *The Nietzsche Legacy in Germany 1890–1990* (1992). On Nietzsche in France, see Douglas Smith's *Transvaluations* (1996).

Existentialism

There are many introductions to, and overviews of, existentialism available. A relatively recent introduction that has attained the status of a classic is David E. Cooper's *Existentialism* (1999). Also useful in discussing Nietzsche's place in relation to existentialism are the introduction in Kaufmann's *Existentialism from Dostoevsky to Sartre* (1975), Macquarrie's *Existentialism* (1972), Nathan Oaklander's *Existentialist Philosophy* (1992) and Steven Crowell's entry on existentialism for the *Stanford Encyclopedia of Philosophy* (2010). For a comprehensive contemporary survey, see *The Continuum Companion to Existentialism* (Reynolds *et al.* 2011).

Jaspers's most important work on Nietzsche is his *Nietzsche: An Introduction to the Understanding of His Philosophical Activity* (1965). On the question of the relationship between Sartre and Nietzsche, see Daigle's "Sartre and Nietzsche" (2004). Camus' most sustained critical discussion of Nietzsche is to be found in the section "Absolute Affirmation" in *The Rebel* (1971). For a discussion of Camus' relationship to Nietzsche, see Duvall's "Camus Reading Nietzsche" (1999). Kaufmann's major work on Nietzsche is his *Nietzsche: Philosopher, Psychologist, Antichrist* (1974). For

Kaufmann on Nietzsche's relation to existentialism, see also the introduction in *Existentialism from Dostoevsky to Sartre* (1975) and the essay "Nietzsche and Existentialism" in *Existentialism, Religion and Death* (1976).

Heidegger references or discusses Nietzsche in many places, but his most sustained study is the four volumes of lectures (also published in English translation in a two-volume edition), *Nietzsche* (Heidegger 1979–87). Concise summaries of many of the important themes of Heidegger's reading of Nietzsche are contained in the essays "The Word of Nietzsche: God is Dead", in *The Question Concerning Technology and Other Essays* (1977) and "Who is Nietzsche's Zarathustra?", in *Nietzsche* II (1984). For a clear, critical discussion of Heidegger's interpretation of Nietzsche, see Schrift's *Nietzsche and the Question of Interpretation* (1990).

Poststructuralism

For a general introduction to poststructuralism, see James Williams's *Understanding Poststructuralism* (2005). The best outline of Nietzsche's relation to poststructuralism is Schrift's *Nietzsche's French Legacy* (1995). This book devotes chapters to Derrida, Foucault, Deleuze and Cixous, and also discusses Lyotard and the anti-Nietzscheanism of Ferry, Renaut and Descombes. Schrift's *Nietzsche and the Question of Interpretation* (1990) also contains useful sections on Foucault's and Derrida's interpretations of Nietzsche. On the history of Nietzsche's reception in France, see Smith's *Transvaluations* (1996). For a selection of interpretations broadly associated with poststructuralism, and the Nietzsche interpretations in vogue in Europe in the 1960s and 1970s, see the edited collection *The New Nietzsche* (Allison 1985). I have explored Nietzsche's influence on two poststructuralist thinkers not dealt with in these pages, Lyotard and Baudrillard, in my book *Nihilism in Postmodernity* (Woodward 2009).

Politics

Nietzsche's writings relevant to politics are collected in *Political Writings of Friedrich Nietzsche* (Nietzsche 2008), which includes a very useful introduction outlining Nietzsche's political context (Cameron & Dombowsky 2008). Ansell-Pearson's *An Introduction to Nietzsche as Political Thinker* (1994), which I have referenced frequently in Chapter 3, is a good starting-point for further research (although there have been many new developments in the area since it was written). Other general treatments of the topic include Conway's *Nietzsche and the Political* (1997b) and Mark Warren's *Nietzsche and Political Thought* (1988). Strong's *Friedrich Nietzsche and the Politics of Transfiguration* (2000) is a classic that sparked contemporary interest in Nietzsche and politics. Useful articles may by found in the edited collections *Nietzsche, Power and Politics* (Siemens & Roodt 2008) and *Nietzsche, Feminism and Political Theory* (Patton 1993).

For explorations of the darker side of Nietzsche's politics, see the collection *Nietzsche, Godfather of Fascism?* (Golomb & Wistrich 2002). The case for Nietzsche being an "unpolitical" thinker is made by Kaufmann (1974) and Leiter (2010). On Nietzsche's aristocratism, see Detwiler's *Nietzsche and the Politics of Aristocratic Radicalism* (1990). Nietzsche's relation to liberalism is discussed in Connolly's *Political Theory and Modernity* (1993) and Owen's *Nietzsche, Politics, and Modernity* (1995). For the debated issue of Nietzsche's relation to democracy, see Hatab's *A Nietzschean Defense of Democracy* (1995) and Appel's *Nietzsche contra Democracy* (1999). Klossowski's reading of Nietzsche's politics can be found in "The Vicious Circle as a Selective Doctrine", in *Nietzsche and the Vicious Circle* (2005: ch. 6) and in his paper "Circulus Vitiosus" (2009). A good example of the creative way in which Nietzsche's politics were developed by the French is Lyotard's paper "Notes on the Return and Kapital" (1978). Lukács's highly critical reading of Nietzsche is to be found in his *The Destruction of Reason* (1980). On Habermas and Nietzsche, see the edited collection *Habermas, Nietzsche, and Critical Theory* (Babich 2004), and on Adorno and Nietzsche, see Karin Bauer *Adorno's Nietzschean Narratives* (1999).

Feminism

For a general introduction to feminism, see Peta Bowden and Jane Mummery's *Understanding Feminism* (2009). There are several very useful collections of essays on Nietzsche and feminist issues. These are *Nietzsche, Feminism and Political Theory* (Patton 1993), *Nietzsche and the Feminine* (Burgard 1994) and *Feminist Interpretations of Friedrich Nietzsche* (Oliver & Pearsall 1998a).

Aschheim's *The Nietzsche Legacy in Germany* has some useful sections on early German Nietzschean feminism (1992: 60–63, 85–93). R. Hinton Thomas's *Nietzsche in German Politics and Society, 1890–1918* (1983) contains a chapter on this topic. Diethe's *Historical Dictionary of Nietzscheanism* (2006) contains many useful entries on early Nietzschean feminists, while her *Nietzsche's Women* (1996) deals with the women in Nietzsche's life.

The key text by Kofman's discussed here is "Baubô: Theological Perversion and Fetishism" (1998). While she has written much on Nietzsche, her other text that has been influential in anglophone scholarship is *Nietzsche and Metaphor* (1993). Irigaray's major text on Nietzsche is *Marine Lover of Friedrich Nietzsche* (1991). Her earlier study *Speculum of the Other Woman* (1985) contains a more critical reading of Nietzsche's eternal return. A further text, "Ecce Mulier? Fragments" (1994), is a parody of Nietzsche's *Ecce Homo*. Oliver's main text discussed here is *Womanizing Nietzsche* (1995). For another important study by a contemporary anglophone scholar, see Oppel's *Nietzsche on Gender* (2005).

Theology

For an analysis of Nietzsche's views on religion in general, see Young's *Nietzsche's Philosophy of Religion* (2006). Christianity is defended from Nietzsche's attack in David Bentley Hart's *The Beauty of the Infinite* (2003) and Stephen N. Williams's *The Shadow of the Antichrist* (2006). For further perspectives on Nietzsche and theological issues, see the edited collection *Studies in Nietzsche and the Judaeo-Christian Tradition* (O'Flaherty *et al.* 1985), Tyler T. Roberts's *Contesting Spirit* (1998) and Fraser's *Redeeming Nietzsche* (2002).

Golomb's *Nietzsche and Zion* (2004) is the major study of the influence of Nietzsche on Buber and other early Zionists. The edited collection *Nietzsche and the Gods* (Santaniello 2001) contains Tillich's "The Escape from God" and an essay on Buber and Nietzsche. A good introduction to radical theology is Hamilton and Altizer's *Radical Theology and the Death of God* (1966). For further on Altizer's views, see his *The Gospel of Christian Atheism* (1966). For further reading see Vahanian's *The Death of God* (1961) and, for a variety of historical views influencing radical theology (including those of Blake, Hegel, Kierkegaard, Nietzsche, Barth and Tillich), the edited collection *Toward a New Christianity: Readings in the Death of God* (Altizer 1967).

Vattimo's primary work discussed here is his initial statement of his rediscovery of Christianity, *Belief* (1999). His most theoretical work in this vein is his *After Christianity* (2002). See also Vattimo and Caputo's *After the Death of God* (2007), Vattimo and Girard's *Christianity, Truth, and Weakening Faith* (2010) and Vattimo and Rorty's *The Future of Religion* (2005). For Caputo's version of weak theology, see his book *The Weakness of God* (2006), as well as his contributions to *After the Death of God* (Vattimo & Caputo 2007). On the recent interest in Paul in continental philosophy, see the edited anthologies *St Paul Among the Philosophers* (Caputo & Alcoff 2009), and *Paul, Philosophy, and the Theopolitical Vision* (Harink 2010).

Posthumanism

For a collection of texts that gives a general overview of posthumanism, see *Posthumanism* (Badmington 2000). For a lively and humorous introduction to transhumanism, see Regis's *Great Mambo Chicken and the Transhuman Condition* (1990). Frank Theys's documentary *Technocalyps* (2006) is also a useful introduction. For more in-depth information about transhumanism, see the articles on the websites of Nick Bostrom (www.nickbostrom.com) and Max More (www.maxmore.com). The debate regarding Nietzsche and transhumanism mentioned in Chapter 6 can be accessed in the *Journal of Evolution & Technology* 21(2) (http://jetpress.org [accessed August 2011]). For Ansell-Pearson's views on Nietzsche and transhumanism, see his *Viroid Life* (1997). Foucault's thesis on "the end of man" can be found in *The Order of Things* (1994). For an analysis of Nietzsche's influence on Foucault's thesis, see Schrift's *Nietzsche and the Question of Interpretation* (1990: 78–81).

Naturalism and science

On Nietzsche as a naturalist, see the edited collection *Nietzsche* (Leiter & Richardson 2001). For an alternative perspective, see Cox's *Nietzsche: Naturalism and Interpretation* (1999). Although not discussed directly in this book, Richard Schracht and Maudemarie Clark have also presented influential naturalistic interpretations of Nietzsche. See in particular Richard Schacht's "Nietzsche's *Gay Science*, or, How to Naturalize Cheerfully" (1988), and Clark's *Nietzsche on Truth and Philosophy* (1990). For the application of naturalism in specific areas of Nietzsche's thought, see Maudemarie Clark and David Dudrick's "The Naturalisms of *Beyond Good and Evil*", Christa Davis Acampora's "Naturalism and Nietzsche's Moral Psychology" and Christopher Janaway's "Naturalism and Geneaology", all in the edited collection *A Companion to Nietzsche* (Ansell-Pearson 2006b).

For an overview of Nietzsche's relation to science, see the edited collection *Nietzsche and Science* (Moore & Brobjer 2004), especially Brobjer's chapter, "Nietzsche's Reading and Knowledge of Natural Science: An Overview" (2004). For a more extensive examination of the influence of current science on Nietzsche's thinking, see Small's *Nietzsche in Context* (Small 2001).

For a broad coverage of many themes regarding Nietzsche's relation to science, see the edited volumes *Nietzsche, Theories of Knowledge, and Critical Theory: Nietzsche and the Sciences I* (Babich & Cohen 1999a) and *Nietzsche, Epistemology, and Philosophy of Science: Nietzsche and the Sciences II* (Babich & Cohen 1999b). Babich's main work on Nietzsche's usefulness to philosophy of science is *Nietzsche's Philosophy of Science* (1994).

Finally, for general indication of recent trends in Nietzsche scholarship, see the edited collections *A Companion to Nietzsche* (Ansell-Pearson 2006b) and *The Oxford Handbook of Nietzsche* (Gemes & Richardson forthcoming).

Bibliography

Acampora, C. D. 2006. "Naturalism and Nietzsche's Moral Psychology". See Ansell-Pearson (2006b), 314–33.

Adorno, T. W. 1978. *Minima Moralia: Reflections from Damaged Life*. London: Verso.

Adorno, T. W. & Max Horkheimer [1944] 1997. *Dialectic of Enlightenment*, J. Cumming (trans.). London and New York: Verso.

Agamben, G. 2005. *The Time That Remains: A Commentary on the Letter to the Romans*, P. Dailey (trans.). Stanford, CA: Stanford University Press.

Allison, D. B. 1985. *The New Nietzsche: Contemporary Styles of Interpretation*. Cambridge, MA: MIT Press.

Altizer, T. J. J. 1966. *The Gospel of Christian Atheism*. Philadelphia, PA: Westminster Press.

Altizer, T. J. J. (ed.) 1967. *Toward a New Christianity: Readings in the Death of God*. New York: Harcourt, Brace & World.

Andler, C. 1920–31. *Nietzsche, sa vie et sa pensée* [Nietzsche, his life and his thought], 6 vols. Paris: Bossard.

Ansell-Pearson, K. 1991. *Nietzsche* contra *Rousseau: A Study of Nietzsche's Moral and Political Thought*. Cambridge: Cambridge University Press.

Ansell-Pearson, K. 1994. *An Introduction to Nietzsche as Political Thinker: The Perfect Nihilist*. Cambridge: Cambridge University Press.

Ansell-Pearson, K. 1997. *Viroid Life: Perspectives on Nietzsche and the Transhuman Condition*. London: Routledge.

Ansell-Pearson, K. 2006a. *How to Read Nietzsche*. London: Granta.

Ansell-Pearson, K. (ed.) 2006b. *A Companion to Nietzsche*. Oxford: Blackwell.

Ansell-Pearson, K. 2009. Review of Ernst Bertram, *Nietzsche: Attempt at a Mythology*. *Journal of Nietzsche Studies* **38**.

Ansell-Pearson, K. 2011. "New Directions in Research: Nietzsche". In *The Continuum Companion to Existentialism*, J. Reynolds, F. Joseph & A. Woodward (eds). London: Continuum.

Ansell-Pearson, K. & D. Large (eds) 2006. *The Nietzsche Reader*. Oxford: Blackwell.

Antiseri, D. 1996. *The Weak Thought and its Strength*. Aldershot: Avebury.
Appel, F. 1999. *Nietzsche contra Democracy*. Ithaca, NY: Cornell University Press.
Aschheim, S. E. 1992. *The Nietzsche Legacy in Germany 1890–1990*. Berkeley, CA: University of California Press.
Assoun, P.-L. 2006. *Freud and Nietzsche*, Richard L. Collier (trans.). London: Continuum.
Babich, B. E. 1994. *Nietzsche's Philosophy of Science: Reflecting Science on the Ground of Art and Life*. Albany, NY: SUNY Press.
Babich, B. E. (ed.) 2004. *Habermas, Nietzsche, and Critical Theory*. Amherst, NY: Humanity Books.
Babich, B. E. & R. S. Cohen (eds) 1999a. *Nietzsche, Theories of Knowledge, and Critical Theory: Nietzsche and the Sciences I*. Dordrecht: Kluwer.
Babich, B. E. & R. S. Cohen (eds) 1999b. *Nietzsche, Epistemology, and Philosophy of Science: Nietzsche and the Sciences II*. Dordrecht: Kluwer.
Badiou, A. 2003. *Saint Paul: The Foundation of Universalism*, R. Brassier (trans.). Stanford, CA: Stanford University Press.
Badmington, N. (ed.) 2000. *Posthumanism*. New York: St Martin's Press.
Baeumler, A. 1932. *Nietzsche, der Philosoph und Politiker*. Leipzig: Reclam.
Barth, K. [1922] 1968. *The Epistle to the Romans*, 6th edn, E. C. Hoskyns (trans.). Oxford: Oxford University Press.
Barth, K. [1927] 2010. *Church Dogmatics*. Peabody, MA: Hendrickson.
Barthes, R. 1972. "The Structuralist Activity". In *Critical Essays*, R. Howard (trans.), 213–20. Evanston, IL: Northwestern University Press.
Bataille, G. 1988. *The Accursed Share: An Essay on General Economy*, vol. 1, R. Hurley (trans.). New York: Zone Books.
Bataille, G. 1989. *My Mother; Madame Edwarda; and, The Dead Man*, A. Wainhouse (trans.). London: Marion Boyars.
Bataille, G. [1945] 2004. *On Nietzsche*, B. Boone (trans.). London: Continuum.
Baudrillard, J. 2003. *The Spirit of Terrorism and Other Essays*, C. Turner (trans.). London: Verso.
Bauer, K. 1999. *Adorno's Nietzschean Narratives*. Albany, NY: SUNY Press.
Beam, C. 1998. "Sartre vs. Nietzsche: Will to Power, Platonism, and Pessimism". http://www.pengkolan.net/ngelmu/filsafat/index.php?nomor=27
Behler, E. 1996. "Nietzsche in the Twentieth Century". In *The Cambridge Companion to Nietzsche*, B. Magnus & K. M. Higgins (eds), 281–322. Cambridge: Cambridge University Press.
Bertram, E. [1918] 2009. *Nietzsche: Attempt at a Mythology*, R. E. Norton (trans.). Champaign, IL: University of Illinois Press.
Best, S. & D. Kellner 1997. *The Postmodern Turn*. New York: Guilford Press.
Blanchot, M. [1988] 2006. *The Unavowable Community*. Barrytown, NY: Station Hill Press.
Bostrom, N. 2001. "Transhumanist Values" (version of 18 April 2001). www.nickbostrom.com/tra/values.html (accessed August 2011).
Bostrom, N. 2005. "Transhumanist Values". *Review of Contemporary Philosophy* **4**. www.nickbostrom.com/ethics/values.pdf (accessed August 2011).
Bowden, P. & J. Mummery 2009. *Understanding Feminism*. Chesham: Acumen.
Brandes, G. 1914. *Friedrich Nietzsche*. London: Heinemann.
Brinton, C. 1941. *Nietzsche*. Cambridge, MA: Harvard University Press.
Brobjer, T. H. 2004. "Nietzsche's Reading and Knowledge of Natural Science: An Over-

view". In *Nietzsche and Science*, G. Moore & T. H. Brobjer (eds), 21–50. Aldershot: Ashgate.

Buber, M. 1900. "Ein Wort über Nietzsche und die Lebenswerte" [A word on Nietzsche and life values]. *Die Kunst im Leben* 1(2): 13.

Buber, M. [1923] 1970. *I and Thou*, W. Kaufmann (trans.). New York: Charles Scribner's Sons.

Burgard, P. J. (ed.) 1994. *Nietzsche and the Feminine*. Charlottesville, VA: University Press of Virginia.

Cameron, F. & D. Dombowsky 2008. "Introduction". In F. Nietzsche, *Political Writings of Friedrich Nietzsche*, F. Cameron & D. Dombowsky (eds). Basingstoke: Palgrave Macmillan.

Camus, A. [1951] 1971. *The Rebel*, A. Bower (trans.). Harmondsworth: Penguin.

Camus, A. [1942] 2000. *The Myth of Sisyphus*, J. O'Brien (trans.). Harmondsworth: Penguin.

Caputo, John D. 2006. *The Weakness of God: A Theology of the Event*. Bloomington, IN: Indiana University Press.

Caputo, J. D. & L. M. Alcoff (eds) 2009. *St Paul Among the Philosophers*. Bloomington, IN: Indiana University Press.

Clark, M. 1990. *Nietzsche on Truth and Philosophy*. Cambridge: Cambridge University Press.

Clark, M. & D. Dudrick 2006. "The Naturalisms of *Beyond Good and Evil*". See Ansell-Pearson (2006b), 148–67.

Colli, G. & M. Montinari (eds). 1967– . *Kritische Gesamtausgabe: Werke*, 40 vols. Berlin: de Gruyter.

Connolly, W. E. 1993. *Political Theory and Modernity*. Ithaca, NY: Cornell University Press.

Conway, D. W. 1997a. *Nietzsche's Dangerous Game: Philosophy in The Twilight of the Idols*. Cambridge: Cambridge University Press.

Conway, D. W. 1997b. *Nietzsche and the Political*. London: Routledge.

Cooper, D. E. 1999. *Existentialism: A Reconstruction*, 2nd edn. Oxford: Blackwell.

Cox, C. 1999. *Nietzsche: Naturalism and Interpretation*. Berkeley, CA: University of California Press.

Crowell, S. 2010. "Existentialism". *Stanford Encyclopedia of Philosophy*. http://plato.stanford.edu/entries/existentialism/ (accessed August 2011).

Cybulska, E. M. 2000. "The Madness of Nietzsche: the Misdiagnosis of the Millennium?" *Hospital Medicine* 61: 571–5.

Daigle, C. 2004. "Sartre and Nietzsche". *Sartre Studies International* 10(2): 195–211.

Danto, A. 2005. *Nietzsche as Philosopher*, exp. edn. New York: Columbia University Press.

Deane, D. 2006. *Nietzsche and Theology: Nietzschean Thought in Christological Anthropology*. Aldershot: Ashgate.

Deleuze, G. [1962] 1983. *Nietzsche and Philosophy*, H. Tomlinson (trans.). New York: Columbia University Press.

Deleuze, G. 1994. *Difference and Repetition*, P. Patton (trans.). New York: Columbia University Press.

Deleuze, G. 2001. *Pure Immanence: Essays on A Life*, A. Boyman (trans.). New York: Zone Books.

Derrida, J. 1973. *Speech and Phenomena, And Other Essays on Husserl's Theory of Signs*, D. B. Allison (trans.). Evanston, IL: Northwestern University Press.

Derrida, J. 1978. *Writing and Difference*, A. Bass (trans.). London: Routledge.
Derrida, J. 1979. *Spurs: Nietzsche's Styles*, B. Harlow (trans.). Chicago, IL: University of Chicago Press.
Derrida, J. 1986. *The Ear of the Other: Otobiography, Transference, Translation*, A. Ronell & P. Kamuf (trans.), C. V. McDonald (ed.). New York: Schocken Books.
Derrida, J. 1997. *The Politics of Friendship*, G. Collins (trans.). London: Verso.
Derrida, J. 1998. *Of Grammatology*, corrected edn, G. C. Spivak (trans.). Baltimore, MD: Johns Hopkins University Press.
Derrida, J. 2002. *Negotiations: Interventions and Interviews, 1971–2001*, E. Rottenberg (ed. & trans.). Stanford, CA: Stanford University Press.
Descartes, R. 1954. *Descartes: Philosophical Writings*, E. Anscombe & P. T. Geach (ed. & trans.). Edinburgh: Nelson.
Detwiler, B. 1990. *Nietzsche and the Politics of Aristocratic Radicalism*. Chicago, IL: University of Chicago Press.
Diethe, C. 1996. *Nietzsche's Women: Beyond the Whip*. Berlin: Walter de Gruyter.
Diethe, C. 2006. *Historical Dictionary of Nietzscheanism*, 2nd edn. Lanham, MD: Scarecrow Press.
Duvall, W. E. 1999. "Camus Reading Nietzsche: Rebellion, Memory, and Art". *History of European Ideas* **25**: 39–53.
Ferry, L. & A. Renaut 1990. *French Philosophy of the Sixties: An Essay on Antihumanism*, M. H. S. Cattani (trans.). Amherst, MA: University of Massachusetts Press.
Ferry, L. & A. Renaut (eds) 1997. *Why We Are Not Nietzscheans*, R. De Loaiza (trans.). Chicago, IL: University of Chicago Press.
Fink, E. 2003. *Nietzsche's Philosophy*. London: Continuum.
Foster, J. B. 1981. *Heirs to Dionysus: A Nietzschean Current in Literary Modernism*. Princeton, NJ: Princeton University Press.
Foucault, M. 1977a. "Nietzsche, Genealogy, History". In *Language, Counter-memory, Practice*, D. F. Bouchard (ed.), D. F. Bouchard & S. Simon (trans.), 139–64. Ithaca, NY: Cornell University Press.
Foucault, M. 1977b. *Discipline and Punish*, A. Sheridan (trans.). Harmondsworth: Penguin.
Foucault, M. 1978. *The Will to Knowledge: The History of Sexuality 1*, R. Hurley (trans.). Harmondsworth: Penguin.
Foucault, M. 1989. *Foucault Live: Collected Interviews, 1961–1984*, S. Lotringer (ed.), J. Johnston (trans.). New York: Semiotext(e).
Foucault, M. 1990. "Nietzsche, Freud, Marx". In *Transforming the Hermeneutic Context: From Nietzsche to Nancy*, G. L. Ormiston & A. D. Schrift (eds), 59–68. Albany, NY: SUNY Press.
Foucault, M. 1994. *The Order of Things: An Archaeology of the Human Sciences*. New York: Vintage.
Fraser, G. 2002. *Redeeming Nietzsche: On the Piety of Unbelief*. London: Routledge.
Friedman, M. (ed.) 1964. *Worlds of Existentialism: A Critical Reader*. New York: Random House.
Gaiger, J. 1998. "Lebensphilosophie". In *The Routledge Encyclopedia of Philosophy*, vol. 5, E. Craig (ed.). London: Routledge.
Gemes, K. & J. Richardson forthcoming. *The Oxford Handbook of Nietzsche*. Oxford: Oxford University Press.
Gillespie, M. A. & T. B. Strong (eds) 1988. *Nietzsche's New Seas*. Chicago, IL: University of Chicago Press.

Golomb, J. 2004. *Nietzsche and Zion*. Ithaca, NY: Cornell University Press.

Golomb, J. & R. S. Wistrich (eds) 2002. *Nietzsche, Godfather of Fascism?: On the Uses and Abuses of a Philosophy*. Princeton, NJ: Princeton University Press.

Golomb, J., W. Santaniello & R. Lehrer 1999. *Nietzsche and Depth Psychology*. Albany, NY: SUNY Press.

Granier, J. 1966. *La Probleme de la Verite dans La Philosophie de Nietzsche*. [The problem of truth in the philosophy of Nietzsche]. Paris: Seuil.

Groenwald, A. J. 2007. "Interpreting the Theology of Barth in Light of Nietzsche's Dictum 'God is dead'". *HTS Teologiese Studies/Theological Studies* 63(4): 1429–45.

Grosz, E. 1994. *Volatile Bodies: Toward a Corporeal Feminism*. St Leonards: Allen & Unwin.

Gutting, G. 2008. "Michel Foucault". *Stanford Encyclopedia of Philosophy*. http://plato.stanford.edu/entries/foucault/#4 (accessed August 2011).

Habermas, J. 1987. *The Philosophical Discourse of Modernity*, F. Lawrence (trans.). Cambridge, MA: MIT Press.

Hadot, P. 2010. "Introduction to Ernst Bertram, *Nietzsche: Attempt at a Mythology*", P. Bishop (trans.). *The Agonist* III(1): 52–84. www.nietzschecircle.com/AGO-NIST/2010_03/translationHadot.html (accessed August 2011).

Hamilton, W. & T. J. J. Altizer 1966. *Radical Theology and the Death of God*. Indianapolis, IN: Bobbs-Merrill.

Harink, D. (ed.) 2010. *Paul, Philosophy, and the Theopolitical Vision: Critical Engagements with Agamben, Badiou, Žižek, and Others*. Eugene, OR: Cascade Books.

Hart, D. B. 2003. *The Beauty of the Infinite: The Aesthetics of Christian Truth*. Grand Rapids, MI: Eerdmans.

Hatab, L. 1995. *A Nietzschean Defense of Democracy: An Experiment in Postmodern Politics*. Chicago, IL: Open Court.

Hayman, R. 1980. *Nietzsche: A Critical Life*. London: Weidenfeld & Nicolson.

Hegel, G. W. F. 1952. *Hegel's Philosophy of Right*, T. M. Knox (trans.). Oxford: Clarendon Press.

Heidegger, M. [1927] 1962. *Being and Time*, J. Macquarrie & E. Robinson (trans.). Oxford: Blackwell.

Heidegger, M. 1977. *The Question Concerning Technology and Other Essays*, W. Lovitt (trans.). New York: Harper & Row.

Heidegger, M. 1979–87. *Nietzsche*, 4 vols, D. F. Krell (trans.). San Francisco: Harper & Row.

Heidegger, M. 1993. *Martin Heidegger: Basic Writings*, D. F. Krell (trans.). New York: HarperCollins.

Heinemann, F. 1929. *Neue Wege der Philosophie*. Leipzig: Queller & Meyer.

Hollingdale, R. J. (ed. & trans.) 1977. *A Nietzsche Reader*. New York: Penguin.

Hollingdale, R. J. 1999. *Nietzsche: The Man and His Philosophy*. New York: Cambridge University Press.

Hovey, C. 2008. *Nietzsche and Theology*. London: T&T Clark International.

Irigaray, L. 1981. *Le Corps-à-corps avec la mère*. Montrèal: Plein Lune.

Irigaray, L. [1974] 1985. *Speculum of the Other Woman*, G. C. Gill (trans.). Ithaca, NY: Cornell University Press.

Irigaray, L. [1980] 1991. *Marine Lover of Friedrich Nietzsche*, G. C. Gill (trans.). New York: Columbia University Press.

Irigaray, L. 1994. "Ecce Mulier? Fragments". In *Nietzsche and the Feminine*, P. J. Burgard (ed.), 316–34. Charlottesville, VA: University Press of Virginia.

James, I. 2007. "Klossowski and Deleuze: Parody, Simulacrum and the Power of Return". In *Sensorium: Aesthetics, Art, Life*, B. Bolt, F. Colman, G. Jones & A. Woodward (eds). Newcastle upon Tyne: Cambridge Scholars Publishing.

Janaway, C. 2006. "Naturalism and Genealogy". See Ansell-Pearson (2006b), 337–52.

Jaspers, K. 1955. *Reason and Existence*, W. Earle (trans.). New York: Farrar Straus.

Jaspers, K. [1936] 1965. *Nietzsche: An Introduction to the Understanding of His Philosophical Activity*, C. F. Wellraff & F. J. Schmitz (trans.). Tucson, AZ: University of Arizona Press.

Jaspers, K. 1975. "Kierkegaard and Nietzsche", William Earle (trans.). In *Existentialism from Dostoevsky to Sartre*, W. Kaufmann (ed.). New York: Meridian.

Joyce, J. 1993. *A James Joyce Reader*, H. Levin (ed.). Harmondsworth: Penguin.

Kaufmann, W. 1957. "Jaspers' Relation to Nietzsche". In *The Philosophy of Karl Jaspers*, P. Schilpps (ed.), 407–36. New York: Tudor.

Kaufmann, W. 1968. *Basic Writings of Nietzsche*. New York: Modern Library.

Kaufmann, W. [1950] 1974. *Nietzsche: Philosopher, Psychologist, Antichrist*, 4th edn. Princeton, NJ: Princeton University Press.

Kaufmann, W. (ed.) [1956] 1975. *Existentialism from Dostoevsky to Sartre*. New York: Meridian.

Kaufmann, W. 1976. *Existentialism, Religion and Death: Thirteen Essays*. New York: New American Library.

Kaufmann, W. 1977. *The Portable Nietzsche*. Harmondsworth: Penguin.

Kelly, K. 1994. *Out of Control: The New Biology of Machines*. London: Fourth Estate.

Klossowski, P. [1969] 2005. *Nietzsche and the Vicious Circle*, D. W. Smith (trans.). London: Continuum.

Klossowski, P. [1957] 2007. "Nietzsche, Polytheism and Parody". In *Such a Deathly Desire*, R. Ford (trans.), 99–122. Albany, NY: SUNY Press.

Klossowski, P. 2009. "Circulus Vitiosus", J. D. Kuzma (trans.). *The Agonist* 2(1): 31–47. http://nietzschecircle.com/AGONIST/2009_03/translationKlossowskiKuzma.html (accessed August 2011).

Kofman, S. 1993. *Nietzsche and Metaphor*, D. Large (trans.). Stanford, CA: Stanford University Press.

Kofman, S. 1998. "Baubô: Theological Perversion and Fetishism", T. B. Strong (trans.). See Oliver & Pearsall (1998a), 21–49.

Kristeva, J. 1982. *Powers of Horror: An Essay on Abjection*, L. Roudiez (ed.). New York: Columbia University Press.

Kuzma, J. D. 2009. Preface to P. Klossowski, "Circulus Vitiosus". *The Agonist* 2(1): 31–2. http://nietzschecircle.com/AGONIST/2009_03/translationKlossowskiKuzma.html (accessed August 2011).

Lampert, L. 1993. *Nietzsche and Modern Times: A Study of Bacon, Descartes and Nietzsche*. New Haven, CT: Yale University Press.

Lange, F. A. [1866] 1950. *History of Materialism and Criticism of its Present Importance*, E. C. Thomas (trans.). London: Trübner.

Leiter, B. 2001. "The Paradox of Fatalism and Self-Creation in Nietzsche". In *Nietzsche*, B. Leiter & J. Richardson (eds). Oxford: Oxford University Press.

Leiter, B. 2002. *Routledge Philosophy Guidebook to Nietzsche on Morality*. London: Routledge.

Leiter, B. 2010. "Nietzsche's Moral and Political Philosophy". *Stanford Encyclopedia of Philosophy*. http://plato.stanford.edu/entries/nietzsche-moral-political/#4 (accessed August 2011).

Leiter, B. & J. Richardson (eds) 2001. *Nietzsche*. Oxford: Oxford University Press.

Levy, O. (ed.) 1909–13. *The Complete Works of Friedrich Nietzsche*. Edinburgh: T. N. Foulis.

Löb, W. 1908. "Naturwissenschaftliche Elemente in Nietzsches Gedanken". *Deutsche Rundschau* **173**: 264–9.

Löwith, K. 1997. *Nietzsche's Philosophy of the Eternal Recurrence of the Same*, J. H. Lomax (trans.). Berkeley, CA: University of California Press.

Lukács, G. [1952] 1980. *The Destruction of Reason*, P. Palmer (trans.). London: Merlin Press.

Lyotard, J.-F. 1978. "Notes on the Return and Kapital", R. McKeon (trans.). *Semiotext(e)* **3**(1): 44–53.

Lyotard, J.-F. 1984. *The Postmodern Condition: A Report on Knowledge*, G. Bennington & B. Massumi (trans.). Minneapolis, MN: University of Minnesota Press.

Lyotard, J.-F. 1991. "Can Thought go on Without a Body?" In *The Inhuman: Reflections on Time*, G. Bennington & R. Bowlby (trans.). Stanford, CA: Stanford University Press.

Lyotard, J.-F. 1992. "Missive on Universal History". In *The Postmodern Explained to Children: Correspondence 1982–1985*, J. Pefanis & M. Thomas (ed. & trans.). Sydney: Power Publications.

Lyotard, J.-F. 1993. *Political Writings*, B. Readings & K. Paul (trans.). Minneapolis, MN: University of Minnesota Press.

Macquarrie, J. 1972. *Existentialism: An Introduction, Guide, and Assessment*. Harmondsworth: Penguin.

Magnus, B., K. Ansell-Pearson & A. D. Schrift (eds). 1995– . *Complete Works of Friedrich Nietzsche*, 20 vols. Stanford, CA: Stanford University Press.

Marcel, G. 1952. *Metaphysical Journal*, B. Wall (trans.). London: Barrie & Rockliff.

Mautner, T. 1999. *The Penguin Dictionary of Philosophy*. Harmondsworth: Penguin.

Mittasch, A. 1952. *Nietzsche als Naturphilosoph*. Stuttgart: Kröner.

Moore, G. 2002. *Nietzsche, Biology and Metaphor*. Cambridge: Cambridge University Press.

Moore, G. 2004. "Introduction". In *Nietzsche and Science*, G. Moore & T. H. Brobjer (eds), 1–17. Aldershot: Ashgate.

Moore, G. & T. H. Brobjer (eds) 2004. *Nietzsche and Science*. Aldershot: Ashgate.

More, M. 1990. "Transhumanism: Towards a Futurist Philosophy". *Extropy* **6**. www.maxmore.com/transhum.htm (accessed August 2011).

More, M. 2010. "The Overhuman in the Transhuman". *Journal of Evolution & Technology* **21**(1): 1–4.

Müller-Lauter, W. 1999. "The Organism as Inner Struggle: Wilhelm Roux's Influence on Nietzsche". In *Nietzsche: His Philosophy of Contradictions and the Contradictions of His Philosophy*, D. J. Parent (trans.). Champaign, IL: University of Illinois Press.

Nancy, J.-L. [1982] 1991. *The Inoperative Community*, P. Connor (ed.), P. Connor, L. Garbus, M. Holland & S. Sawhney (trans.). Minneapolis, MN: University of Minnesota Press.

Nehamas, A. 1985. *Nietzsche: Life as Literature*. Cambridge, MA: Harvard University Press.

Nietzsche, F. 1996a. *Selected Letters of Friedrich Nietzsche*, 2nd edn, C. Middleton (ed. & trans.). Indianapolis, IN: Hackett.

Nietzsche, F. 1996b. *Philosophy in the Tragic Age of the Greeks*, M. Cowan (trans.). Washington, DC: Gateway Editions.

Nietzsche, F. 2000. *The Pre-Platonic Philosophers*, G. Whitlock (ed. & trans.). Champaign, IL: University of Illinois Press.

Nietzsche, F. 2008. *Political Writings of Friedrich Nietzsche*, F. Cameron & D. Dombowsky (eds). Basingstoke: Palgrave Macmillan.

Oaklander, N. L. 1992. *Existentialist Philosophy: An Introduction*. Englewood Cliffs, NJ: Prentice Hall.

O'Flaherty, J. C., T. F. Sellner & R. M. Helm (eds) 1985. *Studies in Nietzsche and the Judaeo-Christian Tradition*. Chapel Hill, NC: University of North Carolina Press.

Oliver, K. 1995. *Womanizing Nietzsche: Philosophy's Relation to the "Feminine"*. London: Routledge.

Oliver, K. & M. Pearsall (eds) 1998a. *Feminist Interpretations of Friedrich Nietzsche*. University Park, PA: Pennsylvania State University Press.

Oliver, K. & M. Pearsall. 1998b. "Introduction: Why Feminists Read Nietzsche". See Oliver & Pearsall (1998a), 1–17.

Oppel, F. 1993. "'Speaking of Immemorial Waters': Irigaray with Nietzsche". In *Nietzsche, Feminism and Political Theory*, P. Patton (ed.), 88–109. London: Routledge.

Oppel, F. 2005. *Nietzsche on Gender: Beyond Man and Woman*. Charlottesville, VA: University of Virginia Press.

Owen, D. 1995. *Nietzsche, Politics, and Modernity: A Critique of Liberal Reason*. London: Sage.

Patton, P. (ed.). 1993. *Nietzsche, Feminism and Political Theory*. London: Routledge.

Pickus, D. 2003. "The Walter Kaufmann Myth: A Study in Academic Judgement". *Nietzsche-Studien* **32**: 226–58.

Prigogine, I. & I. Stengers 1985. *Order Out of Chaos: Man's New Dialogue with Nature*. London: Flamingo.

Ratner-Rosenhagen, J. 2006. "'Dionysian Enlightenment': Walter Kaufmann's *Nietzsche* in Historical Perspective". *Modern Intellectual History* **3**(2): 239–69.

Rée, P. [1877] 2003. *The Origin of the Moral Sensations*, R. Small (ed.). Champaign, IL: University of Illinois Press.

Regis, E. 1990. *Great Mambo Chicken and the Transhuman Condition: Science Slightly Over the Edge*. New York: Perseus.

Reynolds, J., F. Joseph & A. Woodward (eds) 2011. *The Continuum Companion to Existentialism*. London: Continuum.

Richardson, J. 2004. *Nietzsche's New Darwinism*. Oxford: Oxford University Press.

Robbins, J. W. 2004. "Weak Theology". *Journal for Cultural and Religious Theory* **5**(2): 1–4.

Roberts, T. T. 1998. *Contesting Spirit: Nietzsche, Affirmation, Religion*. Princeton, NJ: Princeton University Press.

Rose, G. 1978. *The Melancholy Science: An Introduction to the Thought of Theodor W. Adorno*. Basingstoke: Macmillan.

Rybalka, M., O. F. Pucciani & S. Gruenheck 1981. "An Interview with Jean-Paul Sartre?" In *The Philosophy of Jean-Paul Sartre*, P. A. Schilpp (ed.), 2–51. La Salle, IL: Open Court.

Safranski, R. 2003. *Nietzsche: A Philosophical Biography*. London: Granta.

Salomé, L. 2001. *Nietzsche*, S. Mandel (ed. & trans.). Champaign, IL: University of Illinois Press.

Santaniello, W. (ed.) 2001. *Nietzsche and the Gods*. Albany, NY: SUNY Press.

Sartre, J.-P. 1956. *Being and Nothingness*, H. E. Barnes (trans.). New York: Washington Square Press.

Sartre, J.-P. 1960. *The Transcendence of the Ego: An Existentialist Theory of Consciousness*, F. Williams & R. Kirkpatrick (trans.). New York: Hill & Wang.

Sartre, J.-P. 1965. *Nausea*, R. Baldick (trans.). Harmondsworth: Penguin.

Sartre, J.-P. 1975. "Existentialism is a Humanism". In *Existentialism from Dostoevsky to Sartre*, W. Kaufmann (ed.). New York: Meridian.

Sartre, J.-P. 1990. *Écrits de jeunesse* [Youthful writings], M. Contat & M. Rybalka (eds). Paris: Gallimard.

Saussure, F. de [1959] 1986. *Course in General Linguistics*, C. Bally & A. Sechehaye with A. Riedlinger (eds), R. Harris (trans.). La Salle, IL: Open Court.

Sax, L. 2003. "What was the Cause of Nietzsche's Dementia?" *Journal of Medical Biography* 11: 47–54.

Schacht, R. 1988. "Nietzsche's *Gay Science*, or, How to Naturalize Cheerfully". In *Reading Nietzsche*, R. C. Solomon & M. Higgins (eds), 68–86. Oxford: Oxford University Press.

Schnädelbach, H. 1984. *Philosophy in Germany 1831–1933*, E. Matthews (trans.). Cambridge: Cambridge University Press.

Schrift, A. D. 1990. *Nietzsche and the Question of Interpretation: Between Hermeneutics and Deconstruction*. New York: Routledge.

Schrift, A. D. 1995. *Nietzsche's French Legacy: A Genealogy of Poststructuralism*. New York; London: Routledge.

Schrift, A. D. 2005. *Twentieth-Century French Philosophy: Key Themes and Thinkers*. Oxford: Blackwell.

Shaw, T. 2007. *Nietzsche's Political Skepticism*. Princeton, NJ: Princeton University Press.

Siemens, H. W. & V. Roodt (eds) 2008. *Nietzsche, Power and Politics*. Berlin: Walter de Gruyter.

Simmel, G. [1907] 1991. *Schopenhauer and Nietzsche*, H. Loiskandl, D. Weinstein & M. Weinstein (trans.). Champaign, IL: University of Illinois Press.

Sinnerbrink, R. 2007. *Understanding Hegelianism*. Chesham: Acumen.

Small, R. 2001. *Nietzsche in Context*. Aldershot: Ashgate.

Smith, D. 1996. *Transvaluations: Nietzsche in France 1872–1972*. New York: Oxford University Press.

Smith, D. W. 2005. "Klossowski's Reading of Nietzsche: Impulses, Phantasms, Simulacra, Stereotypes". *Diacritics* 35(1): 8–21.

Smith, D. W. 2005b. "Translator's Preface". In P. Klossowski, *Nietzsche and the Vicious Circle*, D. W. Smith (trans.). London: Continuum.

Sorgner, S. 2009. "Nietzsche, the Overhuman, and Transhumanism". *Journal of Evolution & Technology* 20(1): 29–42.

Spengler, O. [1918] 1932. *The Decline of the West*, C. F. Atkinson (trans.). London: Allen & Unwin.

Stack, G. J. 1983. *Lange and Nietzsche*. Berlin: de Gruyter.

St Aubyn, F. C. 1968. "A Note on Nietzsche and Camus". *Comparative Literature* 20(2): 110–15.

Stoekl, A. 1979. "The Death of Acephale and the Will to Chance: Nietzsche in the Text of Bataille". *Glyph* 6: 42–67.

Strong, T. B. [1975] 2000. *Friedrich Nietzsche and the Politics of Transfiguration*. Champaign, IL: University of Illinois Press.

Theys, F. (dir.) 2006. *Technocalyps*. Votnik.

Thomas, R. H. 1983. *Nietzsche in German Politics and Society 1890–1918*. Manchester: Manchester University Press.

Tillich, P. [1952] 2000. *The Courage to Be*. New Haven, CT: Yale University Press.
Tillich, P. [1945] 2001. "The Escape from God". In *Nietzsche and the Gods*, W. Santaniello (ed.), 173–80. Albany, NY: SUNY Press.
Vahanian, G. 1961. *The Death of God: The Culture of Our Post-Christian Era*. New York: George Braziller.
Vattimo, G. 1997. *Beyond Interpretation: The Meaning of Hermeneutics for Philosophy*, D. Webb (trans.). Stanford, CA: Stanford University Press.
Vattimo, G. 1999. *Belief*, L. D'Isanto & D. Webb (trans.). Stanford, CA: Stanford University Press.
Vattimo, G. 2001. *Nietzsche: An Introduction*. Stanford, CA: Stanford University Press.
Vattimo, G. 2002. *After Christianity*, L. D'Isanto (trans.). New York: Columbia University Press.
Vattimo, G. & J. D. Caputo 2007. *After the Death of God*, J. W. Robbins (trans.). New York: Columbia University Press.
Vattimo, G. & R. Girard 2010. *Christianity, Truth, and Weakening Faith: A Dialogue*, P. Antonello (ed.), W. McCuaig (trans.). New York: Columbia University Press.
Vattimo, G. & R. Rorty 2005. *The Future of Religion*, S. Zabala (ed.). New York: Columbia University Press.
Wahl, J. 1951. *Le Malheur de la conscience dans la philosophie de Hegel*. [The unhappiness of consciousness in the philosophy of Hegel]. Paris: Presses Universitaires de France.
Warren, M. 1988. *Nietzsche and Political Thought*. Cambridge, MA: MIT Press.
Wexelblatt, R. 1987. "Camus' *Caligula* and Nietzsche". *Lamar Journal of the Humanities* 13(1): 27–36.
White, A. 1990. *Within Nietzsche's Labyrinth*. New York: Routledge.
Wiley, C. 2009. "I Was Dead and Behold, I am Alive Forevermore: Responses to Nietzsche in 20th Century Christian Theology". *Intersections* 10(1): 507–17.
Williams, J. 2005. *Understanding Poststructuralism*. Chesham: Acumen.
Williams, S. N. 2006. *The Shadow of the Antichrist: Nietzsche's Critique of Christianity*. Grand Rapids, MI: Baker.
Wilson, C. 2004. *Dreaming to Some Purpose*. London: Century.
Wininger, K. J. 1998. "Nietzsche's Women and Women's Nietzsche". See Oliver & Pearsall (1998a), 236–51.
Woodward, A. 2009. *Nihilism in Postmodernity: Lyotard, Baudrillard, Vattimo*. Aurora, CO: Davies Group.
Woodward, A. (ed.) 2011. *Interpreting Nietzsche: Reception and Influence*. London: Continuum.
Young, J. 2006. *Nietzsche's Philosophy of Religion*. Cambridge: Cambridge University Press.
Young, J. 2010. *Friedrich Nietzsche: A Philosophical Biography*. Cambridge: Cambridge University Press.
Žižek, S. 2009. *The Fragile Absolute: Or, Why is the Christian Legacy Worth Fighting For?*, 2nd edn. London: Verso.

Index